Social Stratification in Central Mexico, 1500-2000

SOCIAL STRATIFICATION IN CENTRAL MEXICO 1500–2000

HUGO G. NUTINI AND
BARRY L. ISAAC

UNIVERSITY OF TEXAS PRESS
AUSTIN

Printed in the United States of America
First edition, 2009
Requests for permission to reproduce material from
this work should be sent to:
Permissions
University of Texas Press
P.O. Box 7819
Austin, TX 78713-7819
www.utexas.edu/utpress/about/bpermission.html

∞ The paper used in this book meets the minimum requirements of ANSI/NISO Z39.48-1992 (R1997) (Permanence of Paper).

Library of Congress Cataloging-in-Publication Data
Nutini, Hugo G.
Social stratification in central Mexico, 1500–2000 / Hugo G. Nutini and Barry L. Isaac. — 1st ed.
p. cm.
Includes bibliographical references (p.) and index.
ISBN 978-0-292-72351-1
1. Social stratification—Mexico—History. 2. Mexico—Social conditions. I. Isaac, Barry L. II. Title.
HN120.Z9S637 2009
305.5′1209724—dc22 2008042037

contents

acknowledgments

This book is based on ethnographic fieldwork in Central Mexico, totaling some 180 months from 1958 to 2008, in addition to archival and library research. Thus, we are indebted to an unusually large number of individuals and institutions. For funding, we thank the National Science Foundation, the Wenner-Gren Foundation for Anthropological Research, the National Endowment for the Humanities, the American Philosophical Society, the Pittsburgh Foundation, the National Geographical Society, and the University of Pittsburgh (Center for Latin American Studies, Center for International Studies, College of Arts and Sciences, Central Research Development Fund, Center for Social and Urban Research).

We are grateful to the many archival facilities in Mexico, the United States, and Europe that we have consulted during the past fifty years. In Mexico, we thank the Archivos de los Estados de Tlaxcala and Puebla, the Archivos de las Ciudades de Tlaxcala and Puebla, the Archivo de la Ciudad de Teziutlán, the Archivos de las Ciudades de Córdoba and Orizaba, many parochial archives in those regions (over thirty in the Tlaxcala-Pueblan Valley, seven in the Sierra de Puebla, and five in the Córdoba-Orizaba region), the Archivo General de la Nación, the Archivo del Museo Nacional de Antropología e Historia, the Archivo de Asuntos Agrarios, the Archivo de la Sociedad Nacional de Geografía, and the Archivo de la Sociedad de Genealogía y Heráldica. Archives consulted in the United States include the New York Public Library, the National Archives, the Bancroft Collection at the University of California, Berkeley, Library, the Ayer Collection at the Newberry Library in Chicago, the Peabody Museum Library at Harvard University, and the University of Texas at Austin Library. In Europe, we consulted archives in Spain (Archivo de Indias, Biblioteca Nacional, Archivo Militar), Italy (Biblioteca de la Citta di Firenze and the Vatican Archives' Propaganda Fide, archivio segreto), France (Bibliothéque Nacional), and England (British Museum).

We could not possibly single out all the other institutions and individuals who helped us during the half century of fieldwork and archival research that went into the writing of this book. At best, we can express our appreciation to those who made the most significant contributions. We are grateful to the Instituto Nacional de Antropología e Historia for administrative support and to the state authorities of Tlaxcala, Puebla, and Veracruz for administrative and material support. We thank the bishops of the dioceses of Tlaxcala and Córdoba and the archbishop of the diocese of Puebla for facilitating our research in the local parochial archives and for helping to create goodwill among parish priests and local religious hierarchies. We are grateful for the openness and willingness of countless municipal authorities in the states of Tlaxcala, Puebla, and Veracruz that made our lives easier and facilitated our fieldwork. Of course, we could not have accomplished the fieldwork without the kindness and generosity of the inhabitants of hundreds of communities in the Tlaxcala-Pueblan Valley, the Sierra de Puebla, and the Córdoba-Orizaba region, as well as Mexico City, over the past five decades. They took us into their households and made us participants in their lives, and we often established deep bonds.

Others who gave generously of their time and expertise to facilitate the writing of this book include the following: Alan R. Sandstrom, Robert M. Laughlin, and an anonymous reviewer provided criticisms that greatly improved the final product; Katherine A. Lancaster at the University of Pittsburgh provided invaluable editorial and technical support; Jorge Angulo Villaseñor and Jaime Litvak King offered good advice on library resources in Mexico City. The artist Jaime Sánchez of Córdoba, Veracruz, produced the maps.

Social Stratification in Central Mexico, 1500–2000

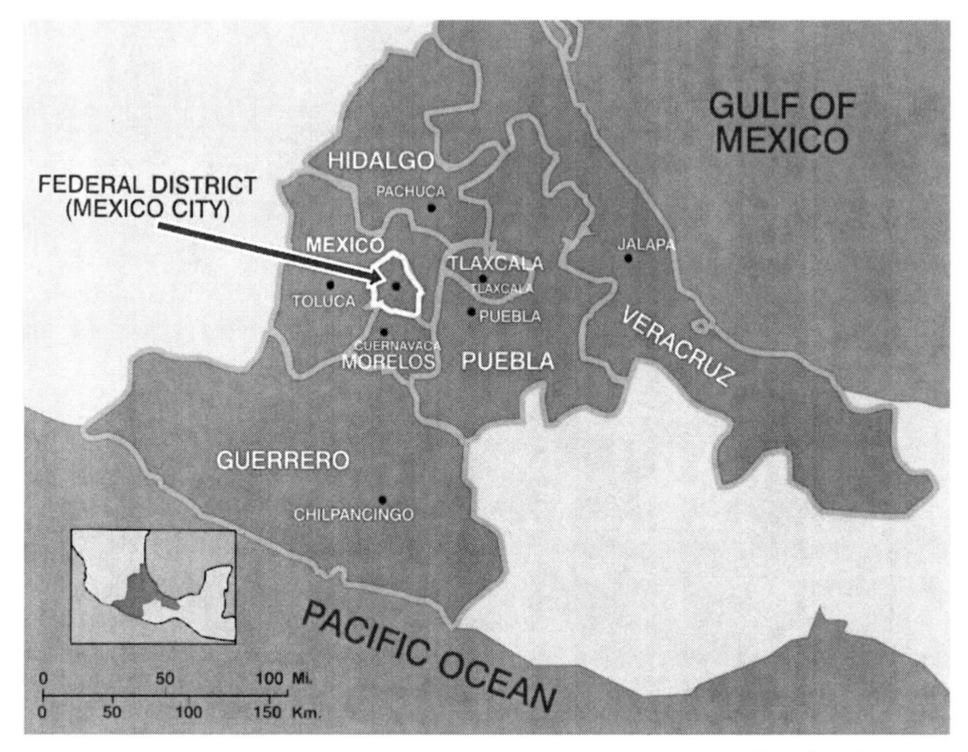

MAP 1. Central Mexico

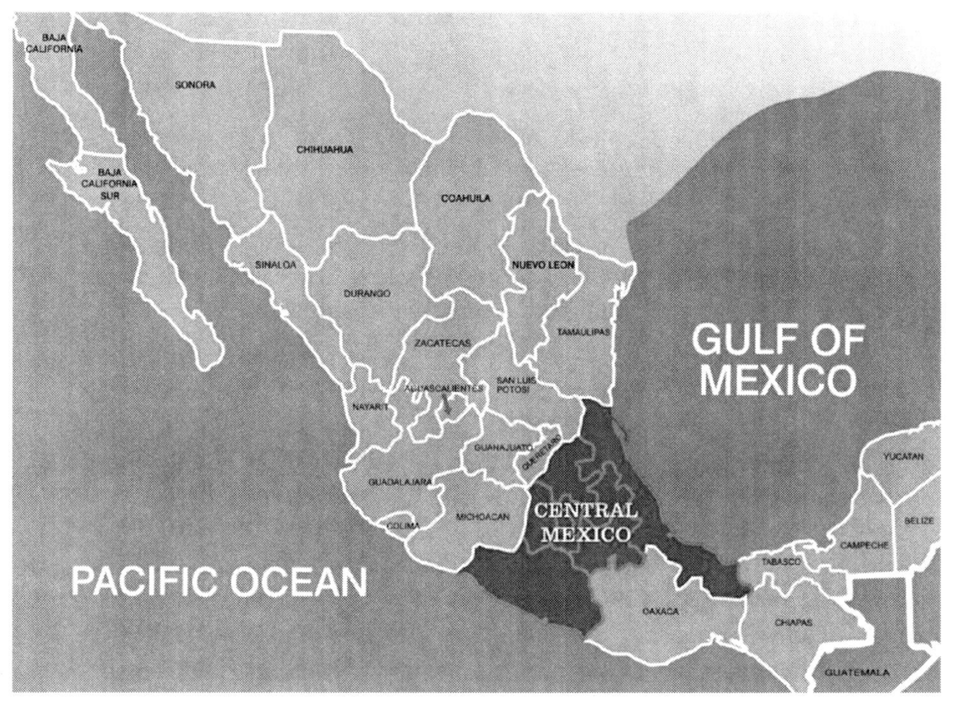

MAP 2. Central Mexico within the Country of Mexico

INTRODUCTION

This book presents the first longitudinal and comprehensive overview of social stratification in Central Mexico, embracing the time span from just before the Spanish Conquest up to the present (1500–2000). Central Mexico was the heartland of the Aztec Empire when the Spaniards arrived in 1519, and it is still the country's economic and political motor. It comprises the present states of Guerrero, México, Morelos, Hidalgo, Tlaxcala, Puebla, and Veracruz, as well as the Federal District (Distrito Federal), which includes Mexico City (see Maps 1 and 2). Although Central Mexico encompasses only 11.3 percent of the national territory, its 41.5 million inhabitants in 2000 constituted 42.6 percent of the national population of 97.5 million (INEGI 2003: 5–9).

We combine historical and ethnographic materials to construct our portrait of this core area. Students of Mexican anthropology and history will be familiar with Nutini's more than forty-five years of ethnographic work in the area, some fifteen of them devoted specifically to social class (see Nutini 1995, 2004, 2005). His rich experience is complemented by Isaac's historical research on the Aztec and early colonial periods, as well as his firsthand observations of Mexican politics and economics, especially among the lower-middle and working classes of Mexico City, during the past twenty years. In short, our approach is eminently anthropological, combining structured interviews and participant observation, but it also reaches deeply into history.

In both Mexico and the United States, the social stratification system that frames every individual's worldview and life chances remains poorly understood, even among highly educated people. This is so because—in the words of William Lloyd Warner (1960: v), a pioneer in the study of social stratification—"no teacher teaches us the hard facts of our social-class system." Indeed, the topic of social class has become the last taboo in the United States, in education as well as in politics, while in Mexico the subject has lost the prominence that it enjoyed in the social sciences there during the 1970s and early 1980s. Even international agencies typically avoid using the concepts of class and stratification, because these terms are thought to evoke dangerous "notions of conflict, privilege, and exploitation" (Portes and Hoffman 2003: 42).

Thus Warner's lament remains largely true today. We hope that this book will serve to fill that educational gap, because neither the past nor the present is intelligible in Central Mexico—or, for that matter, elsewhere in our hemisphere—unless we understand its evolving social stratification system, which has shaped its politics, economics, and racial-ethnic relations. Especially important is the transition from a legally defined, hereditary estate system to the more fluid class structures of the present day (see below and Chap. 1). Yet, while the stratification system has undergone fundamental changes during the period of this study, these changes have always been incomplete, even in response to changes in official policies. In fact, an important lesson we hope to convey in this book is that political regimes, even the strong ones of the twentieth century, have only a limited ability to alter national social systems.

Central Mexico is an especially interesting and instructive region for a longitudinal study of social stratification. Historically, the area saw the rise of the Aztec Empire in 1430 and its dramatic overthrow by a Spanish-led force of rebelling Aztec subjects in 1521. Upon the ruins of the former empire, the Spaniards established a multiethnic and multiracial colonial state that endured for three centuries. When Mexico won its independence from Spain in 1821, one of its first official acts was the abolition of the colonial *casta* system of racial classification that had attempted to separate the "mixed" (Indian-African-European) majority from both the light-complexioned ruling stratum and the indigenous peasantry. Legally, at least, the whole structure of hereditary estate stratification (see below) that had been in force throughout the colonial period was struck down, leaving only classes as macro-social building blocks. In practice, remnants of the estate system endured in a few locales, known as "refuge regions," until late in the twentieth century.

In 1910–1920 Central Mexico was an important crucible of the great Mexican Revolution. The area's most famous revolutionary, Emiliano Zapata, helped to transform the struggle into a genuine social revolution that aimed to change the country's economic and social systems, as well as its political structure. An eventual outcome of the social aspect of the Revolution was the extensive agrarian reform carried out by President Lázaro Cárdenas in the 1930s. The essence of that reform was the expropriation of large landholdings, typically without reimbursement, and their redistribution to peasant communities.

Agrarian reform brought the downfall of Mexico's landed aristocracy, which had been the undisputed ruling class since independence in 1821. By the 1950s, over 80 percent of the remaining aristocrats had relocated to Mexico City, where they flourished for another decade as a prestige class, even though they had lost their political influence and much of their wealth. Most important, they served as the model of high society for the rising plutocrats, who had become wealthy in manufacturing, commerce, and finance. During the 1980s, this new plutocracy displaced the aristocracy as the dominant class of the country's superordinate social stratum.

The prosperity enjoyed by Central Mexico's plutocrats during the 1980s and 1990s stood in sharp contrast to the increasing hardship experienced by the urban lower classes, which had become the area's majority social component during the 1970s. The lower stratum's paltry incomes were eroded by sharp devaluation of the Mexican peso in 1982 and 1995, driving up the prices of most consumer goods. At century's end, the urban lower classes also were facing two new problems: (1) a "neoliberal" reform that abolished, reduced, or redirected many of the federal social welfare programs that had subsidized their livelihoods; and (2) job displacement as the result of globalization.

Our account of these momentous developments is divided into two parts. Part One (Chaps. 1–3) concerns the period from the Spanish Conquest of 1521 to the Revolution of 1910. Of course, we did not set out to write a narrative history of Central Mexico. Rather, our aim is simply to depict the main features of the estate system that existed both before and after the Conquest, the nature of stratification on the haciendas that dominated the countryside for roughly four centuries, and the importance of race and ethnicity in both the estate system and the class structures that accompanied and followed it. Part Two (Chaps. 4–8) portrays the class structure of the postrevolutionary period (1920 onward), emphasizing the demise of the landed aristocracy, the formation of new upper and middle classes, the explosive growth of the urban lower classes, and the final phase of the Indian-mestizo transition (from ethnic to class stratification) in the countryside.

Chapter 1 introduces the concepts *estate* and *class*. Estates, rather than classes, were the primary hierarchical social divisions from the emergence of the world's first states about five thousand years ago until the late eighteenth century. Estates were legally defined strata, each with its own rights, privileges, and duties and each associated with particular occupations. The basic estates were nobility and commonalty, but finer distinctions were usually present also. Estate membership was typically hereditary, in the sense of a lifelong identity ascribed at birth, and ambiguities of assignment were minimized by estate endogamy, or marriage within one's birth stratum. Estate stratification provided the dominant social framework for both Spain and the Aztec Empire in 1521, the time of the Spanish Conquest of Central Mexico. Classes can be distinguished within major estates, but classes did not become the major building blocks of national societies until the overthrow of estate-based legal systems. In Europe, the French Revolution of 1789 is usually seen as the watershed in this regard. In Mexico, the corresponding date is 1822, the year following the overthrow of Spanish colonial rule.

That the classes of class-based societies are not legally defined has important ramifications for both the members of these societies and the social scientists studying them. For the former, social mobility is now possible to an extent that would have been unimaginable in estate-based polities. Thus, upward social (class) mobility is a major life goal of many individuals and families, and the fear of downward mobility is always present. For the social scientist, the legal indeterminacy and social mobility of class-based societies means that there is no "fixed" definition of the basic stratificational unit, the class or set of classes.

Chapter 1 lays out some tools for conceptualizing this complexity, the most important being the distinction between *real* and *nominal* classes. Real classes are existential divisions recognized or acted upon by the members of the society, whereas nominal classes are strictly analytical distinctions drawn by the researcher. As we shall see, a complete analysis of present-day Central Mexico requires using both concepts.

Chapter 2 explores the factors of race and ethnicity in the stratification of Central Mexico, covering the entire five-hundred-year period. Spanish colonial society was divided into three social estates that were initially defined on the basis of physical race: Spanish conquerors-rulers, Indian commoners, and African slaves. This system's racial basis eventually created administrative chaos, as widespread interbreeding resulted in a demographic majority of mixed people who could not be assigned automatically or unambiguously to any of the original three estates.

During the 1630s or early 1640s, the colonial regime tried to rescue the estate system by creating an intermediate estate of *castas* for mixed-race people, distinguishing up to sixteen named categories. For instance, the Spanish-African mixture was called *mulato* (from *mulo*, or mule), while the mulato-Spanish combination was *morisco* (from *moro*, or Moor), and morisco-Spanish parentage resulted in a *salta atrás* (throwback). The Catholic Church was required to maintain separate vital registries for Spaniards, Indians, and castas, but even this new classification system was soon overwhelmed by the increasingly convoluted family histories. After about 1750, many parishes effectively compressed their registries into two books, one for Indians and one for non-Indians—the two catchall census categories that are still used today. The entire estate system, along with its racial classifications, was finally abolished in 1822, following independence from Spain in 1821.

The racial and ethnic situation in Central Mexico remains complex today. First, no more than 10 percent of the present population is still classified as Indian in national censuses, and only a small fraction of 1 percent identify themselves as Afro-Mexican. Second, there is no strict correlation between social classes and either ethnicity or race at the regional or national level. At the same time, the upper social stratum is typified by light skin color and other European physical traits, and standards of beauty and physical appearance are still essentially European. Racial/ethnic discrimination remains widespread but is often very subtle. For instance, parents at all social levels typically favor their light-skinned offspring, and upwardly mobile individuals often try to accentuate their European heritage or appearance.

Chapter 3 covers the period of the hacienda's dominance over the countryside (roughly 1570–1940). Haciendas were large farms and ranches typically administered by small staffs of trusted employees (*empleados de confianza*) who managed much larger numbers of wage workers. The hacienda was the fourth of a succession of rural institutions designed to harness Indian labor for Spanish enterprises. The first was slavery, from which Indians were largely exempted (except as judicial punishment or debt indenture) in 1542. The second was the *encomienda*, a grant of Indians who owed both labor and material tribute (tax) to the Spanish grantees (*encomenderos*). The encomienda was the major mechanism of exploiting Indian labor from the 1520s to 1549, when the institution was redefined legally as requiring tribute but not labor.

To replace the labor that could no longer be recruited through the encomienda, in 1550 the colonial administration introduced the third mechanism: the *repartimiento* (lit., "division," "dividing up"). Up to 2 percent of the adult men of an Indian village were to be assigned to work on Spanish enterprises at any one time but for no more than one week continuously and no more than four (nonconsecutive) weeks per year. These restrictions quickly rendered the repartimiento inadequate, as the number of Spanish enterprises multiplied while the Indian population continued to shrink. Increasingly, *hacendados* (hacienda owners) recruited Indian laborers directly, offering them cash wages and permanent residence on the haciendas, which excused them from repartimiento duties. The repartimiento was becoming a dead letter in the countryside by 1632, when agrarian work was excluded from its purview. Thereafter, haciendas recruited their laborers through a combination of wage incentives and various types and degrees of coercion. As noted above, the hacienda system continued to dominate the countryside until the 1930s, when President Lázaro Cárdenas (1934–1940) expropriated vast amounts of hacienda land and redistributed it to peasant villagers.

Chapter 4 is devoted to the four classes of Central Mexico's upper stratum: aristocracy, plutocracy, political class, and the apex of the upper-middle class. Together, they constitute less than 1 percent of the population today (see Table 0.1). At its height the aristocracy never amounted to more than 2 to 3 percent of the national population, and its proportion had dwindled to about 0.5 percent by independence in 1821 and to a minuscule 0.25 or so on the eve of the Revolution of 1910 (Nutini 2004: 11). It is even smaller today, comprising some 750 households, or a total population of about 5,000 individuals—roughly 0.005 percent of the national population of 97.5 million and 0.01 percent of Central Mexico's 41.5 million inhabitants in 2000.

The plutocracy arose from the middle classes after the 1910–1920 Revolution, especially in the period 1920–1950. From the outset, its investments were mainly in industry, commerce, and finance rather than the agrarian enterprises that were the aristocracy's economic foundation. Map 3 shows, in fact, that there was relatively little overlap between the new plutocracy's cities of origin and those in which the old aristocracy had been based.

The plutocracy is Mexico's present ruling class. Unlike the political class, which holds elected or appointed offices and actually exercises the functions of government, the ruling class exerts a strong, often determinative, behind-the-scenes influence on both those who govern and those who obey, without holding formal political positions. Countrywide, the

TABLE 0.1
Present (2000) Social Classes of Central Mexico, by Approximate Percentage

Strata and Classes	Approximate Percentage Representation[a]	
Upper stratum[b]		< 1
Middle stratum		32–40
upper middle	ca. 2	
solid middle	10–15	
lower middle	20–25	
Lower stratum		55–65
working class	30–35	
marginal class	25–30	

[a] Adapted from Nutini 2004, 2005.
[b] No meaningful percentage breakdown can be provided for the four components of the upper stratum, each of which constitutes far less than one percent of the total population. The four components are aristocracy, plutocracy, political class, and prestige-UMC.

plutocracy numbered about 2,000 households, or some 13,000 to 14,000 individuals, in 2000 (Nutini 2004: 44–49). Most of the country's wealthiest plutocrats have their main residences and/or principal investments in Central Mexico, especially in Mexico City.

The political class consists of present and former political officeholders, and the most influential members of this class have held high federal offices in Mexico City. The political class has always been small, comprising about 1,500 households (perhaps 7,000 to 10,000 individuals) at any time. From 1929 until 2000, they were almost entirely affiliated with the Partido Revolucionario Institucional (PRI), which was so dominant that it was widely referred to as the "official party" during that period.

The smallest component of the upper stratum is the apex of the upper-middle class, which we call the prestige-UMC. Before the Revolution of 1910, these elite families provided social support to the aristocracy, principally by swelling the number of guests in attendance at aristocratic social functions. Although wealthy and prominent in their own right, these families had neither the aristocracy's huge wealth nor its distinguished ancestry. Nevertheless, through long association with the aristocracy, the prestige-UMC assimilated a large proportion of its refined manners, tastes, and behavior. When the aristocracy fled the provincial cities after the Revolution, the prestige-UMC became the local upper class and served as the model for upwardly mobile provincial families, including the nascent provincial plutocracy.

Chapter 5 discusses the middle stratum, in which we distinguish three classes: upper middle (excluding the prestige-UMC), solid middle, and lower middle. We analyze each according to phenotype (observable "racial" traits), occupation, income, housing, formal education, kinship organization, *compadrazgo* (ritual kinship), class consciousness, and religiosity. Here, we comment only on the first three aspects, as our aim is simply to provide some initial guidance.

Members of the upper-middle class consider themselves and are generally regarded by others as "white," although the class includes some individuals of light mestizo appearance ("mixed," showing some Indian and/or African ancestry) and about 5 percent with dark mestizo features. The solid-middle class presents the obverse phenotypic profile: predominantly mestizo, usually light skinned but including many individuals with noticeable Indian/African or European phenotypes. The lower-middle class, like the adjacent working class in the lower stratum, is overwhelmingly mestizo, and many of its members have very prominent Indian and/or African features. There are also a few *criollos* (very light-skinned mestizos) and a sprinkling of individuals with a fully European physical appearance in these two classes. Thus, while there is a very striking increase in the proportion of European features as one goes up the social class scale in Central Mexico, there is sufficient variation within each class to prevent "race" (phenotypic perceptions) from playing a determinant role in interclass relations.

Among the upper-middle class are many business owners and (in provincial cities) farmers, as well as top-ranking professionals (primarily lawyers, physicians, accountants, and engineers). The solid-middle class is more varied in terms of occupation. It includes many professionals (mostly physicians, lawyers, engineers, architects, dentists, accountants, and agronomists), owners of medium-sized businesses and farms, middle-level bank officials, and well-placed government bureaucrats. The lower-middle class includes some relatively well paid blue-collar workers,

MAP 3. Mexico's Major Hacendado Cities (ca. 1910) and Plutocratic Centers (1920s–1940s)

especially independent tradesmen (e.g., electricians, mechanics, plumbers) and those holding unionized factory jobs, but it consists mainly of white-collar workers (e.g., teachers, nurses, store clerks, office workers) and owners of small businesses. The latter are a mixture of white-collar and blue-collar workers, actually, as they typically work actively in their own service-oriented enterprises, such as small retail outlets, bars, butcher shops, bakeries, beauty salons and barbershops, tanneries, upholstery shops, and parts and repair shops (automotive, hydraulic, agricultural).

In provincial cities, the upper-middle class has an annual disposable household income of U.S.$100,000 to $200,000 (in 2000 dollars); in Mexico City, the range peaks at about U.S.$300,000. Solid-middle-class income ranges from about U.S.$150,000 annually to as low as U.S.$15,000. In the lower-middle class, two trends are readily evident. First, its most affluent members are business owners, whose 2002 incomes in the Córdoba, Veracruz, area were in the U.S.$7,800 to $36,000 range (see Nutini 2005). Second, this class's blue-collar workers often earn more than its white-collar employees. For instance, schoolteachers earned about U.S.$2,250 to $5,000 and shop clerks around U.S.$1,050 to $1,800 in the

Córdoba area in 2002, while independent tradesmen netted U.S.$4,200 to $6,600 and unionized factory workers made about U.S.$3,800 to $7,200 (Nutini 2005).

Chapter 6 covers the urban lower classes. Mexico's population has been predominantly urban and nonagricultural since the late 1960s. The majority of this urban population belongs to the lower stratum, in which we distinguish two classes: a working class and a marginal class (see Table 0.1). Generally, the working class holds relatively steady, blue-collar jobs in the formal economy, while the marginal class's employment is sporadic and/or in the informal (unlicensed, untaxed) economy. Many members of the marginal class are periodically self-employed service providers (plumbers, carpenters, masons, etc.) or street vendors, while many others (especially women) are home-based pieceworkers for the garment, toy, plastics, electronics, and other industries.

There is a great deal of movement of people between these types of employment and much fluidity of membership between the two lower classes, making generalizations difficult. Not only might today's wage-working shop laborer be tomorrow's self-employed street vendor, or vice versa, but different members of the same household may be engaged in quite different modes of livelihood. What is indisputable, though, is that the hallmark of the urban lower classes is their poverty. Accordingly, much of Chapter 6 is devoted to a discussion of the origins, persistence, and measurement of urban poverty, as well as the survival strategies that enable the masses of poor people to cope with their precarious economic situation.

Chapter 7 concerns the most profound cultural, ethnic, and stratificational transformation in twentieth-century Mexico: the Indian-mestizo transition in the countryside and provincial towns. (In this context, *mestizo*—from *mestizar*, "to mix"—denotes Mexico's dominant culture.) This ongoing transition involves the final breakdown of vestigial estate stratification rooted in colonial-era ethnic relations and its replacement by social class stratification along national lines. It also entails a nationalization of identity, from traditional Indian villager to modern Mexican (or regional) citizen. Ethnic self-awareness has not disappeared, of course; in fact, it is often revitalized in reconfigured form in response to regional or national political agendas. Nevertheless, for millions of people who formerly made economic, political, religious, and lifestyle choices primarily within the framework of village-Indian identity, social participation in general has become mainly a matter of class and geography, not ethnicity.

The cultural transformation that lay at the very heart of the Indian-mestizo transition was and is more complex. Of course, it involved such readily observable changes as the adoption of contemporary national-urban clothing, housing, furniture, tools, machinery, occupations, and so on, and the acquisition of some degree of fluency in Spanish. More important, though, it entailed the demise of most of that syncretic amalgam of Spanish, indigenous, and African elements that emerged during the seventeenth century as "Indian" culture and then persisted, albeit with constant adaptations, through much of the twentieth century. A crucial element of this transformation was the change from a deeply sacred to a much more secular approach to life.

Chapter 8 features an aspect of social stratification that has received all too little attention. We refer to this as *expressive culture* (or behavior), or simply *expression*. The defining quality of expression is that its motivation is basically noninstrumental, or nonutilitarian. A universal of human culture, it is readily observable in such domains as art, music, play, games, manners, etiquette, dress, and adornment, although it can be part of virtually any type of behavior or aspect of culture. For instance, it often colors such utilitarian arenas as religion, economics, warfare, and politics, and it also serves as an important boundary marker for social groups (e.g., clubs, lodges, sports teams, schools) and social strata (whether castes, estates, or classes).

In fact, expression is the aspect of social stratification that is most immediately and directly perceived, and it is the primary way in which the members of a social stratum initially recognize one another and, in turn, are recognized as distinctive by nonmembers. More generally, all social groups have expressive arrays, which they share to greater or lesser extents with other such groups. This is true of both real and nominal social classes, although for real classes the arrays are more distinctive, because some parts of them serve as social boundary markers.

Historically, and even as recently as the early to mid-twentieth century, the most elaborate arrays of expressive culture in Central Mexico occurred at the very top and the very bottom of the rural stratification system—among aristocratic hacendados and traditional Indian villagers. The aristocratic expressive array was most elaborate in household accoutrements and skills and in leisure activities, whereas the traditional Indian array was focused on religion. As we point out in Chapter 7, mestizoization of village Indians reduces or even destroys much of their distinctive expressive culture, and much of what remains is highly secularized, even commercialized, and often trivialized as "old-fashioned customs." In Chapters 3 and 8, we note that the elaborate aristocratic expressive array also is fading, along with the demise of the traditional aristocracy and its supportive partner, the prestige-UMC.

The entire Mexican stratification system is rapidly evolving. The traditional system, in which expressive factors were highly significant in social class formation and boundary maintenance, is giving way to an emerging system in which structural factors such as power, wealth, formal education credentials, and occupation are the main determinants of class membership. At the very top, the traditional expressive refinements have been trumped by materialistic conspicuous consumption—everything from ostentatious mansions to private airplanes and the latest sound and visual equipment—requiring an annual disposable income of at least U.S.$1 million. At the very bottom of the national system, traditional village Indians have largely adopted the culture of the national lower classes, and even the formerly pronounced rural rusticity, which was still quite noticeable at midcentury, has largely disappeared.

The Conclusion focuses on two aspects of the present stratification system of Central Mexico. The first is its increasing "classlessness." This term, which apparently was first used with reference to the United States, is not as radical as it might appear at first blush. Basically, it refers to the replacement of real classes by nominal classes in postindustrial societies. The "mass" aspects of these societies—mass formal education, mass production, mass communications, mass geographic mobility—and substantial social mobility have led to an unprecedented extent of cultural blending that buffs out the once-visible boundaries of classes, regions, and adjoining countries.

The second topic is the persistence of a lower-stratum majority or, stated negatively, the failure of the great Mexican Revolution (1910–1920) and subsequent governmental efforts to produce the middle-class majority envisioned by social philosophers and visionary politicians. We discuss the main causes of the persistence of this situation through the end of the twentieth century, as well as some of the early-twenty-first-century forces that will almost certainly ensure its continuation into the foreseeable future.

PART ONE

Historical Overview

one: ESTATES AND CLASSES

Only during the past two hundred years or so have social classes been the major social building blocks of national societies. Earlier societies such as the Aztec Empire and those of western Europe, were divided mainly into hereditary estates. In such societies, classes were distinguishable only within the estate framework.

The Concept of Class

The term *class* has no single, standardized usage in everyday speech or in the social science literature (see Crompton and Scott 2000; Perrucci and Wysong 2003: 6; Whiteford 1960: 21 f.). Nevertheless, there is general agreement that classes are relatively fluid aggregates, with membership that is not strictly inherited. Within that framework, any particular society can be analyzed into different kinds or numbers of classes, according to the analyst's purpose or focus. For example, we might wish to distinguish *real classes*, that is, social groupings that have identifiable real-world consequences in terms of self-identity ("class consciousness") and concerted action. A different approach would distinguish *nominal classes*, which are social divisions designated by the researcher to facilitate analysis; the members of the society being studied either do not recognize these divisions or regard them as general or vague social categories only, not as units of self-identity or social action (Portes 2003).

In this book, we distinguish a combination of real and nominal classes. We present our full rationale for doing so in the Conclusion. For the moment, two guidelines will suffice. First, real classes are readily evident today in the upper stratum of Central Mexico but not, for the most part, in the middle and lower strata. Second, while nominal classes are analytical rather than existential units, they cannot be delineated willy-nilly if they are to be useful for social analysis. Rather, they must be grounded in real-world data and based on a combination (correlation) of two or more variables. In this regard, we follow Pitirim Sorokin's pioneering formulation of social classes as "multibonded"—based on two or more sociocultural dimensions—to distinguish them from "unibonded" groupings such as clubs, unions, political parties, and occupational associations (Sorokin 1947: 271 ff.; also see Stern 1994: 424n).

Another fundamental distinction in the study of social class is that between objective and subjective approaches. Most U.S. and Mexican sociologists employ the objective, or structural, approach. Using individuals (often, only men) as the units of analysis, they typically emphasize occupation, income, and/or wealth as class indicators. Such studies have been popular for several decades, largely because the data for them can be gathered rapidly through surveys (often using mailed questionnaires or published census data) and then quantified easily.

In our view, the objective-structural approach is often unsatisfactory, even sterile, when used alone. First, it yields little or no insight into class formation, change, or persistence. Second, its reliance on surveys using structural variables (e.g., occupation, income, measurable wealth) can easily minimize such important social segments as the intermittently unemployed or workers in the underground economy; for that matter, Mexico's relatively impoverished aristocrats, short on wealth but long on prestigious heritage, would be difficult to place meaningfully through such an approach. Third, because its unit of data gathering and analysis is the individual, the objective-structural approach is at best an awkward tool for dealing with the family or household—the basic social matrix that structures daily living and enculturates children—of contemporary societies. In an approach focused on individuals, how do we decide the social class placement of a household formed around a surgeon and a teacher? or a teacher and a janitor? or a lawyer and her plumber husband (Crompton 2000)?

Fourth, while the structural-objective approach is useful for delineating nominal classes, its inherent methodological individualism does not equip it to uncover real classes, where they indeed exist, or to illuminate their historical significance. As Olivé Negrete and Barba de Piña Chan

(1960: 176) have pointed out with reference to the Mexican Revolution of 1910–1920, one will look in vain for a historical role for the usual nominalist divisions (e.g., an upper-lower or a lower-middle class) based on statistical compilation, "whereas it is easy to establish the role of [such real classes as] the working class, the peasantry, the bourgeoisie [large capitalists], the petite bourgeoisie, [and] large landowners" in that great historical transformation.

We see ourselves as working mainly in a different tradition, one that harkens back to the pioneering work of the anthropologist William Lloyd Warner (1960, 1963). This is an approach that recognizes the importance of objective-structural factors but also emphasizes subjective, or behavioral-ideational, factors such as expressive (nonutilitarian) behavior, family heritage, ritual, symbolism, worldview, prestige seeking, and community ranking. Warner's approach foreshadowed the present-day interest in consumption as an important aspect of social rankings of all types. In his words, "products are not only items of utility for those who buy [them] but powerful symbols of status and social class" (Warner 1960: vii). Not just wealth, income, or consumption but "the 'right' kind of house, the 'right' neighborhood, the 'right' furniture, the proper behavior" (Warner 1960: 23) are crucial to a household's social class placement.

As noted above, we advocate combining the objective and subjective approaches (also see Nutini 2004, 2005). The former is useful for delineating nominal macro-aggregates that provide the researcher with a way to depict community or national patterns (Portes 2003), whereas the latter is essential for locating and describing real classes, as well as for depicting the lifestyle differences among nominal classes (see Chaps. 5–8).

The number of classes in a given community or nation is always established by the researcher and can vary according to the problem at hand. This point is most readily apparent at the level of nominal macro-aggregates, where we find wide disparities among researchers. With reference to the United States, for example, Gilbert and Kahl (1987: 326–337) distinguish six classes (capitalist, upper-middle, middle, working, working poor, underclass), whereas Perrucci and Wysong (2003: 27–38) insist that there are only two (privileged and working-class), although they distinguish additional "segments" therein. Even the number of real classes, though, may vary. For instance, the present-day upper stratum of Central Mexico can be characterized as consisting either of four real classes (aristocracy, plutocracy, political class, and upper-middle-class elite) or of three (ruling, political, and prestige), depending on the problem under investigation (see Aron 1966).

Estate Stratification

Estates are legally defined strata, each associated with particular occupations and each having its own enforceable (as well as customary) rights, privileges, and duties. Estate membership is typically inherited—ascribed, in sociological parlance—although there can be considerable mobility within the major estates and subestates, as explained below. Marriage is largely endogamous. Estates are unequal before the law, and the superordinate (top-ranked) estate or subestates typically exercise legal jurisdiction over their own members. Present-day U.S. and Mexican military courts that exercise legal jurisdiction over military personnel, determining punishments for their crimes and infractions of rules, are vestiges of the medieval European estate system. Similarly, the ecclesiastical courts of the Catholic Church once had jurisdiction over all members of the clergy. Though now stripped of their powers over criminal matters in both countries, they continue to adjudicate infractions of Church law.

The basic building blocks of estate stratification are the nobility and the commonalty. Where military conquest initially imposes an estate system or replaces an existing one, almost all the conquered people—except for some of the nobility—are compressed into a new commonalty, regardless of their previous placement. This is precisely what happened in Central Mexico after the Spanish Conquest. In time, though, an enduring estate system will develop intermediate strata, usually called petite estates. In western Europe, for instance, the knightly orders and the clergy came to constitute intermediate estates.

WESTERN EUROPE

Western Europe's two great estates, nobility and commonalty, became internally differentiated through time. Nobles, who accounted for no more than about 10 percent of the total population (Nutini 1995: 378–379), were basically rentiers living off landed property worked by commoners, but some of them also participated in the military and priestly petite estates or held governmental offices. The noble estate became divided into higher and lower nobility (peerage and gentry), as well as a complex series of ranks conferred by hereditary title (from duke to knight). All of them held certain legal privileges in the economic and political realms, although the lower nobility were less favored in this regard.

Commoners were mainly subsistence cultivators, whether as bound tenants (serfs or villeins) on nobles' lands or as freeholders (peasants). The commonalty was not an undifferentiated bloc, however. There were also growing numbers of specialists (some full-time) such as landless farm laborers, urban wage workers or pieceworkers, blacksmiths, potters, petty traders, millers, herders, brewers, vintners, cobblers, diviners, clerks, and scribes. Below, we take up the question of how to typify this internal diversity.

At the bottom were slaves. Although agrarian slavery had vanished from rural Spain nearly five hundred years before the conquest of Central Mexico, slavery continued in all the major Spanish cities during the first half of the sixteenth century (Bonnassie 1991: 101–108, 217, 320; Martín Casares 2000: 26–28, 143). Mostly North African "Berbers" captured in slave raids, West Africans purchased from slave traders, and moriscos (Arab-Spaniards) charged with subversion or heresy, slaves constituted perhaps 1 to 2 percent of the population in most cities (Martín Casares 2000: 15, 115). They were mainly employed in textile and hide production, food preparation, petty commerce, a wide range of artisanry (e.g., smithing, candle making), and household service for nobles (301–319).

Noble privileges in most of sixteenth-century western Europe included tax exemption, exclusive right of landownership, trading concessions, the right to hunt and fish on public land, the right of political participation and officeholding, and the right to bear arms, as well as honorific privileges (e.g., titles, coats of arms, and forms of address such as "mister" or "don"), exclusive right to luxurious dress, and exclusive or preferential access to military orders, the clergy, and universities. In Spain, noble privileges also included exemptions from judicial torture (except in extreme cases, such as subversion), whipping or condemnation to hard labor, drowning as capital punishment (decapitation being substituted), debtors' prison (except for debts to the crown), and legal confiscation of personal weapons, clothing, horses, and homes (Domínguez Ortiz 1973: 40–41). As landowners, European nobles enjoyed such seigneurial privileges as labor services and private taxes from the resident commoners within their lands or districts, as well as legal jurisdiction over them, monopoly of certain commercial activities (usually brewing, winemaking, and mining), and rights of preeminence in public gatherings (e.g., front-row church pews and the lead in processions) (see Nutini 1995: 118–119).

THE AZTEC EMPIRE

Like western European societies, Aztec society was divided basically into two hereditary, mostly endogamous estates: nobility and commonalty (Hicks 1999; Berdan 1982: 45–55). Estimates of the size of the Aztec nobility range from 5 to 17 percent of the total population (Hicks 1999: 419). By birthright, nobles (but rarely noble women) monopolized the upper levels of government, the military, and the clergy, although some commoners (again, men) achieved the lower ranks of all three of these sectors.

Aztec nobles did not have the monopoly on landownership enjoyed by their western European counterparts, but the higher nobility had large hereditary landholdings and exercised juridical authority over the resident commoners (*mayeque*; sing. *maye*), perhaps equivalent to the European feudal system (Berdan 1982: 59–60; but also see Lockhart 1992: 97–99). The lesser nobility—families not in the direct line of city-state rulership—had smaller landholdings and fewer subordinate commoners, and there were some relatively poor nobles "who worked their own fields with the help only of a son or an in-law and who had authority over only a handful of commoner families" (Hicks 1999: 410–411). Lesser nobles also served in the lower rungs of local government. Higher and lesser nobles were tried in separate courts, as were the various ranks of soldiers, government officials, and the commonalty (Durán 1994: 192–193).

By law, the nobility enjoyed sumptuary privileges—rights to certain luxury goods or exclusive behaviors—denied to commoners, typically on pain of death. For instance, only nobles could wear cotton clothing and certain adornments (woven designs, gold jewelry, precious stones, and certain flowers and feathers), own two-story houses, wear gilded sandals within the great cities, or enter the interior rooms of the royal palace (Durán 1994: 208–211). Male nobles also had privileged access to the temple schools that taught the fields of knowledge necessary for entrance or success in the higher tiers of government, the military, or the priesthood: reading and writing, rhetoric, religion and philosophy, history, governance, and martial arts (tactics and elite weaponry) (Berdan 1982: 88–90; Smith 1998: 137–138).

Aztec commoners were mainly free peasants and the serf-like mayeque who cultivated small plots of land in which they held hereditary rights based on kinship or long-term residence. Sometimes they supplemented farming with part-time work as artisans (e.g., potters, carpenters, mat makers, weavers), specialized laborers (e.g., porters, salt makers, mineral lime makers), or providers of services (e.g., midwives, sorcerers, diviners, marketplace traders) in the local economy (Berdan 1982: 34–35). There was also an undetermined but probably small number of full-time commoner specialists in some of these occupations. Both commoner and noble women also typically worked part-time at spinning maguey or cotton thread and weaving it into cloth with which to make clothing (maguey for commoners, cotton for nobles). In addition, commoner women spun thread from cotton or maguey, sometimes issued to them by the state, as part of their households' tax obligation.

A few commoner boys were nominated to attend noble temple schools, enabling them to become priests. A much larger number of commoner men served in the lower rungs of local government as messengers, overseers, neighborhood heads, and the like. According to Durán, "[The Aztec] nation had a special functionary for every activity. . . . There were even officials in charge of sweeping" (1994: 309; also see Berdan 1982: 103–104). These official functions were too numerous and often too humble to be staffed by the empire's small number of nobles.

At the bottom of the commonalty were a relatively small number of slaves. Overwhelmingly, they were urban, rather than rural, and worked in household service; very few worked in agriculture or other types of production, although slave women—like other Aztec women—were spinners and weavers. Many of the people who are referred to as slaves in the literature were in fact indentured commoners working off a debt or loan (having pawned themselves), or they were criminals making restitution for petty crimes against those who were now their masters. Others, though, had been purchased by professional merchants in foreign slave markets and resold within the empire; a few entered these markets as punishment for serious crimes. Apparently, none of the male slaves originated as soldiers captured in battle; instead, male captives were sacrificed to the gods. In contrast, women and children captured in battle became slaves, but they were not the usual targets of capture (Berdan 1982: 46, 61–63; Shadow and Rodríguez 1995). It would be possible to regard slaves as constituting a separate petite estate, but we have chosen to include them among commoners because their slave status was not hereditary and because they were relatively few in number, overwhelmingly commoners in origin, and often in only temporary bondage (pawn, indenture).

Between the two Aztec great estates, nobility and commonalty, there were three important petite estates: professional merchants, elite artisans (feather weavers, gold- and silversmiths, precious-stone workers), and distinguished soldiers. The first two belonged to hereditary guilds that enjoyed some of the legal privileges otherwise reserved for nobility, such as their own courts, insignia, right to human sacrifice, and exclusive residential areas (Berdan 1982: 26–33; 1986: 283–288). Neither the merchants nor the artisans were nobles, but neither were they were like ordinary commoners. Both were closely identified with the nobility. The merchants dealt in noble sumptuary goods and the raw materials for making them (e.g., gold, jade, tropical feathers), which they obtained outside of the empire, that is, from beyond the reach of the tax system. They resold these goods and materials in marketplaces, for purchase by nobles and elite artisans or by commoners who were taxed in terms of these items. When operating beyond the frontiers, merchants occasionally traded in the name of the Aztec king, sometimes with goods provided by him, and also served as his spies and explorers (Isaac 1986: 331–338). The luxury artisans made their sumptuous goods exclusively for the nobility, either on commission or through sale in marketplaces (Brumfiel 1987).

The third petite estate, distinguished soldiers who had captured at least four enemies on the battlefield, was organized into three sodalities, each of which was internally graded (with distinctive insignia and dress) to allow further advancement through military distinction (Berdan 1982: 64–65). Although membership was open to all soldiers who took at least four prisoners, nobles had a much better chance of achieving this goal because they alone did the front-line, hand-to-hand combat that presented the best opportunities for making a capture. Men who advanced within the sodalities, whether nobles or commoners, could be elevated to military command positions or even to high civil office, such as judge. The distinguished commoners could not become nobles, however, no matter how brilliant their military or civil performance (65).

Class Stratification

In contrast to estates, classes are not legally defined as distinctive social bodies, even where they sharply divide the society. Indeed, the hallmark of class stratification is official (de jure) legal equality throughout the polity—even if certain ethnic, racial, or economic segments continue to be denied full equality in local practice (de facto). It follows that a class system allows much greater social mobility, as there are no official legal barriers to overcome or formal permissions necessary for the transition.

At the same time, classes and estates share two important traits: a high degree of endogamy and a strong correlation with particular occupations. The first is relatively easy to explain. Majority endogamy continues in class systems, which have no legal prescription for it, because most individuals (and their parents) prefer marriage to people who are like themselves. Indeed, those are the people they are most likely to know well.

The long-term association of particular classes and particular occupations requires a bit more explanation. In the preindustrial era, training for adult occupations began early, within the birth household and/or through apprenticeship, because all jobs that would render a living had high skill requirements. This was as true of farming as of other occupations, as the tiller needed in-depth edaphic, climatic, botanical, and other knowledge to produce crops reliably. Even something as seemingly simple as crop storage required finely honed skills and judgment: grain or hay stored before its moisture content had dropped sufficiently either molded (becoming poisonous in some cases) or was at risk of spontaneous combustion. Nonfarming occupations had to be learned through childhood apprenticeship, which could last up to twelve years (Epstein 1991: 142; Santiago Cruz 1960: 29), because product quality and quantity were both determined by the skilled hand and trained eye of the producer.

At first blush, it is surprising that a correlation between class and occupation has persisted even after the extensive deskilling and reskilling of all kinds of work as the result of the industrial revolution of the early nineteenth century and the cybernetic revolution of the late twentieth century. On reflection, though, it is apparent that the class-occupation linkage remains strong because barriers to, as well as opportunities for, entry to certain kinds of work continue to be set through education in the fullest sense—from informal enculturation in the home to the extent, kind, and locale of formal training or schooling. Education in this broad sense determines the individual's type and level of *cultural capital*—his or her effective fund of knowledge, skills, and adaptive attitudes—that can be expected to open certain social doors but, typically, not others (after Bourdieu 1973; Bourdieu and Passeron 1990).

Familial and formal education are closely and causally related, of course: familial enculturation includes the role models presented to the child in the form of parental occupations, which in turn strongly influence parental financial ability and willingness to provide certain forms or extents of formal preparation for adulthood. In both the United States and Mexico today, for instance, young people with university degrees (baccalaureate, or *licenciatura*) typically face far different occupational prospects than do their age peers who lack such credentials or who did not finish high school, or *preparatoria*. Attaining a postgraduate credential (master's degree or Ph.D.) usually greatly magnifies the difference. Even in Mexico, where university tuition and fees are very low, attending college usually means reduced income in the present to meet the ongoing cost of living—which is why family (especially parental) financial support greatly enhances the possibilities of graduation.

Furthermore, there is a significant difference in both the necessary financial outlay and the eventual occupational payoff for students who can attend a prestigious and costly private university (such as the Universidad Iberoamericana or Harvard) and those who can attend only the lesser state or municipal institutions (see Jiménez G. and Márquez R. 2003; Nutini 2005; Perrucci and Wysong 2003: 207–237). Students with few financial resources often have no choice but to attend the latter in order to reduce their expenses by continuing to live at home, even if they qualify for admission to a private university or a more prestigious public institution in a distant city.

Wealthier students reap two advantages by earning credentials from more prestigious institutions, apart from the supposed or actual superiority of the instruction they receive. First, they have access to more lucrative or exclusive employment opportunities and, usually, higher earnings. Second, prestigious universities enable them to establish friendships and build social networks among both peers and professors who are similarly or better placed economically and politically. In other words, their very attendance at prestigious institutions virtually ensures a significant increase in their *social* capital (after Bourdieu 1973; Bourdieu and Passeron 1990).

Classes within Estates

We are now prepared to discuss the internal divisions within the great estates of both medieval western Europe and the Aztec Empire of Central Mexico on the eve of the Spanish Conquest. Wrestling with this question enables a deeper understanding of both estates and classes as modes of stratification. We will deal first with the Aztec case, for which Hicks (1999) provides a penetrating analysis.

THE AZTEC EMPIRE

Hicks (1999) distinguishes upper, middle, and lower classes that crosscut the Aztec great estates that were the principal units of the stratification system. We should emphasize two points at the outset. First, in saying that these classes crosscut the estate system, we mean that the middle class, for instance, is intermediate between the upper and lower classes—not between the great estates. Second, in contrast to the grand and petite estates, about which the Aztecs were loquacious (see Sahagún 1979), Hicks' classes are nominal, researcher-designated divisions that almost certainly were not real or otherwise meaningful units to the Aztecs themselves. Nevertheless, they are very useful for understanding the dynamics of Aztec stratification.

The Aztec upper class (probably all nobles) would have been very small, because "in no stratified society does it amount to more than one or two percent of the population" (Hicks 1999: 411). The Aztec middle class would have comprised 12 to 18 percent of the Central Highlands population—"small when compared to the more prosperous countries in the world today, but in line with estimates for preindustrial states" (419). Combining these figures for the upper and middle classes leaves some 80 to 86 percent of the Aztec population, mainly peasants, in the lower class. In addition to peasants, the lower class would have contained a minority of nonagricultural specialists—diviners, healers, artisans who produced commoner goods (such as mats, pottery, and stone tools), marketplace vendors, and the like—many of whom probably performed their specialties part-time. All members of the lower class were commoners, but some commoners were not members of the lower class.

Hicks (423) argues that "there is always a middle class in any system of . . . stratification, because an upper class cannot get along without it." This is so because the middle class performs specialized duties and produces prestige goods that the upper class is either unable or unwilling to provide for itself. In the Aztec case, the largest component of the middle class "was probably a sort of generic 'nobles' of modest resources, the lesser political officials" (419)—neighborhood heads, public works supervisors, tax collectors, local magistrates, warehouse accountants, and the like (414). Many commoners also performed these roles, however, and the commoner "steward" who stood between lord and peasant "is almost the quintessence of all that is middle class." He allowed his upper-class lord to maintain a suitable social distance from his lower-class workers and spared him "the drudgery of dealing personally with each of the households subordinate to him" (414).

The middle class also included the petite estates of elite artisans and merchants, as well as nonelite provincial merchants and marketplace traders and all the woodcarvers, potters, and painters (including manuscript writers) who produced sumptuary goods for the nobility (415). The priests who officiated at small-town or minor temples or who served as schoolteachers "most likely were of middle-class status," as were some diviners and astrologers "who were consulted for all sorts of undertakings" (417). Other diviners apparently were in the lower class and served their peers, perhaps part-time; midwives seem to have been similarly split between the middle and lower classes (418). Finally, the middle class included the petite estate of distinguished soldiers (418–419), some of whom were of lower-class, commoner origin.

WESTERN EUROPE

For medieval western Europe, we lack a similarly detailed account of nominal classes that crosscut the grand estates but are confident that the basic outlines would be similar in both proportion and composition to what Hicks (1999) provides for the Aztec Empire. The western European upper class, located within the noble estate, would have comprised 1 to 2 percent of the total population, while a lower class of commoners constituted 80 to 85 percent, leaving 15 to 20 percent of the population in the middle class. As in the Aztec case, the middle class would include the lesser nobles who, along with distinguished commoners, served as stewards and low-level political functionaries (see Nutini 1995: 9–17, 362–366). Also in the middle class would be the members of the military petite estate, the bourgeoisie (large merchants, small-scale traders, artisans and manufacturers, and other urban specialists), and the lower ranks of the priesthood.

The most dynamic of the upper-class components was the bourgeoisie. It did not emerge from the commoner estate as a distinctive middle-class entity until the late 1400s, but by the late 1700s it had given rise to western Europe's first self-conscious real class—the *haute bourgeoisie*, or plutocracy (Nutini 1995: 97, 363). In less than three hundred years, this class would become the overwhelmingly dominant upper-class component in both continental Europe and Mexico.

The members of medieval western Europe's upper class (a segment of the upper nobility) sorted and resorted themselves into relatively fluid groupings that we can characterize (after Aron 1966) as the political class (holders of important public office), the ruling class (powerful families who strongly influenced politics but did not hold political office), and the prestige class (exalted aristocrats who set the standards of elite fashion, taste, and behavior). Although all three classes were drawn from the same social pool (the noble great estate), the political and prestige classes were easily identifiable for the duration of the estate system; the ruling class was more difficult to define precisely, because its membership often was altered by social mobility and because it overlapped with the prestige class. Once the estate system was replaced by class stratification, the ruling and political classes became harder to differentiate, as their membership became much more fluid as well as overlapping. Furthermore, both classes tended to merge with the haute bourgeoisie/plutocracy, which eventually displaced the old aristocratic prestige class as well (Nutini 1995: 121–136; 2004: 8–15).

The lower class would have included the great bulk of the commonalty, which was mainly agrarian. Often simply called "the peasantry," the agricultural population was actually internally diverse. *Class* seems an inappropriate term for characterizing this diversity, though, because the main distinctions reflected degrees of political freedom or political bondage involving service to the powerful lords who held ultimate title to agrarian real estate. We refer to the free cultivators (not legally bound to remain or serve), the villeins (loosely bound in contractual tenure for service), and the serfs (totally bound, unable to leave without the lord's permission, which—even if granted—required cash payment). Given their legal foundation, these three lower-class components are best characterized as agrarian subestates of the commonalty. The lower class also would have contained a minority component of such part- or full-time specialists as diviners, healers, midwives, potters, cobblers, and marketplace traders.

COMPARISON

In both medieval western Europe and the Aztec Empire, the upper class was drawn from the noble estate, and the lower class was part of the commoner estate. Membership in either was ascribed according to birth, but upper-class membership was also in part achieved, in the sense that neither entry nor permanence was automatic. The Aztec upper class, like its counterpart in western Europe, probably contained distinctive political and ruling classes, but we are not certain that a separate Aztec prestige class existed. In both cases, the middle class had members from both of the great estates and, probably, a preponderance of lower nobles, and it served the interests of the upper class and provided "a buffer shielding it from the much more numerous lower class" (Hicks 1999: 423).

Finally, we should reissue a caveat with regard to the classes we have delineated in both western Europe and the Aztec Empire. So long as estates were the basic societal building blocks, the three large classes (upper, middle, lower) we have discussed are purely nominal, researcher-determined aggregates. Only the political, ruling, and prestige classes we distinguished within the upper class of western Europe—and, potentially, in Aztec society—would have been existential or social-action bodies (i.e., real classes). For all but the minuscule upper class, the existential units of social stratification would have been the grand and petite estates.

Class Formation, Persistence, and Demise

We shall now draw together several threads that run through this chapter by looking briefly at the social and cultural forces that give rise to real classes and determine their persistence or demise. We exclude nominal classes here because their origin is not problematic; they are generated by researchers, not by forces inherent in the sociocultural matrix.

Earlier, we argued against the temptation to delineate social classes, whether real or nominal, exclusively on the basis of structural variables. Instead, we advocated using a combination of structural and behavioral-ideational variables, these latter including expressive culture, family tradition, ritual, worldview, and the like. Nevertheless, the historical perspective employed throughout this book reveals the great importance of structural factors, especially financial wealth, in class formation and demise. Stated more formally, the *necessary condition* for the emergence and persistence of a real social class is a distinctive structural profile. The *sufficient condition*, though, is the conjunction of that structural base and a distinctive behavioral-ideational (cultural) profile.

The most important aspect of the latter profile is its expressive array, that is, its repertoire of basically noninstrumental culture/behavior. We have already introduced this concept; here, we want to add only that class-specific expression can be as subtle as manner of walking, voice inflection, speaking vocabulary, and gestures. In its entirety, the expressive repertoire is the core of the individual's class-specific cultural capital.

For all individuals, mastery of the appropriate cultural capital is required for full social acceptance within their current class. In turn, such acceptance allows individuals to expand or reinforce their social networks within the class. These networks constitute one's social capital, examples of which include the mutual-aid networks that are crucial to the survival of the very poor (see Chap. 6) and the political and financial networks that reinforce the wealth and power of the very rich (see Chap. 4).

Acquisition or mastery of the requisite cultural capital becomes increasingly expensive as one goes up the social scale. Thus, disposable wealth is a requisite for upward mobility, which requires the acquisition of at least the most readily observable portions of the target class's expressive array, such as house size and location, home furnishings, wardrobe, club memberships, and leisure activity equipment (see Chaps. 5, 8). A certain level of disposable wealth is also necessary for maintaining social standing in all but the very bottom, marginal class, and any long-term decrease in the required financial wherewithal—whether absolute or relative—eventually leads to downward mobility for individuals or even whole classes.

The necessary conjunction of structural and cultural dimensions in the formation and persistence of real classes is easily illustrated by the fate of Central Mexico's landed aristocracy during the twentieth century (see Chaps. 3, 4). In 1900, the aristocracy still enjoyed the structural requisites to constitute the regional and national ruling class, as well as the wherewithal to sport the prestigious cultural refinements that made it the prestige class that was admired and/or emulated by all other social sectors. The first blow to their exalted standing came during the 1930s and 1940s, when aristocrats lost most of their land to agrarian reform. Families who had not previously diversified their investments to include urban rental properties and commercial holdings subsequently lacked the capital to rescue themselves through large-scale investment in Mexico's expanding modern sectors (finance, manufacturing, commerce); some even scorned such nonagricultural investments, insisting that only landed wealth—which agrarian reform made impossible to amass in the requisite quantities—was a legitimate economic base for their class.

Thus, Central Mexico's aristocratic class had experienced a sharp and *absolute* decline in wealth by the mid-twentieth century. During the second half of the century, the surviving aristocrats experienced a *relative* economic decline that was even more devastating to their superordinacy, as their remaining wealth paled in comparison to the huge new fortunes accumulated by plutocrats in the financial, manufacturing, and commercial sectors from the 1940s onward. These newly rich plutocrats rapidly displaced the traditional aristocrats as the regional and national ruling class but continued to emulate them as the prestige class for several decades. By century's end, though, the aristocracy was rapidly losing even this standing, as the plutocratic expressive array came to include features that were far beyond the aristocracy's financial ability. In short, the remnant aristocracy now lacks not only the economic clout to constitute a ruling class but also the disposable income required to set the standards for upper-class culture. Accordingly, it is a dying social class, as its succeeding generations either descend into the upper-middle class or become plutocrats, whether through intermarriage or, finances permitting, by emulating plutocratic investment strategies and expressive culture.

That real classes must have distinctive cultural profiles has large implications for their future in Central Mexico, which is becoming a "mass society"—with mass communication, mass formal education, mass geographic mobility, and so on—in which cultural boundaries of all sorts are eroded and blurred. These boundaries seem to erode first in the middle and lower strata. They persist longer in the upper stratum, which is not only better equipped financially to insulate itself with a costly lifestyle but also more internally cohesive, in part because of its smaller demographic size and in part because it has high incentive to guard its political power against intrusion.

two: RACE AND ETHNICITY

The Spanish Conquest brought together three distinct populations: indigenous "Indians," Europeans, and African slaves. The region's indigenous population numbered at least three million in 1521 (Smith 1998: 62). But by 1620 introduced diseases (especially smallpox, measles, and typhus) had reduced this figure by perhaps 90 percent. In comparison, the initial European influx was minuscule. At Tenochtitlan, the Aztec capital city, Hernán Cortés commanded only about 900 Spanish soldiers alongside the "more than 150,000" Indians who volunteered from the rebelling provinces of the rapidly imploding Aztec Empire (Cortés 1971: 206–207, 249). Within a year or so, there were perhaps as many as 2,200 Spaniards in all of Mexico (Nueva España, or New Spain) and only about 7,000 by 1530. By 1600, roughly eighty years after the Conquest, Spaniards—not only *peninsulares*, those born in Spain, but also creoles, those born in New Spain—numbered 70,000 (Nutini 1995: 156–157). Many of these creoles, in fact, had Indian mothers but nevertheless were accepted as "Spanish" (Marín 1999: 172–173; Castillo 2001: 151–173; Mörner 1967: 68–70).

The Spanish colonial administration went to great lengths to institute estate stratification in New Spain. Originally, they established three great estates, with Spaniards (and a few other Europeans) at the top, the masses of Indian commoners in the middle, and slaves (both African and Indian) at the bottom. Indian nobles—especially those who cooperated with the Spaniards—occupied a petite estate between the Spaniards and the other Indians. Interbreeding soon eroded the neat boundaries of this scheme, creating ambiguities that made it increasingly difficult to administer (Mörner 1967: 68 ff.). Nevertheless, a version of it survived until Mexico's independence from Spain in 1821. In fact, the system's inherent racism motivated many men of color to join the fight against Spanish rule (1810–1821).

The Three Racial Estates of the Sixteenth Century

AFRO-MEXICANS

The African component of colonial Central Mexico has received its scholarly due only in the past twenty years, and it turns out to have been much more important than previously thought. African slaves were present from the moment of the Spanish Conquest of Central Mexico, having been brought from Cuba by the Spanish expeditions (Aguirre Beltrán 1972: 19). Importation greatly increased after 1542, when Indian slavery was largely abolished, and by 1553 there were some 20,000 African slaves in Mexico. Over roughly the next two hundred fifty years, perhaps 200,000 were imported to the colony (Vincent 2001: 277; Palmer 1976: 30).

Many of these slaves were destined for the sugarcane plantations around Córdoba and Orizaba, in the eastern part of Central Mexico, or for the silver mines in northern Mexico, but substantial numbers were also brought to the Central Highlands as industrial, commercial, agricultural, or domestic slaves (Carroll 2001; Cope 1994; Martínez Montiel 1995; Mondragón 1999; Naveda 1987; Palmer 1976; von Mentz 1999). In fact, "the urban areas received a greater proportion of slaves than the rural areas" (Palmer 1976: 45). For instance, African slaves were sold in the city of Puebla as early as 1545, and by 1574 this eminently "Spanish" city had an equal number (about 500) of Spaniards and *negros* (blacks), "as well as many mulattoes" of mixed African-Indian parentage (Paredes and Lara 1995: 34–35). In 1570 Mexico City had 11,736 (38 percent) of the 30,569 blacks in the entire colony. An undetermined number of them had been born in Mexico and were therefore Afro-Mexicans rather than Africans (Mondragón 1999:49). By 1612 the capital reportedly had some 50,000 blacks and mulatos (mainly, African-Indian mixtures), about 15,000 "Spaniards" (including creoles, some of mixed Spanish-Indian parentage), and about 80,000 Indians (Palmer 1976: 46). Assuming these figures are accurate, Mexico City's population was 34.5 percent black/mulatto and 10.3 percent "Spanish" in that year.

As noted above, the colony's "negro" category included both African- and Mexican-born persons by the mid-sixteenth century. Furthermore, this included an undetermined number of mixed-race individuals who were arbitrarily classified as "negro," rather than "mulato," and the classification was to become increasingly inconsistent and often arbitrary in the next few decades. Accordingly, we use the term *Afro-Mexicans* (after Palmer 1976)—in preference to either the Spanish *negros* or the English *Africans* or *blacks*—except in reference to slaves imported directly from Africa.

From the late 1520s onward, Afro-Mexicans were an important component of all of New Spain's urban centers (Mondragón 1999: 65), especially its two leading cities: Mexico City (formerly Tenochtitlan) and Puebla (founded by the Spaniards in 1531). These Afro-Mexicans performed a surprising number of functions. By the 1540s or earlier, the homes of rich Spaniards in Mexico City each had twenty or more resident Afro-Mexican slaves who performed every imaginable domestic service—baker, barber, butler, coachman, cook, footman, maid, page, stable hand (51 f.). Nuns from rich families even took some slave servants with them into the convents, and some priests also had such servants (65).

Apart from their utilitarian function, Afro-Mexican slaves were a component of the expressive displays of wealthy Spaniards, who often strutted about the city accompanied by their slave retinues. On these occasions, the slaves, like their owners, "would . . . wear beautiful clothing and the slave women [would wear] jewels, necklaces, armlets or wristlets"—at least until 1571, when a law prohibiting such finery to either slave or free Afro-Mexicans was enacted (Mondragón 1999: 58). Church attendance was no exception, and slave attendants were "in charge of carrying the pillow or cushion upon which the lady knelt, her prayer book and her fan" at Mass. Even within the home, slave children "had an ornate function . . . and served as a kind of pet" (65).

Urban slavery was not limited to domestic service, however. Many Afro-Mexican slaves labored in the textile (mainly wool) workshops, or *obrajes*, that began springing up in all of Central Mexico's major cities in the 1530s (Mondragón 1999: 66–67; Paredes and Lara 1995: 45–64). The importance of Afro-Mexican laborers, both slave and free, in these enterprises greatly increased after 1595, when a royal edict prohibited (but did not entirely stop) Indian employment in both obrajes and sugar mills (Viqueira and Urquiola 1990: 112–122). Urban slaves were sometimes also used in the construction of roads, bridges, churches, and public buildings; others worked for religious orders as servants in their churches, convents, monasteries, colleges, missions, and farms. There were even slaves working in the royal mint in Mexico City (Mondragón 1999: 68). Still others worked as laborers or as apprentices in urban artisan trades, although they were restricted in some guilds and closed out of others (see Carrera Stampa 1954; Santiago Cruz 1960).

Colonial Mexico always allowed for the manumission of African and Afro-Mexican slaves, and there were already freed persons residing in the present state of Puebla during the 1520s. In fact, three freedmen were among the first residents of the city of Puebla (Paredes and Lara 1995: 65). Their numbers greatly increased from about 1550 onward, to an estimated 8,000 by 1592 and 15,000 to 20,000 by 1650 (Palmer 1976: 178). Most of them were freed by provision of their masters' last wills and testaments. Other masters allowed certain slaves to purchase their freedom at an arbitrary price ranging from nominal to much above market value. There were several possible avenues for earning the requisite money (Palmer 1976: 175–177). Slaves who were rented out by their masters were entitled to a portion of their earnings. Perhaps some slaves grew vegetables for sale in gardens near their quarters. Slaves with craft skills probably sold some of the items they made. It was also possible for a slave to purchase his or her freedom by installments with money earned as a servant or laborer. Finally, in a few cases a slave's freedom was purchased by sympathetic kin or even by neighbors "who wanted to make a charitable gesture" (Palmer 1976: 175).

As Palmer (1976: 177) states, "The true measure of a society's attitude toward manumission lies in the type of slaves that were freed." Colonial Mexico did not suffer by this measure, as it always regarded freedom as a right—albeit, an earned right—for its slaves. On the negative side, though, we are confronted by three facts that prevent us from painting an overly positive picture. First, some slaves were manumitted when they became too old or infirm to be good workers (175), saving their owners the cost of their maintenance. Second, the many restrictive laws defining the Afro-Mexican estate typically made no distinction between free and slave persons. Third, the Afro-Mexican free population was overwhelmingly skewed toward women and children. One study of the free population of Mexico City in the period 1580–1650 revealed that 72 percent were women and children, and only 8 percent were men aged sixteen to thirty-five, their prime working years (176–177). Another study, covering Mexico City for the years 1576–1577, showed the Afro-Mexican free population to be not only 70 percent female but also 86 percent mulatto. These figures indicate both that slave owners largely "freed or permitted to be freed their mulatto mistresses and children" and that "Spaniards looked more favorably upon the attainment of freedom by the mulatto," who was regarded as "genetically superior to his brother of pure African descent" (178–179).

One caveat is in order regarding the "mulato" category: some of them may not have been the children of Spanish masters and slave mothers but of Afro-Mexican fathers and Indian mothers. During the 1570s, the Spanish term *mulato* could designate this latter mixture in both Puebla and Michoacán (Chávez 1995: 110; Paredes and Lara 1995: 52). In these cases, though, the free mulatto would have been freeborn, not manumitted, because children inherited slave status only from the mother—and Indians were free after the New Laws of 1542 prohibited Indian slavery.

The free Afro-Mexican population was mostly urban, with the highest concentrations in Mexico City, Puebla, and Veracruz (Palmer 1976: 178). Their occupations included domestic servant, laborer, porter, cobbler, barber, marketplace vendor, peddler, and artisan. Guild rules severely restricted their participation in the skilled trades, however. They and all other persons of mixed descent were excluded from the silkworker, gilder, painter, and schoolteacher guilds and were allowed to become journeymen (skilled laborers) but not masters (employers) in the glovemaker, press operator, hatmaker, and needlemaker guilds. Only the candlemaker and tanner guilds allowed Afro-Mexicans to become masters (Palmer 1976: 180; cf. Carrera Stampa 1954: 226–243, Mondragón 1999: 53–54; Santiago Cruz 1960: 19–20, 34–35).

The Afro-Mexican population was the target of other special restrictions, such as the sumptuary laws intended to maintain the boundaries of the estate system. For instance, a law of 1571 (quoted in Mondragón 1999: 58) specified, "No black woman free or slave, or *mulata*, can wear gold, pearls, or silk," unless she was married to a Spaniard, in which case she "can wear gold earrings, with pearls, and a choker, and on the skirt a velvet border." Even if the wife of a Spaniard, though, she could not wear any garment except a shawl that reached "much below the waist." The penalty for violating these rules was having the prohibited items "taken off her" by the authorities.

The foregoing decree was intended to deny to Afro-Mexican women a highly visible part of the Spanish estate's female expressive array. A law of 1582 did likewise with regard to the Indian estate (quoted in Mondragón 1999: 54). It specified that neither a *mestiza* (a woman with an Indian mother and an other-race father) nor an Afro-Mexican woman (whether *mulata* or *negra*) could "go about dressed as an Indian woman." The penalty was more severe in this case: imprisonment, one hundred lashes in public, and a half-peso fine.

Taken together, these two sumptuary laws separated women into three great estates—Spanish, Indian, and Other (Afro-Mexican and mixed)—on the basis of permissible expressive culture. The laws reinforced a notion of social but not genetic race, as neither the Spanish nor the Indian population was genetically "pure" by this time (see Castillo 2001: 79 ff.). Furthermore, the third estate, which we call "Other" for want of an equally succinct term, included mixed-race women as well as the Afro-Mexicans specifically designated as "negras" (blacks). In the final analysis, these laws affected the entire population, not just women, because a mixed-race child typically inherited the legal status of its mother by this time. For instance, children of Spanish fathers and other-race (or mixed-race) mothers were now only rarely reared as "Spaniards" and absorbed into the Spanish estate, as had been the case routinely in the 1520s and 1530s (Castillo 2001: 126; Mörner 1967: 68–70).

An interesting detail of the 1571 sumptuary law is its partial exemption of Afro-Mexican women married to Spaniards. In this light, it is important to emphasize that such a marriage would not automatically free either a slave woman or her children. Spain legislated against such automatic manumission in 1526, and Mexico did so separately in 1527 and again in 1541 (Palmer 1976: 172). Of course, the Spanish husband-father could readily secure official manumission of his wife and/or children, so long as he still owned them. If he had sold his wife or any of their children, however, the matter was more complicated, although a law of 1563 made him the preferential buyer of his slave children, if they were for sale, so long as his intent was to free them (172).

We will not detail the many other special laws to which Afro-Mexicans were subject, in part because many of them were poorly enforced or later overturned (León 1924: 9–11). Of note, though, are the laws intended to protect both Spaniards and Indians from Afro-Mexicans. For instance, Afro-Mexicans were forbidden to bear firearms or swords, except by petition of their owners or employers (Palmer 1976: 185; Mondragón 1999: 54). Indian commoners also fell under this prohibition, as the Spanish feared Indian uprisings, as well as slave revolts—which were numerous, beginning in 1536 (Mondragón 1999: 62–64; Paredes and Lara 1995: 25–28)—and criminal activity by Afro-Mexicans generally. At various times, Afro-Mexicans were forbidden to live in either Spanish or Indian neighborhoods or communities, unless they had official permission to reside with Spanish masters or employers. These laws reflected the Spanish belief that Afro-Mexicans thieved and caused public disturbances in both types of settlements and that they taught "bad customs and vices" to the Indians (Palmer 1976: 182; see also Mondragón 1999: 56).

Also noteworthy is the 1574 royal edict that commanded able-bodied free Afro-Mexicans to pay taxes ("tribute"), which previously had been levied solely on Indians. In part, the edict seems to have been aimed at compelling the free population to seek gainful employment to earn the tax and to establish permanent residences to facilitate tax collection (and administrative control generally). Enforcement was a great problem, however, despite increasingly harsh penalties in successive laws compelling registration. Finally, "in 1612 all freedmen were required to undertake gainful employment with a Spaniard" (Palmer 1976: 184) to facilitate both tax collection and social control.

What do these laws mean in stratificational terms? We have seen that legislation sometimes distinguished between free and slave Afro-Mexicans and sometimes did not. For this reason, we regard these two segments of the population as subestates within a general Afro-Mexican estate rather than as classes, which are not legally defined or enforced.

INDIANS

In the short run, military conquest does not require changing much except the top of the political pyramid. In fact, the cheapest form of colonial domination is indirect rule, whereby the indigenous political system is left in place but brought under colonial authority. Worldwide, most colonial powers known to history have employed indirect rule in conquered areas with preexisting chiefdoms or states. It should not surprise us, then, that the Spanish instituted this form of colonial rule in Central Mexico. Nor did it surprise the Indians, because the Aztecs also had ruled indirectly over most of the roughly five hundred conquered city-states that made up their empire (Smith 1998: 162–185).

In the long run, of course, the post-Conquest cultural outcome involved much more than politics or a mere substitution of one set of rulers for another. Nevertheless, from the standpoint of the Indian population, post-Conquest social stratification is understandable only in two initial contexts, one of which is indirect rule. The other, also a matter of politics, is the legal machinery intended to harness Indian labor and goods to Spanish economic interests.

Initially, the Spanish conquerors envisaged exploiting substantial numbers of Indians through slavery. Spanish law recognized enslavement as the fate of enemy soldiers and their dependents captured in war (Martín Casares 2000: 76 ff., Zavala 1967: 1–7). Accordingly, captured and enslaved Indians were sent to silver mines and obrajes during the first fifteen years after the Conquest (76). This labor mechanism was largely frustrated when the alarming Indian death rate from epidemic diseases prompted the Spanish Crown to abolish Indian slavery in 1542, to avoid aggravating the demographic losses. Nevertheless, colonial Spaniards were still able to implement Spanish laws imposing servitude for debt defaulters and as criminal punishment (Taylor 1979: 100–105; Viqueira and Urquiola 1990: 65–85, 210).

Obrajes for turning raw wool into various types of cloth were established in Central Mexico's major cities at least by the 1530s. They made abundant use of Indian indentured servants, convicted criminals, and war captives, as well as African slaves and Afro-Mexicans (Gibson 1964: 243–246, 252–254; Salvucci 1987; Viqueira and Urquiola 1990). Some of the indentured servants were working off wage advances given them by contract with the obrajes; others, though, were working off third-party debts bought up by obraje owners, who could then compel the original debtors to pay with labor at the going rate, minus deductions for room and board. Judicial punishment, even for capital crimes (Taylor 1979: 100), often took the form of fines, which Indian commoners could not pay; obraje owners paid the fines, in effect buying the workers for the length of time it took them to amortize the sum at the going wage. The Indian workforce also eventually included Chichimec slaves captured in the chronic warfare on New Spain's northern frontier (Frye 1996: 43–53; Zavala 1967: 179–349). Yet others had entered the obrajes as child apprentices or had been remanded there as orphans. "Once inside, they spent the remainder of their lives behind locked or guarded doors" (Gibson 1964: 246).

The locked workshop was, in fact, a prison for most of the labor force, regardless of their legal status. Laws against locked workshops were only partly effective, and the practice continued throughout the colonial period (Gibson 1964: 246). Furthermore, the royal decree of 1595 prohibiting Indians from working in sugar mills or obrajes was poorly enforced in the latter case (Salvucci 1987; Viqueira and Urquiola 1990: 112–122). We should add that even the obraje workers who ostensibly arrived voluntarily were often impelled to do so by destitution. An observation that Salvucci (1987: 111) culled from an official report on obraje recruitment of free-market labor in the eighteenth century is instructive: "He is in this obraje voluntarily, because he had nothing to eat where he came from."

A greater challenge for the Spanish administration was to devise a way to harness the labor of the great majority of Indians, who remained rural and mainly agrarian. The major mechanism for exploiting their labor during the first fifty years of Spanish rule was the *encomienda* (trusteeship), which was established almost immediately after the Conquest (Simpson 1982). There were over six hundred encomiendas in New Spain (Mexico) by 1550 and over one thousand by 1600 (Nutini 1995: 164–168). In its original form, the encomienda assigned Indian high nobles and their associated commoners to particular Spanish grantees, or encomenderos, to whom the commoners owed both labor (prohibited after 1549) and tribute in goods. The assigned Indians were free, not slave, because the encomenderos did not own them "as property" (Gibson 1964: 58). Also, Indian nobles succeeded in exempting from encomienda payments their own traditional slaves (*tlacotin*) and dependent settlers (mayeque), preserving for the moment the pre-Conquest lower social orders.

In 1549, following the deadly epidemics of 1545–1548, the Spanish Crown stripped the encomienda of Indian labor service and in 1550 instituted a new recruitment mechanism, the *repartimiento* (lit., "redistribution," "dividing up"), which remained the dominant means of harnessing labor for Spanish interests, including urban construction projects, until 1632 (Gibson 1964: 220–235). Although the repartimiento came to entail much brutality and compulsion, it was intended to meet Spanish labor needs without further weakening the Indian population. It specified that the Indian governing body of each community had to furnish no more than 2 percent of its male taxpayers in any given week for paid labor nearby and that no individual was to be worked more than four weeks per year, never consecutively. As with the encomienda, Indian nobles initially exempted their dependent settlers and traditional slaves from repartimiento service in order to retain them for their own enterprises. Within thirty years, though, epidemics had so reduced the numbers of ordinary commoners that Indian rulers could not longer permit these exemptions if they were to meet their labor quotas under the repartimiento. Accordingly, the members of both of these special categories passed into the ranks of the *macehualtin* (Sp. *macehuales*), the mass of commoners. Thus, the effect of Spanish colonialism was to "equalize and compress" the bottom rungs of the Indian social stratification system by the end of the sixteenth century (Gibson 1964: 153–154; see also Lockhart 1992: 111–114).

To a lesser extent, the nobles themselves also eventually suffered social compression and equalization, despite their widespread initial participation in indirect rule (Gibson 1964: 153–167, 191–193; Gibson 1973; Lockhart 1992: 30–55; Pérez-Rocha and Tena 2000). At first, those who cooperated—by professing and promoting Christianity and administering towns and encomiendas in Spanish interests—retained their titles, lands, tributes, and subjects, and "many were addressed by the [honorific] title of Don" (Gibson 1967: 143). They also enjoyed certain Spanish sumptuary privileges, such as the right (with viceregal licenses) "to carry swords or firearms, to wear Spanish clothing, [and] to ride horses or mules with saddles and bridles," and some Indian nobles even went to Spain to plead their cases for lands, tribute, titles, or inheritances before the royal court (Gibson 1964: 155).

The indigenous nobility's heyday was brief. The Spanish conquest had brought an abrupt end to the near-chronic warfare that had validated Aztec noblemen's status and enriched outstanding soldiers with plunder and official rewards (Lockhart 1992: 111). Indian nobles also eventually lost their slaves and other dependent workers to Spanish law or social compression, as we have seen. The introduction of Spanish-style municipal councils (*cabildos*) in the 1530s lessened the nobles' powers by standardizing and routinizing local government (Lockhart 1992: 35–55; Gibson 1967: 103–123), and by century's end, service in local government had lost most of its rewards and prestige (Gibson 1964: 193). The nobles' early importance as Christianizers was diminished by the arrival of increasing numbers of Spanish clergy, some of whom were dissatisfied with what had been done in this regard (Pérez-Rocha and Tena 2000: 68). As early as 1550, the Indian nobles' reduced importance to Spanish colonial interests was reflected in their much-reduced success at petitioning to retain their offices, lands, and tributes against Spanish and Indian encroachments (Pérez-Rocha and Tena 2000: 72). By 1600 indigenous noble titles had disappeared from official documents, even from wills that named successors to positions of privilege (Lockhart 1992: 130–131).

The implications of these changes varied by locality and family, however. In some localities, many prominent noble families retained large landholdings and considerable local influence (Chance 2000). In other places, the "process of 'commonerization' [*macehualización*] of the Indian nobility" (Pérez-Rocha and Tena 2000: 68) was clearly evident by the seventeenth century, and the few descendants of nobles who remained wealthy eventually became indistinguishable from other rich people in the colony (Gibson 1964: 198; 1973: 26; Perkins 2007). Even at that, the indigenous population was not homogenized, as classes within it remained evident over much of Central Mexico throughout the colonial period (Ouweneel 1995; Schryer 1900).

In the course of all these changes affecting both nobles and commoners, rich and poor, a new ethnicity was born: *indio* (Indian). Before the Conquest, Central Mexico had a dozen or so major, mutually unintelligible languages and many more minor ones. The political history was one of warring city-states, and even after these units were cowed into submission by the Aztec Empire, self-identity and political allegiance were predominantly "to their local city-state, not the empire" (Smith 1998: 162). Thus there was neither polity-wide nor language-wide self-identity; speakers of Otomí or Náhuatl, for example, identified with their home communities, not with the language community or the polity that had incorporated their city-state.

The new ethnicity "indio" was entirely an artifact of colonialism, having originated in Columbus' mistaken (or feigned) belief that he had circumvented the globe and landed in India. For the next three centuries, Mexico's indigenous population largely avoided the term (Lockhart 1992: 114–115). In the nineteenth and twentieth centuries, though, indigenous peoples often used it to refer to themselves in dealings with outsiders, usually as a form of embarrassed apology for their rusticity or poverty (Friedlander 1975: 72–79). Today, *indio* has largely been replaced by *indígena* (indigene, native) in conversational Spanish, but *indio* continues to be used in historical contexts in both Spanish and English.

SPANIARDS (AND OTHER EUROPEANS)

The early Spanish estate was highly diverse in origin. Culturally, its members reflected the localisms of the mother country. Like the Aztec subjects they conquered, Spaniards "identified with their *patria chica* (local region)" rather than with the state, "which was only a geographic expression," and they saw persons from other towns and provinces as *gringos*, or foreigners (MacLaughlin and Rodríguez 1980: 209–210). Each region had its own language—for example, Basque, Galician, Catalán, Castilian—and only an especially heavy emigration from southern Spain ensured that the official language, Castilian (*castellano*, or Spanish), prevailed in the Americas.

What the immigrants had in common, besides their status as conquerors, was that they were all from Spain. Thus, they were all *españoles* (Spaniards), a distinctive ethnic bloc in the colony. Within twenty years, however, an invidious class distinction arose among them—between peninsulars and creoles—and the breach between these two classes grew ever wider over the next three hundred years, coming to a head in the struggle for Mexican independence (1810–1821).

Socially, the early Spanish estate was sharply stratified. Among the conquistadors and settlers who arrived in the first twenty-five years (1520–1545) were a few members of the upper nobility, perhaps one hundred fifty lesser nobles (*hidalgos*), and many middle-class commoner professionals and artisans (physicians, apothecaries, professional soldiers, carpenters, masons, blacksmiths), as well as poor men seeking a better life (Nutini 1995: 153–157). In time, poor people came to predominate among immigrants, and by 1600 more than one-half of the men and one-sixth of the women emigrated as servants, many of them sponsored by kin already established in Mexico (MacLachlan and Rodríguez 1980: 210; Lockhart and Otte 1976:117–146; von Mentz 1999: 116–119). Some of them eventually prospered in the colony, but most remained poor.

In New Spain, though, they were all members of the superordinate estate, a status symbolized by their legal exemption from taxation—a distinctly noble privilege in Spain. Thus, the early Spanish immigrants became de facto hidalgos, and many actually claimed that status once they had prospered, regardless of their original social standing back home. All Indians, in contrast, were taxed, making them like the commoners of Spain, regardless of their pre-Conquest social status (Nutini 1995: 187–188).

The Spanish estate also absorbed other European immigrants—mostly Portuguese and Italians, with a sprinkling of French, Flemish, English, Germans, and Greeks—perhaps a total of two thousand in the sixteenth century, many entering illegally (Aguirre Beltrán 1972: 240; Israel 1975: 117 ff.). Some were wealthy merchants or skilled professionals, but "a high proportion were poor men, cobblers, barbers, carpenters, hosiers, and even vagabonds" (Israel 1975: 120). Most remained poor artisans or petty merchants, although a few prospered, especially as dealers in contraband. Among these "foreigners," particularly those entering from Portugal after its annexation by Spain in 1580, were many Jews fleeing Spanish persecution. Like the other immigrant groups, most of the Jews arrived and remained poor, making a modest living as "shopkeepers, craftsmen, peddlers, and vagabonds" (Israel 1975: 126). Many of them and their descendants suffered imprisonment, torture, and/or execution for heresy in the next century during the Mexican Inquisition (Israel 1975: 125–126).

It is clear that the common notion that sixteenth-century Spaniards in New Spain were mostly rich ranchers, encomenderos, or miners is wrong. Most, in fact, were urban and poor or middle class, working as bakers, barbers, cartwrights, shopkeepers, peddlers, pack train muleteers, and artisans, including smiths (gold, silver, iron), sword makers, tailors, weavers, embroiderers, and cobblers (von Mentz 1999: 119). Furthermore, by the 1530s, the colony had "numerous white vagabonds who styled themselves hidalgos . . . and who refused to work, living [instead] by plundering the Indians" (Israel 1975: 11). In 1531, in an effort to induce them to take up farming or other legitimate livelihoods, the Spanish Crown offered incentives for white settlement in its newly founded city, Puebla. Nevertheless, "Spanish vagabondage remained a problem of some seriousness throughout the seventeenth century" (Israel 1975: 77).

The Spanish estate's upper class was highly urban and increasingly concentrated in Mexico City and Puebla, although most maintained country houses as well (Kiczu 1999: 28; Nutini 1995: 176). Residence was a readily visible marker of their estate status, because Indians, Afro-Mexicans, and other nonwhites were forbidden to construct houses within Spanish quarters. When Mexico City was rebuilt on the ruins of Tenochtitlan, a 13- by 13-block zone in the center—*la traza* (lit., "the trace" or "boundary line")—was reserved for Spanish residences. "The rich and illustrious lived within *la traza,*" while Spaniards of lesser means "built outside it or far from the 'white city,' even in the [Indian] neighborhoods" (Mondragón 1999: 45). Many traza houses were virtual palaces or forts, with "turrets, barbicans, battlements, and embrasures" (46). The ground floor housed slaves and servants—a score or more of each in the richest homes—while the upper floor was reserved for the owners and their extended family, sometimes dozens of them. The rear patio contained corrals, stables, storehouses, and hay barns (45; Nutini 1995: 204). These houses and their large retinues of slaves and servants were utilitarian, of course, but their ostentation was part of the elite expressive array, along with equestrian games, the sponsorship of religious ceremonies, and the use of East Asian products such as silks, porcelains, and spices (Nutini 1995: 200–208).

Surprisingly, few descendants of the conqueror generation were among New Spain's elite by 1600. Rather, the great fortunes and prestige that allowed upper-class entrée were gained in international commerce and high government service, the latter being rewarded by grants of Indians and lands. Encomenderos, large farmers or ranchers, and silver mine concessionaires certainly were local elites, but "those who did not diversify their investments . . . fell by the wayside" (Kiczu 1999: 20) in the struggle for colony-wide preeminence. The upper class reinforced its wealth and exclusivity by endogamous marriage, often between first cousins or even uncle and niece, so that marriage dowries would circulate within their own group or family (Kiczu 1999: 30). Elite intermarriage (usually of women) with indigenous nobles had ceased by 1600 (Nutini 1995: 181). Even today, the descendants of the colonial elite have a European physical appearance (Nutini 1995: 209).

The *Castas* of the Seventeenth to Nineteenth Centuries

The tripartite estate system established in the early sixteenth century could endure only so long as most individuals could be assigned unambiguously to one or another of the three categories. By 1600 interbreeding had made such assignment problematic in many cases. The colonial administration tried to save the system by defining an intermediate estate of *castas* for interracial persons. At the time, the Spanish word *casta* (as well as the English *caste*) had not yet acquired its denotation of rigid social stratification; rather, it was the equivalent of today's *lineage*, *kind*, or *race*.

Initially, there had been only two major recognized products of interestate unions: *mestizo/-a* and *mulato/-a*. The former term was usually, but not always, reserved for the offspring of a Spanish man and an Indian woman; the latter almost always referred to children of mixed Spanish and African or Afro-Mexican unions. (Spanish uses the –*o* ending for male or unspecified gender and the –*a* ending for female; the gender-inclusive plural takes the –*os* ending.) The casta system was designed to handle the much more complicated situation that arose from the backbreeding and interbreeding of the mixtures themselves. Nicolás León (1924: 9, 21–27) presents the following casta designations:

1. Spanish + Indian = *mestizo* (mixed or crossbred)
2. mestizo + Spanish = *castizo* (Spanish-like, or light-skinned)
3. castizo + Spanish = *español* (Spanish)
4. Spanish + African = *mulato* (from *mulo*, "mule")
5. mulato + Spanish = *morisco* (mixed color; from *moro*, Moor)

6. morisco + Spanish = *salta atrás* (throwback)
7. salta atrás + Indian = *chino* (curly-haired)
8. chino + mulato = *lobo* (wolf)
9. lobo + mulato = *gíbaro* (wild)
10. gíbaro + Indian = *albarrazado* (dyed)
11. albarrazado + African = *cambujo* (reddish black, ref. donkeys)
12. cambujo + Indian = *sambaygo* (from *sambo*, a type of monkey)
13. sambaygo + mulato = *calpan mulato* (derivation of *calpan* unclear)
14. calpan mulato + sambaygo = *tente en el aire* (up in the air)
15. tente en el aire + mulato = *no te entiendo* (I don't understand you)
16. no te entiendo + Indian = *hay te estás* (there you are/have it)

No specific date can be given for the implementation of the casta system. What we do know is that the major churches in Mexico City were keeping a separate casta marriage register in 1646 (Cope 1994: 25). There was always considerable regional variation in both categories and names (see Aguirre Beltrán 1972: 166–179; Castillo 2001: 129–141; Marín 1999: 39–40), and the full list of fifteen or sixteen castas probably was not employed anywhere. Usually, only five to seven categories were used—*español, castizo, morizco, mestizo, mulato, indio,* and *negro*—to designate "a hierarchical ordering of racial groups according to their proportion of Spanish blood" or likeness (Cope 1994: 24). Even at that, there was no legal consistency with regard to the system, as some laws applied to specific castas while others lumped all mixed-bloods together, using *castas* as an umbrella term (Cope 1994: 161). The system also had an important and curious omission: there was no widely accepted category for the offspring of the most frequent kind of intercasta union, mestizo-mulato. Apparently, the children of these unions "were drawn into the social network of one parent or the other, whichever was more advantageous" (Cope 1994: 84).

"Mestizo" (mixed), as a category, was slow to take on its eventual meaning. Immediately after the Conquest, the offspring of Spanish men and Indian women were regarded as "Spaniards" or "creoles" (American-born Spaniards), but that practice quickly faded for out-of-wedlock children. In fact, the term *mestizo* originated in the 1530s to single out the latter as "persons of Spanish-Indian descent who were not full members of either group" (Cope 1994: 14–15). It is worth emphasizing, along with Aguirre Beltrán (1972: 245), that this early division between creoles and mestizos was based on culture—on whether or not their parents were married—and not on biology. By 1560, there were at least two thousand people classified as mestizos, compared to one thousand or more mulattoes, in New Spain (Gibson 1964: 380).

By about 1600, *mestizo* had become the general term for persons of mixed Indian-Spanish heritage, whether of legitimate or illegitimate birth. Like Spaniards, mestizos paid no tribute (tax)—which both Indians and, after about 1580, free Afro-Mexicans had to pay—and initially shared with Spaniards the designation *gente de razón* (intelligent people; lit., "people with reason"). As their numbers increased, however, mestizos were often lumped with New Spain's other interracial groups, and many laws lumped them together with "blacks, mulattoes, chinos, and zambos" (Cope 1994: 19). For instance, the punishment for using fraudulent scales for weighing meat was a twenty-peso fine for Spaniards and one hundred lashes for Afro-Mexicans, mulattoes, and mestizos. To take another example, mestizos, as well as other castas, were prohibited from joining certain artisan guilds or from advancing beyond apprentice or journeyman in them (Cope 1994: 19).

At the same time, not all mestizos were regarded or treated equally. By 1600 colonial officials often differentiated two groups of mestizos: the "typical" ones, who were said to be "illegitimate, lazy, [and] parasitic"; and the good "sons of Spaniards," who "acted as allies of the colonials" (Cope 1994: 20). Some of the latter served in important positions, both private (e.g., stewards for Spanish encomenderos or farmers) and public (e.g., *gobernadores* [governors] of Indian communities); furthermore, after 1588, mestizos of legitimate birth were allowed to become priests (Cope 1994: 20). A third mestizo group is invisible to the historical record, as they and their descendants blended into the Indian population, whose "demographic recovery" in the late seventeenth century may be attributable in part to such mestizo absorption. Gibson (1964: 147) wryly suggests that Spanish officials reclassified mestizos as Indians in order to make them taxable (for tribute and/or public works service), and he quotes a 1790 document that refers to "mestizos and half-castes who are also called Indians." We suspect that many other casta individuals had already blended into the Indian estate, just as many more were to do in the next century.

In fact, by the 1770s the casta system as it had been envisaged more than a century earlier was dead. Indicative is the city of Puebla, whose 1777 census showed the following breakdown of its 56,168 inhabitants (Marín 1999: 66–67): Spaniards (31.8 percent), Indians (21.4 percent), castizos (4.1 percent), mestizos (16.1 percent), mulatos (4.6 percent), negros (0.01 percent), and "other castas" (21.9 percent). Two aspects of this distribution are striking. First, the negros (Afro-Mexicans)—whose numbers had equaled those of Spaniards in this city two hundred years earlier (Paredes and Lara 1995: 34–35)—had virtually disappeared, having been absorbed into other categories. Second, more than one-fifth of the city's population could no longer be classified precisely and were lumped into the catchall category "other castas." In the city's hinterland, meanwhile, about 80 percent of the population was still confidently classified as Indian (Marín 1999: 69).

In urban Puebla, the classification system had become so ambiguous that parishes could no longer maintain the mandated separate registry books for Spaniards, Indians, and people of color (*gente de color quebrado*, or equivalent terms). In fact, after about 1750, "more and more parishes came to abandon the tripartite focus of the Books" (Marín 1999: 89). Even the parishes that retained the three books took to entering the names of both castas and Spaniards into whichever of the two non-Indian books was at hand, resulting in chaos and "numerous personal offenses" (89).

Some parishes went a step further, keeping only two books. For instance, Puebla's Sagrario parish abandoned its *Libro de negros, chinos y pardos* (Book of Blacks, Curly-hairs, and Dark-skins) in 1790 and also renamed its *Libro de españoles* (Book of Spaniards) the *Libro de españoles, castizos y mestizos* (Book of Spaniards, Spaniard-like, and Mixed-Breeds); in this latter were entered the life-cycle events of all parishioners who could not be confidently recorded in the *Libro de indios* (Book of Indians) (Marín 1999: 90). This was not really a dramatic change, because even the creoles—the most common kind of "Spaniards"—whose parents had been in the colony for a few generations were almost certainly of mixed racial heritage by this time. "Thus, the difference between a Creole . . . and a mestizo, castizo, or mulatto was, in reality, only a matter of degree"; some creoles were darker than some mestizos, and "there were mestizos who without doubt could have passed for Indians" (Marín 1999: 173; see also Castillo 2001: 151–173). Meanwhile, the apparently uncomplicated persistence of the *Book of Indians* in both urban and rural parishes reflected a transcendent tendency, namely, Mexico's population was increasingly being lumped into the two catchall census categories, Indian and non-Indian, that are still used today (Marín 1999: 45; see also Lewis 2000).

Puebla's church records for the years 1780–1831 also show that there was still a strong correlation between occupation and both estates and social classes, notwithstanding the blurring and blending of castas. Marín (1999: 152–157) scaled occupations into a hierarchy of six "groups"—excluding farmers, merchants, the military, and the priesthood—and then looked for correlations among six castas: peninsular Spaniard, creole Spaniard, *cacique* (high-ranking Indians), mestizo, mulatto, and Indian (commoners). In rough summary, his occupational groups were as follows:

I. High government officials.
II. Minor and local government and church lay officials, professionals (e.g., physicians, lawyers), large business owners, and so on.
III. Semiprofessionals and skilled artisans, small business owners, entertainers, and so on.
IV. Lesser government and church employees, some artisans (less prosperous?), specialized laborers, and *arrieros* (pack train muleteers).
V. Unskilled workers, small-scale merchants, service people, and servants.
VI. Agricultural workers.

Within each group, Marín (1999) rated the representation of the six castas relative to their demographic profile in the total sample (see Table 2.1). Group I was entirely a Spanish domain, although split between peninsulars and creoles (which Marín treats as separate "castas"); surprisingly, peninsulars—constituting only 2.7 percent of Marín's sample—still held 41 percent of these high positions. Peninsulars and creoles were "dominant" and "strong," respectively, in Group II, but caciques had an "equitable" (equivalent to their demographic profile) representation there too. In Group III, creoles were "dominant," and both peninsulars and caciques were "weak." In Group IV, creoles and caciques had "equitable presence," both mestizos and mulattoes had "strong presence," and commoner Indians had "weak" representation. Group V was "dominated by [commoner] Indians," but mestizos also had "equitable presence," while both caciques and mulattoes had "strong presence." Group VI was also "dominated by [commoner] Indians," although mulattoes had "weak presence"; no others were represented there (157).

This association of casta and occupational classes dovetails with the fact that social mobility was quite limited in Puebla at the time. In the period 1780–1810, 77 percent of the men in Marín's sample (taken from

TABLE 2.1
Castas and Occupations in Puebla, 1780–1821

Occupational Groups[a]	Castas[b] PEN	CR	CAC	MES	MUL	IND
I	D	D				
II	D	S	E			
III	W	D	W			
IV		E	E	S	S	W
V			S	E	S	D
VI					W	D

Source: After Marín 1999: 152–157.

[a] For "Occupational Groups" and "Castas," see text. Letters in the body of the table show representation of each casta in proportion to its demographic profile in the sample population: D = dominant, E = equitable, S = strong, W = weak.

[b] PEN = peninsular Spaniards; CR = creole Spaniards; CAC = caciques (high-ranking Indians); MES = mestizos; MUL = mulattoes; IND = Indians (other than caciques).

marriage records) had occupations in the same grouping as their fathers. For the period 1780–1831, 96 (58 percent) of the 167 sets of brothers in the sample were involved in "identical economic activities," and 55 (47 percent) of the 117 brother-sister pairs "had the same occupation as their brother-in-law," while 25 (39 percent) of the 64 sets of sisters "married men with the same occupation" (Marín 1999: 158–159).

Three trends are clear. First, a version of the casta system—although a very different one from that originally envisaged—remained intact through the end of the eighteenth century. Second, the correlation of casta and occupation was pronounced at both the top and the bottom of the occupational hierarchy, with implications for both income and prestige. Third, the late colonial middle and working classes bridged the divisions of casta, race, and ethnicity. Creole Spaniards, caciques and commoner Indians, mestizos, and mulattoes all worked in Puebla's lower-middle-class Group IV occupations, and the working-class Groups V and VI included caciques and commoner Indians, mestizos, and mulattoes (Marín 1999: 157).

We are confident that a study of other urban centers of the period would yield similar results (see Castillo 2001; Cope 1994; von Mentz 1999) but with one important addendum: working-class Spaniards. In Mexico City, for instance, there had been substantial numbers of poor Spaniards in the working class a century earlier (Cope 1994: 22–23).

The casta system was not officially abolished until 1822, following Mexican independence from Spain (González N. 1970; MacLachlan and Rodríguez 1980: 330–331). The creole elite who sparked that struggle had openly appealed to the castas' desire for social equality (Vincent 2001: 44 ff.), and many mulattoes and mestizos fought in the ensuing wars. Many served under Vicente Guerrero, a mulatto or Afro-mestizo who became Mexico's second president (and for whom the present state of Guerrero is named). Independence wiped out the laws that had codified ethnic and racial discrimination, abolishing official recognition of the estate stratification system that had been erected on that foundation. Of the casta terminology, only *mestizo* and *indio* survived to denote sociocultural categories for the whole country. The other terms retained only local currency, if that, or passed into the general lexicon as terms for dark skin color (Nutini 1997).

Within a decade of independence, the old creole elite had taken full control again, expelling the despised peninsulars in 1829. The Reform period (La Reforma) of midcentury again shook their grip on power (see Chap. 3), but they did not lose their supremacy until the great Mexican Revolution of 1910–1920. In many ways, the Revolution was a replay of the war of independence, as the popular leaders of both struggles championed Mexican nationality and nationalism to mobilize forces against a Eurocentric elite (Knight 1994). The several decades leading up to the Revolution had seen the rise of *mestizofilia*—the idea that the mixture of races and/or cultures is desirable—among Mexican intellectuals (Basave 1992), and this "Mestizo Mexico" ideology helped to legitimate both the Revolution and the political, economic, and artistic reforms that followed it, as we shall see later.

Of course, the 1910–1920 Revolution did not abolish social stratification, despite socialist rhetoric and the subsequent redistribution of land to the rural poor (see Chap. 3). Nor did it abolish ethnic or racial discrimination (Gall 1999; Gillian 1976; Margolies 1975; Martínez Maranto 1995; Romer 1998; T. Sierra 1999). In fact, as Basave (1992: 142) writes, "the correlation between race and class . . . persists in goodly measure," and "the presence of Indian traits . . . is still inversely proportional to socioeconomic level."

Race, Ethnicity, and Class in the Twentieth Century

GENERAL FEATURES

Late-twentieth-century Central Mexico presents an often bewildering conflation of cultural, ethnic, and somatic traits in the categorization of individuals and groups, but we can distinguish certain general parameters. First, as one moves up the stratification system, the importance of phenotypic differences—culturally interpreted constellations of physical traits—increases while that of purely cultural differences decreases as criteria for social evaluation and acceptance. Today's plutocrats and the upper-middle class, as well as the descendants of the pre-Revolution aristocracy, regard themselves as ancestrally and phenotypically European. Aristocrats condescend somewhat toward the upper-middle class, though, reflecting a suspicion of greater non-European admixture, and prefer to marry other Mexican aristocrats or upper-class Europeans. The few plutocrats and aristocrats whose physical appearance deviates markedly from the European ideal are "whitened" by the combined effects of wealth and power, and their nonconforming traits may even be interpreted pridefully as "throwbacks" evidencing prestigious ancestral roots in the early colonial period.

Second, even though Mexico is racially (genetically and phenotypically) overwhelmingly Indian, the cultural standards of beauty and ideals of physical appearance are strongly European. These preferences are daily reinforced through television and all forms of graphic advertising, and many people feel impelled to emulate them in order to enhance not only their physical appearance but their ethnic identity as well. For example, many women enhance their European appearance by not shaving their legs, and many men cultivate beards or moustaches for the same reason. Middle-class people also tend to avoid apparel with strong Indian or mestizo associations, such as men's straw hats and women's long skirts or cotton shawls (*rebozos*).

Third, light complexion—combined with the "right" cultural characteristics—gives great advantage in upward mobility, as dark skin color is generally thought to indicate lower-class origin. Not surprisingly, parents of all social classes often give preferential treatment to their lighter-skinned children or those with more European features (Friedlander 1975: 77–79; Nutini 2005: 112, 156n6). Many lower- and middle-class parents also encourage their offspring to marry lighter-skinned persons, usually through selectively giving or withholding approval of certain friends or potential spouses.

Fourth, the superordinate and subordinate classes often regard each other in terms of racial stereotypes. Members of the middle and lower classes view the upper stratum as an undifferentiated white population, while many (perhaps most) upper-class people lump the middle and lower classes together, stressing their Indianness. Aristocrats, furthermore, typically do not distinguish between mestizos and Indians, often referring to them all with such derogatory labels as *la indiada* (that mob of Indians) and *la naquiza* (that bunch of *nacos*; a corruption of Totonaco, the name of an Indian group on the east coast). At the same time, aristocrats tend to idealize Indians who stay in their own communities and remain "uncontaminated" by the modern world. These Indians are regarded as well behaved, courteous, friendly, devout, loyal, respectful, and faithful to their traditions. In contrast are the Indians who have made the painful transition to national culture and society, as they are seen as having been corrupted by incorporation into la naquiza. These aristocratic views of Indians are shared by a sizable segment of the plutocracy and upper-middle class as well, even by the minority of phenotypical mestizos among them. Interestingly, exactly the same distinction between good Indians who remain "in their place" and bad, pushy ones who are "out of place" is reported for Peru (Portocarrero 1999: 43).

ETHNICITY AND CLASS

There is no strict correlation between class and ethnicity in modern Mexico, but this simple fact belies a complex situation. First, ethnic categorization is most important toward the bottom of the system and generally comes into play during social mobility, as individuals and families struggle to rise from Indian to mestizo ethnic status and from the lower to the middle class. A one-generational rise from the predominantly Indian-mestizo lower echelons into the national upper-middle class is highly unlikely and would trigger discrimination based on phenotype ("race," in common parlance) for darker-skinned individuals. A meteoric rise from working class to the national elite is nearly impossible, although President Ernesto Zedillo (1994–2000)—a light-skinned mestizo—is said to have accomplished it (Oppenheimer 1996: 113–118). At any rate, ethnic categorization is least significant at the very top, which is populated mainly by European and light mestizo phenotypes.

Second, in contrast to the United States, foreign ethnic identity is generally lost after the second generation, beyond which social placement and evaluation are based on cultural and phenotypic traits. Such prominent Mexican family names as Bartlett, Clouthier, Chuayflet, Creel, Fox, Hank, Jackson, Massieu, O'Gorman, Slim, and others of obvious non-Hispanic/non-Indian origin regularly appear in the public media but never with the hyphenated ethnic markers (e.g., Arab-Mexican, French-Mexican) that would be used in the United States.

There are basically four operational categories that may be termed ethnic or even racial in Mexico today: (1) *güero* or *blanco* (white), denoting European and Near East extraction; (2) *criollo* (creole), meaning light mestizo in this context but actually of varying complexion; (3) *mestizo*, an imprecise category that includes many phenotypic variations; and (4) *indio*, also an imprecise category. These are nominal categories, and neither *güero/blanco* nor *criollo* is a widely used term (see Nutini 1997: 230). Nevertheless, there is a popular consensus in Mexico today that these four categories represent major sectors of the nation and that they can be arranged into a rough hierarchy: whites and creoles at the top, a vast population of mestizos in the middle, and Indians (perceived as both a racial and an ethnic component) at the bottom.

This popular hierarchy does not constitute a stratificational system or even a set of social classes, however, because its categories are neither exhaustive nor mutually exclusive. While very light skin is indeed characteristic of the country's elite, there is no "white" (güero) class. Rather, the superordinate stratum is divided into four real classes—aristocracy, plutocracy, political class, and the crème of the upper-middle class—or, for some purposes, into ruling, political, and prestige classes (see Chap. 4). Nor is there a mestizo class, as phenotypical mestizos are found in all classes, though only rarely among the aristocracy and very frequently in the middle and lower classes. Finally, the bottom rungs are not constituted mainly of Indians, except in some localized areas, such as the Sierra Norte de Puebla (see Nutini and Isaac 1974: 149–203). At the bottom of the national stratification system we find instead an aggregate of rural mestizo and Indian peasants, laborers, artisans, traders, and so on, and an urban working class of both mestizo and Indian extraction, many of whom are in transition from an Indian to a mestizo identity (see Chap. 7). It is important to note that phenotypically as well as genetically mestizos and Indians are very similar. At this level, then, ethnicity is defined entirely in cultural terms, though preference may be given to light-skinned children and mates (see Friedlander 1975).

INDIAN ETHNICITY

The ethnic definition of "Indian" is a perennial tough nut in Mexico, but it is one we must hammer away at, even if we cannot crack it, because ethnicity and class are often wrongly conflated in the case of Indians. No set of criteria has ever been agreed on, and even the ability to speak an indigenous language—the national census criterion since 1960 (Valdés 1995: 22)—does not yield entirely valid or reliable results, as census takers must rely on self-reporting in the absence of any fluency tests to safeguard against false denial or exaggeration of abilities. Nevertheless, most anthropologists think that Indians constitute roughly 10 percent of the national population, based on language, while allowing that there may be up to four times that many who identify themselves as Indian on other criteria (parentage, village history, clothing, housing, etc.) in some rural areas (21; also see Vázquez 1992: 104). The 1990 federal census showed only 7.89 percent (Valdés 1995: 74), a figure we consider too low. Central Mexico—the states of Guerrero, Hidalgo, Mexico, Morelos, Puebla, Tlaxcala, and Veracruz, plus the Federal District—had a 1990 population of 34,871,223 (42.92 percent of the country's total), of whom 2,645,111 (7.58 percent) were said to be speakers of indigenous languages. The greatest concentrations were in Guerrero (13.75 percent), Hidalgo (20.32 percent), Puebla (14.82 percent), and Veracruz (11.32 percent).

Since the Revolution of 1910–1920, Indian ethnicity has been the source of both national pride and political controversy. To forge a new, non-European national identity, postrevolutionary politicians and intellectuals appealed to the idea of Mestizo Mexico, in which only the products and people of Spanish and Indian intermixture could be authentically Mexican. On the face of it, the ideology simply ratified the obvious and designated it as desirable. Making it truly desirable, though, required considerable effort after four centuries during which Indians had been denigrated.

The movement for the rehabilitation of the nation's Indian roots became known as *indigenismo* (Indianism), and anthropology in all its forms had a major role in it (see Villoro 1950). Archaeologists would recover, restore, and reconstruct the ruins of the great civilizations of the Classic Period (ca. 300–900 C.E.), often with the help of physical anthropologists, to reconstruct ancient demography, disease profiles, diet, and so on; linguists would study and preserve indigenous languages; ethnographers would salvage the survivals of pre-Conquest cultures, and ethnohistorians would place them in context. All these efforts would be in service to and funded by the new national state. To this day, anthropologists enjoy popularity and prestige in Mexico that are unparalleled in any other country.

Indigenismo succeeded in forging a new intellectual and political culture that indeed honors the country's Indian roots in many ways, but it fell out of favor among intellectuals after about 1970. A younger generation of anthropologists has sharply criticized its predecessors for having played a key role in an official indigenismo that had total ethnic assimilation as its ultimate goal (see Bonfil Batalla 1996; Castellanos 1994; Friedlander 1975; Lomnitz-Adler 2001: 228–262; Machuca 1998; Medina 1998; García Mora and Medina 1983/1986; Robins 1994). The Indians who were extolled by official indigenismo were the Aztec nobility (the quintessential "noble savages") and the long-dead Indians of the Classic Period whose great artworks filled museums and whose temples and pyramids became national icons (Figs. 2.1, 2.2). Today's Indian, in contrast, was viewed as a downtrodden remnant in need of salvation by way of assimilation into the national mestizo culture—"the redemption of the Indian through his disappearance" (Bonfil Batalla 1996: 115). The great artistic output inspired by indigenismo in painting, fiction, and cinema has also been criticized, partly on the same grounds but also for having both stereotyped the mestizo and marginalized the Indian. As Doremus (2001: 401) writes, "Discourses on the Indian . . . generally lacked indigenous voices." This is especially noticeable in movies, in which Indians were portrayed by actors with European features and light complexions such as Dolores del Río or Pedro Armendáriz (Doremus 2001: 398). Finally, after nearly a century of national efforts to glorify Mexico's Indian roots, many Indians still live in acute poverty (see Valdivia 1996/1999), a political embarrassment in a country that has accepted the Indian as a key icon (see Figs. 2.3, 2.4).

FIGURE 2.1. Indigenismo, I: Life-sized, Europeanized statue of founding Aztec king Itzcoatl in downtown Mexico City. Photo by Barry Isaac.

FIGURE 2.2. Indigenismo, II: Ancient rain god Tlaloc and Aztec period designs on a fountain in Chapultepec Park, Mexico City. Photo by Barry Isaac.

FIGURE 2.3. Impoverished, mestizoizing Nahua peasant family in the *tierra templada* of Veracruz state; house has *tabla* (plank) walls and corrugated metal and tarpaper roofs. Photo by Hugo Nutini.

FIGURE 2.4. Rainy season street scene in impoverished, mestizoizing Nahua village in the Sierra Norte de Puebla, in northeastern Puebla state. Photo by Barry Isaac.

Indigenismo transformed selected aspects of Indian culture and selected personages, especially Aztec kings, into national icons but did not resolve the problem of how to define present-day Indian ethnicity. Anthropology made a great contribution to this issue, though, by redefining the Indian's national placement and destiny in terms of culture instead of biology (Doremus 2001: 381). At the same time, anthropologists have never agreed on just which cultural features or perceptions are definitive of modern Indian ethnicity. The three major anthropological approaches to date can be summarized as follows: Indians are people with a predominantly pre-Hispanic culture, Indians are people whose culture has perceptible pre-Hispanic influence, or Indians are people who identify themselves as Indians and are integrated into communities of self-identifying Indians.

The first approach is exemplified by Judith Friedlander's community study in rural Morelos, *Being Indian in Hueyapan* (1975). Friedlander was surprised to encounter "Indian" villagers with a culture that makes them "virtually indistinguishable from non-Indian [rural Mestizo] Mexicans" (xv). From the grammar and vocabulary of their native Náhuatl to their foods, clothing, kinship terminology, medicines, and religion, villagers displayed an "Indian" culture that is heavily impregnated with European traits (85–100). It contains "mere traces of a destroyed cultural heritage

. . . [that] have virtually nothing to do with . . . daily life" (xviii). In short, Hueyapeños are not really Indians at all, if we define Indian ethnicity in terms of bearing unaltered pre-Hispanic culture. In fact, "their Indianness is not a distinct cultural entity but, rather, a reflection of the culture of a highly stratified contemporary society" (xv)—of class, in other words. Hueyapeños still identify themselves as Indians because they continue to think "in terms of a concept of Indian that was constructed during early colonial times when it was valid to describe . . . [them] as culturally distinct," even though "the Spanish subsequently destroyed the Hueyapeños' culture." The Hueyapeños fail to distinguish "between their 'culture,' which has been changing, and their 'class,' which has remained virtually the same"—at the bottom—since the Spanish Conquest (72).

The second approach to defining Indian ethnicity—Indians are people whose culture reveals indigenous roots—is exemplified by Guillermo Bonfil Batalla's highly popular *México Profundo: Reclaiming a Civilization* (1996). In his view, there are two Mexicos today: an authentic "deep Mexico" rooted in indigenous cultures and an "imaginary Mexico" based on imported (first European, then U.S.) culture and development projects. Bonfil Batalla rejects the concept of Mestizo Mexico, arguing instead that "there has never been a process of convergence, but, rather, one of opposition" (61). He recognizes cultural mixture, of course, but dismisses its importance to the definition of Indian ethnicity. The presence of European cultural traits "does not in itself indicate weakness or loss of authenticity within Indian cultures," because the basic question is not "the proportion of 'original' traits as opposed to 'foreign' traits" but "who exercises control over those traits: those who participate in the culture, or the members of the dominant society" (137). So long as the traits are integrated into a cultural complex that displays identifiable indigenous elements, we are dealing with Indian Mexico. Thus, "a wooden plow, brought by the [Spanish] invaders, is today as legitimate and 'authentic' a part of many Mesoamerican [Indian] cultures as are corn and tortillas" (137). So-called mestizos "are the contingent of 'de-Indianized' Indians" who have succumbed to "the pressure of ethnocide" (17) disguised as modernization, national integration, or economic development. "This . . . process, de-Indianization, has been called 'mixture' [*mestizaje*], but it really was, and is, ethnocide" (24). When these pressures reach the breaking point, the community's self-identity changes from Indian to mestizo, but its authentic identity remains the same: "Such communities are now Indian without knowing that they are Indian" (46).

Surprisingly, Bonfil Batalla and Friedlander reach mirror-opposite conclusions from the same database. Friedlander argues that the Hueyapeños are not Indians, even though they say they are, because cultural syncretism has robbed their pre-Hispanic elements of authenticity. Bonfil Batalla argues that many people who identify themselves as mestizos—or at least deny an Indian identity—are still Indians, because their culture still evidences many pre-Hispanic elements, the authenticity of which is not damaged by the European-Indian syncretism. In our view, though, these scholars' divergence is much less important than the key feature they share: they reserve for themselves the right to decide who is authentically Indian and who is not, irrespective of whether the designees agree.

The third position was articulated succinctly by Alfonso Caso (1948: 245): "Every individual who feels that he pertains to an Indian community [and who] conceives himself as an Indian, is Indian," though a community had to meet certain biological, linguistic, and cultural criteria to qualify as an "Indian community": predominance of non-European "somatic elements," preferential use of an indigenous language, and a "strong proportion" of "indigenous elements" in its "spiritual and material culture." Individual and group self-identity was the key element for Caso: "a group that has no sentiment that it is indigenous cannot be considered as such, even though it has abundant [Indian] somatic and cultural traits" (1948: 246).

In principle, we agree with Caso, with two caveats. First, as Doremus (2001: 381) points out, for many purposes Indians are not in fact granted self-definition but instead are defined by census takers, government officials, and anthropologists. Second, if self-identity trumps all other criteria—as Caso ends up postulating (cf. Villoro 1950: 200)—then ethnicity, Indian or otherwise, is disconnected from any *specific* cultural content, potentially conflating it with other kinds of group identities. For instance, a member of a political party is expected to accept "the same ethical, esthetic, social and political ideals as the group," to participate in its "collective sympathies and antipathies," and to become "in goodly degree a collaborator in its actions and reactions"—to use Caso's (1948: 245) words in describing Indian ethnicity—but we would not regard political party identity as an ethnicity. In our view, rather, ethnicity is a historically grounded sense of peoplehood revolving around a particular cultural constellation or tradition that is thought to set one social group (village, region, nation-state) apart from others. The particular cultural content varies by time and place, of course, and we deal with this point in Chapter 7, which concerns the transition from Indian to mestizo.

Comparing all three positions—Friedlander's, Bonfil Batalla's, and Caso's—we can say that the effective operational contrast is between ethnic self-identity (Caso) and researcher-designated ethnicity (Friedlander, Bonfil Batalla). The former is a realist-existential approach; the latter, a nominalist approach. Both are required for a complete picture. For instance, understanding the ethnic and social class placement of today's self-identifying "Indians" requires connecting them (nominally) with a pre-Hispanic population that never used the term. To take another example, regional analysis is usually possible only through the nominalist approach, which looks for common denominators that may or may not be acknowledged as such by contemporary people. We will not belabor this contrast, as it is precisely analogous to the one we laid out in Chapter 1 with reference to real and nominal social classes.

Having posed ethnicity as a historically grounded group identity, we rush to caution that the group (or any member of it) is not constrained by the empirical historical record as a historian or social scientist would define or interpret it. Rather, ethnic traditions are always subject to reinterpretation in an ongoing adaptation to changing circumstances. A good example of such reinterpretation comes from the town of Mexquitic, San Luis Potosí, which was founded by the Spanish in 1591 and populated by fifty families brought from Tlaxcala to help the Spanish subdue the area's nomadic Guachichil hunter-gatherers. When David Frye came to study the Tlaxcalans' descendants in 1982, though, they denied their Tlaxcalan roots. Instead, they presented themselves as descendants of the Guachichil, the very hunter-gatherers whom the Spanish had brought the ancestral Tlaxcalans there to displace. The identity switch had occurred because the Guachichil purportedly "were never conquered and therefore cannot be painted with those stereotypes that depict Indians as base, servile, defeated" (Frye 1996: 69). Furthermore, the town was now said to have been founded not by the Spanish but by San Miguel, its patron saint, who appeared on the site "because that was the place where God had ordained that a pueblo should be built" (Frye 1996: 192).

The small community of El Coyolillo near Jalapa, Veracruz, provides a second example of the fluidity of ethnic identity. Most of its inhabitants are descendants of African slaves imported to work on sugarcane plantations, but there is no local memory or tradition of this historical origin

(Martínez Maranto 1995: 531). Rather, the people attribute their Afro-Mexican physical traits either to a supposed influx of "Cubans" fleeing violence during Mexico's 1910–1920 Revolution or to divine whim, according to which *diós pinta como quiere* (God colors however he wants to).

Finally, we have Luis Vázquez's book, *Ser indio otra vez: La purepechización de los tarascos serranos* (1992) (To Be Indian Again: The Purepechization of the Highland Tarascans), about ethnic "re-Indianization" in highland Michoacán state. His book shows clearly that ethnicity within the modern nation-state is greatly shaped, even created, by politics. In 1971, the Ley Federal de Reforma Agraria (Federal Agrarian Reform Law) was amended to "explicitly recognize the agrarian community as a legal holding institution over [the] lands, waters, and forests" to which it could lay historical claim (Vázquez 1992: 114–115). The oldest documentable historical claims, of course, are those of Indian communities in the early colonial period, for which archival evidence can be mustered. The result was a rebirth of Indian ethnicity, complete with the revival of a long-obscure ethnic name, Purépecha—whose pre-Hispanic meaning probably was "commoner," equivalent to *macehual* in Náhuatl (see Lockhart 1992: 114–115; Vázquez 1992: 112n23)—to replace "Tarasca," the designation given them by the Spanish. Even some previously self-identified mestizo communities reconnected with their past, becoming Purépecha to take advantage of the new law (Vázquez 1992: 129–130). Purépecha ethnicity is now widespread in highland Michoacán and has been successfully employed to organize claims to rural resources, especially timber.

Conclusion

When Spain conquered Central Mexico in 1521, Spanish society—like the rest of Europe—was structured by estate stratification, and the conquerors set out to structure New Spain likewise. The system they instituted was necessarily very different from that of their homeland, however. While the Spanish polity contained a welter of local languages and identities, as well as Old and New Christians (the latter being recent converts from Islam or Judaism), there was an overriding sense of racial oneness from top to bottom, except for the relatively small number of African slaves in the port cities and a few recalcitrant Moors in Granada. Spanish nobles and commoners were born on the same soil, rooted in a shared political macro-history, and indoctrinated in the same official religion.

Central Mexico presented a radically different scenario. There, the Spaniards were a minuscule demographic fraction—no more than seventy thousand even by 1600—in a conquered overseas province with millions of subjects who were of markedly different race and culture/ethnicity. Furthermore, African slaves and their offspring soon equaled Spaniards in numbers in the major cities.

Not surprisingly, the estate system instituted in Central Mexico (and elsewhere in New Spain) was based on race, which initially coincided with political status: Spanish rulers, Indian commoners, and African slaves. Within twenty years, though, interbreeding across estates had caused ambiguities of classification, at first producing a generation of Spanish-Indian mestizos and Spanish-Indian-African mulattoes and then a confusion of blended heritage that not even the elaborate casta system could keep straight. Even a macro-classification into Spanish/casta/Indian became impossible to apply unambiguously in the cities, resulting increasingly in a dual division between Indians and non-Indians. After the estate system was officially abolished at Mexican independence in 1821, the Indian/non-Indian division remained in place as an ethnic distinction within a system of class stratification. During the late nineteenth century, though, the Mestizo Mexico ideology, which embraced both biological and cultural mixture as the essence of Mexican authenticity, arose among intellectuals and then became the official outlook after the Revolution (Basave 1992).

As official policy, Mestizo Mexico did not embrace diversity but rather sameness—except for the white elite, of course. The residual "Indian problem" was to be resolved by assimilating the Indian minority into national/mestizo culture, and a huge effort was expended on public education and "cultural missions" to that end (Aguirre B. and Pozas A. 1973; Caso et al. 1973; de la Fuente 1973; Sierra 1973). Less subtle methods were also used. In the 1920s, for instance, Indian men were prohibited by law from wearing their distinctive clothing in certain cities, as is documented at least for San Luis Potosí (Frye 1996: 38) and Mexico City (Bazán 2003). To avoid being fined or jailed while visiting these cities, Indian men had to shed their pajama-like white bottoms and buttonless pullover white tops (Friedlander 1975: 93–94) and don European-style pants and shirts. To this day, Indian migrants to major cities face ethnic discrimination. The greatest abuse is heaped on Indian children by non-Indian children at school—heavily in primary school, less in the secondary grades, and viciously again in certain universities and technical schools (Romer 1998).

Discrimination against Indians also occurs in the countryside and towns. Chiapas usually comes to mind in this regard (see Gall 1999), but discrimination is not absent from Central Mexico, where the Sierra Norte de Puebla preserved a clear separation of Indians and mestizos until late in the twentieth century. For instance, in the town of Zacapoaxtla, Puebla, Isaac observed the following in the mid-1960s: an Indian being physically assaulted for failing to yield the sidewalk to a mestizo; Indians standing in the back of the town's cinema, even when plenty of unoccupied seating was available; Indian men watching games in the pool hall and pushing the balls around unoccupied tables but never actually playing the game and quickly moving away from the tables when a mestizo approached. While these obvious signs of ethnic abuses have abated, Indians are still at great disadvantage in the area's legal systems (Sierra 1999).

Given the continuing racial and ethnic discrimination, it is easy to take the cynical view that the Revolution was a fraud, that indigenismo was a farce, and that Mestizo Mexico is a fantasy—as many intellectuals have concluded. Our experience in the United States leads us to a more generous view of Mexico's accomplishments in this regard. For example, we could not say of Mexico, as Sherry Ortner (1998: 4) has correctly said of the United States, that ideas about race and ethnicity have such "enormous cultural salience" that "they tend to swamp everything else" in discussions of socioeconomic differences; or that "class, race, and ethnicity are so deeply mutually implicated" in ordinary discourse "that it makes little sense to pull them apart" (9); or that "there is no class . . . that is not always already racialized and ethnicized" (10). To the contrary, while race and ethnicity are certainly categories in popular Mexican thought, occasionally erupting into public discourse, they are not major determinants of social class or even of most other forms of social placement (e.g., occupation, educational access) in Mexico today.

It is true that the Spanish introduced a race-based estate system in New Spain and that racism was integral to the preindustrial worldview—and did not have to await either capitalism or economic development, contrary to the rhetoric of certain Marxian social scientists in the late twentieth century (see Gall 1999: 78–79; Portocarrero 1999: 29n4). It is also true that Spanish and Portuguese colonialists had or developed a kind of racism distinct from what the British implanted in the United States. In the latter case, races were supposed to remain pure, and race mixture (especially of whites and African Americans) was, until very recently, viewed with such horror that any hint of mixed-race ancestry automatically assigned the person to the darker group. The Spanish-Portuguese view does not afford a complete contrast—"it is good to be mixed, but the whiter, the better" (Portocarrero 1999: 28)—but it did allow the development of an ideology of mestizofilia that would have been unthinkable in the Anglo-American tradition of a century ago and to a great extent even today. Certain Andean countries evidenced some form of mestizofilia in the mid-twentieth century (Portocarrero 1999: 27–28), but nowhere has the idea become so deeply embedded in both popular thought and official policy as in Mexico, much to that country's credit, we believe.

three: HACIENDAS AND THEIR WORKERS

For nearly four hundred years—from about 1570 to 1940—two socio-economic institutions dominated the Central Mexican countryside: the hacienda and the agrarian village. At first, only Spaniards owned haciendas. But by the beginning of the twentieth century hacendados had become a heterogeneous group that included a few non-Spanish Europeans and U.S. citizens, in addition to the heirs of the original owners and a much larger number of aristocratized mestizo elites. Economically, the great hacienda was an entrepreneurial, market-oriented institution for the entirety of its existence; its periodic unprofitability or withdrawal inward reflected adverse circumstances—political unrest, highway banditry, deteriorated roads, market slumps, labor scarcity—rather than the "feudalism" often erroneously attributed to it.

The agrarian village was exclusively Indian in the mid-sixteenth century. Over time, the rural population became mestizoized, both biologically and culturally, and from the turn of the twentieth century onward, an increasing number of mestizo villages appeared in the area (see Chaps. 2, 7). Agriculture remained the mainstay of village livelihood, but many villages also had resident artisans (e.g., potters, weavers, mat-makers) or other specialists (e.g., curers, muleteers, petty merchants). Villagers were never entirely self-sufficient, in the sense of being unconnected to the economy beyond it, but they were largely self-sustaining in terms of basic needs at the beginning of the period. From the mid-seventeenth century onward, most agrarian villages drew more heavily on the outside economy—mainly through wage labor but also through the manufacture and sale of artisan goods—to supplement their home-based production system. This dependency accelerated during the twentieth century, even though most hacienda lands were confiscated and distributed to villagers during Mexico's impressive agrarian reform, begun in earnest by President Lázaro Cárdenas (1934–1940).

The Hacienda in Legend

The great hacienda is shrouded in a legendary history that arose to rationalize the 1910–1920 Revolution and then endured to legitimate the postrevolutionary governments to the end of the twentieth century. Only in recent decades have scholars made significant headway toward a more objective view of the hacienda. While we gladly leave to others the scholarly battle to replace legendary with factual history, we must sketch out some of the main points of revisionist scholars (see, e.g., Buve 1984a; Jarquín Ortega 1990; Leal and Menegus 1995; Meyer 1986; Miller 1995; Nickel 1987, 1989a, 1989b, 1996).

The legend has two important components. The first portrays the hacienda as a precapitalistic "feudal patrimony" whose owners "sought a low, safe return on their capital" and, accordingly, greatly underutilized their vast resources—"the very reverse of entrepreneurs" (Brading 1980b: 11). Because haciendas occupied a large part of the countryside, their purported feudal inefficiencies, underutilization, and ostentatious wastefulness are said to have made them a major obstacle to Mexico's economic development. We have already pointed out that the hacienda was, to the contrary, an entrepreneurial institution from the start.

The second component holds that hacienda workers were everywhere half-starved, servile *peones* (laborers, peons) who lived on the hacienda and were bound to it by hereditary indebtedness so great that neither they nor their descendants could ever hope to get free. The major mechanism of indebtedness, the legend holds, was the hacienda's *tienda de raya* (company store), at which the food rations that were part of the workers' compensation had to be purchased at exorbitantly high prices, enriching the hacendado while hopelessly inflating the workers' debts. In addition, hacendados and their managers were everywhere free to imprison, flog, or even kill their workers with impunity.

For southeastern Mexico (Tabasco, Chiapas, Yucatán) and the Valley of Oaxaca, these features of the legend are almost certainly factually correct, at least during the Porfiriato (the dictatorship of Porfirio Díaz,

1876–1910). In Central Mexico, though, they are true for some haciendas but not for many others, even during the Porfiriato. In virtually every feature, in fact, the Mexican hacienda showed great differences not only by region (North, Center, Southeast) but also by time period (colonial, early independence, the Porfiriato), type of crop or product (e.g., maguey or sugarcane vs. grains or livestock), and owners' management styles (a continuum, apparently, from benign paternalism to ruthless cruelty). More controversial are differences in the relative incidence, relative intensity, and implications of various labor practices, especially the means of recruitment and retention, as well as working conditions. In fact, so great is the variation that it is hard to generalize about haciendas even in Central Mexico. Nevertheless, we can offer the following points.

1. Hacienda workers in Central Mexico were less oppressed by debt peonage—bondage because of debts owed to their employers—than were their counterparts in the Southeast (Tabasco, Chiapas, Yucatán) but more oppressed than many workers in the North, where employers feared their escape across the border into the United States. Most researchers have been surprised at the low incidence and intensity of debts among workers on Central Mexican haciendas (see Couturier 1976: 190–192; Gibson 1964: 252–255; Katz 1974: 6–9; Konrad 1980: 229–238; Konrad 1990; Mertens 1989: 163–167; Nickel 1987:48, 79, 91–95, 100–105; Rendón G. 1989: 84–90; Warman 1980: 57, 61). Although debt tended to increase during the Porfiriato in some areas, it apparently decreased in others (Buve 1984b: 207–108; Katz 1974: 28–29; Leal and Menegus 1995: 113–114; Mertens 1989: 164, 196; Nickel 1987: 116–117, 134; Rendón G. 1989: 86–89). Researchers have also uncovered great differences in the extent to which debts were inherited or in whether defaulting debtors were pursued legally or extralegally (e.g., Herrera Feria 1990: 146–147; Rendón G. 1989: 85–87).

   At the same time, it is important to keep in mind Richard Salvucci's (1987) cautionary statements about worker debt, which are as applicable to the hacienda as to the textile obrajes that he studied. Debt peonage "was complex and subtle," he cautions. "The method left no bruises and produced no complicated account books, but its dimensions were cunning" (116–117). Worker indebtedness to the enterprise does not necessarily indicate peonage, so long as workers have a reasonable possibility of liquidating their debts, but neither does the fact that debts are small—as was the case for many obraje and hacienda workers—necessarily rule out debt peonage. A common practice in both obrajes and haciendas was to require guarantors (*fiadores*), that is, kin or friends who were legally obligated to repay the debt if the debtor was unable or unwilling to do so (116). Default or flight to avoid repayment broke trust not only with the employer but also with the guarantor(s), an excruciating cost. Collection by means of squeezing guarantors was a cheap substitute for hunting down runaway debtors.

2. While many Central Mexican haciendas had tiendas de raya, they did not always fit the stereotype, even (perhaps especially) on the eve of the 1910–1920 Revolution. For instance, the ranching hacienda San Juan Hueyapan, in Hidalgo, had a tienda de raya, but it was rented out, which meant that "the hacienda did not participate directly in the benefits of the workers' debts. Furthermore, only a small percentage of the peons [laborers] owed money and . . . quantities were small" (Couturier 1976: 191). In fact, many such stores were rented out, rather than operated directly, by Central Mexican haciendas on the eve of the Revolution (Margolies 1975: 29–30; Nickel 1987: 167–168; Rendón G. 1989: 89–90). Many other haciendas, such as the large Santa Clara/Santa Ana sugar plantation, in eastern Morelos, had no tienda de raya by that time: "The hacienda had no company store nor any other method of tying people down through debts" (Warman 1980:61). Finally, the rations that were part of resident workers' pay were often, perhaps typically, reckoned at or below market value in Central Mexico, whether dispensed through the tienda de raya or issued directly (Mertens 1989: 185–187; Nickel 1987: 102–103, 171–172; Nickel 1989b: 37).
3. Resident laborers (*peones acasillados*) were neither the most numerous nor the most downtrodden or servile of hacienda employees in Central Mexico. Temporary workers were typically the most numerous by far, and they typically had fewer job benefits than the residents. There were also typi-

cally several grades of employees, as we shall see in the case studies. Second, at least by 1900 and often earlier, the resident laborers on many Central Mexican haciendas enjoyed substantial job benefits. In virtually all cases, they were given rent-free housing and a small plot of cultivable land. Among other benefits, which varied among haciendas (and were no doubt absent on many), were merit bonuses, old age pensions for workers and widows, a school for workers' children, free weekly or monthly medical attention, gifts of food and/or clothing for religious festivals, and free funeral mass and burial (Couturier 1976: 148; Mertens 1989: 172–173, 182–185; Nickel 1989b: 34–35, 38–39; Rendón G. 1989: 82; Warman 1980: 57–58). Third, there is considerable evidence that resident laborers in Central Mexico saw themselves as a privileged labor sector, by the standards of their day (Katz 1974: 27–28, 45; Nickel 1987: 98; Warman 1980: 59–62). Fourth, the resident laborers were nowhere, apparently, the first group to join the Revolution of 1910—not even in Morelos, where the struggle began in Central Mexico—and in some cases they remained loyal to the haciendas throughout it (Couturier 1976: 178, 186; Katz 1974: 45; Knight 1991; Leal and Menegus 1995: 41–48; Nickel 1989b: 18–19; Nickel 1988; Warman 1980: 110–111). We shall return to this last point in the case studies.

4. Physical abuse of workers apparently was universal in the Southeast (Tabasco, Chiapas, Yucatán), especially during the Porfiriato, but was typical of only certain parts of Central Mexico. The highlands of Puebla and Tlaxcala stand out in this regard (see Herrera Feria 1990; Katz 1974; Nickel 1996: 272 ff.). Many haciendas there had their own jails for laborers who were disobedient or whose behavior (e.g., adultery) offended the hacendados. That such abusive practices were not universal in Central Mexico is attested by Couturier's (1976: 131–164, 190–192) detailed account of the huge ranch in Hidalgo and Warman's (1980: 55–61) exemplary study of the Morelos sugar plantation. It is important to establish context for the anecdotal reminiscences of abuse that are sprinkled through the literature on haciendas (e.g., Lewis 1951:94–96; Medellín 1988: 75). Warman (1980: 58) writes, for example, "Physical punishment was not practiced, except in

the occasional outburst of evil temper from some administrator; moreover, there was no jail or fine for *realeños* [resident laborers]." Also: "Physical punishment was neither frequent nor necessary; blows, always a result of the chief's [administrator's] temperament, are remembered as something exceptional, not as an institutional corrective" (61).

5. In Central Mexico, it was the textile industry—not the hacienda—that sustained the most exploitative and brutal working environment (Ramírez R. 1984). The conditions of many late-nineteenth- and early-twentieth-century industrial clothing mills equaled those of the wool workshops of the sixteenth through eighteenth centuries in terms of viciousness. Tens of thousands of workers and their families were virtually imprisoned in company towns in the Puebla-Tlaxcala region (Ramírez R. 1984). Working conditions apparently were better in the other great textile center, the Córdoba-Orizaba region of Veracruz, but still sufficiently bad that worker unrest was high in the decade preceding the Revolution (Anderson 1974; Rajchenberg 1995). Furthermore, around 1900 it was the textile mill—not the hacienda—of highland Central Mexico that typically paid in scrip redeemable only at the company store, where goods were sold at grossly inflated prices.

In summary, Charles Gibson's (1964: 256) observation for the colonial period in Central Mexico may have considerable validity into the early twentieth century: "Hacienda labor might appear moderate in comparison with other circumstances of the colonial period, and harsh only in comparison with a twentieth-century liberal ideal." As we have indicated previously, though, this observation would not hold for the Southeast or the Valley of Oaxaca, where working and living conditions were often horrendous.

The Colonial Hacienda, ca. 1570–1820

The rise of the hacienda can be understood only in terms of the conjunction of two extreme circumstances: the dramatic demise of the indigenous population and the increasing financial desperation of the Spanish Crown. The former amounted to the greatest demographic catastrophe ever recorded, as Indians succumbed to introduced European and African diseases against which they had little natural immunity or tolerance. For instance, by 1570 the Valley of Mexico population was only one-fifth the size it had been exactly fifty years earlier, on the eve of the Spanish Conquest; and by 1650 "four-fifths of the 1570 population had been eliminated" by disease (Konrad 1980: 335).

Often, the surviving Indians regrouped into a reduced number of settlements, leaving large tracts of lands officially "vacant, unowned, or unappropriated" and thus available for Spanish appropriation "without injury" to Indians (Gibson 1964: 282). In part to complete the process of land clearance and in part to facilitate administration, the colonial government also concentrated Indian remnant populations into new or existing communities known as *congregaciones* (congregations), each with an official allocation of farming lands from which to meet subsistence and tribute requirements. Some of the now-vacant land was granted to individual Spaniards as rewards for service, typically with restricted inheritability (only one generation beyond the original grantee) so as to prevent the rise of independent power bases in New Spain. As the Spanish Crown became increasingly desperate for funds to pay for its European military ambitions, however, it yielded to the temptation of outright sale of vast amounts of these lands, creating the first haciendas.

At first, the haciendas provisioned themselves with Indian labor mainly through the repartimiento, supplemented by African slaves and some freely contracted Indian wage workers. According to Gibson (1964: 246), "Agricultural work was well adapted to repartimiento; it was relatively unskilled . . . ; it could be adjusted to seasonal demands; and excess laborers could be channeled into other employment." Nevertheless, hacendados soon came to prefer private wage labor over the repartimiento, even though the cost was approximately the same under both systems.

The changing preference involved both the legal structure of the repartimiento system and the Indian demographic catastrophe. The repartimiento was structured to meet Spanish labor needs without disrupting the Indians' economic activities or health. Accordingly, no more than 2 percent of the male Indian taxpayers were to be drawn away from any community in any particular week, and no man was to be worked more than four nonconsecutive weeks per year. Thus the repartimiento could serve Spanish interests only so long as it could draw on a large Indian population. Just as the hacienda was emerging as an important form of Spanish production, the great epidemic (probably typhus) of

1576–1581 killed off perhaps one-third to one-half of the already greatly reduced Indian population. Given this dramatic population reduction, the repartimiento could not possibly meet the increasing labor needs of the proliferating haciendas. The shortfall was so great that it could not feasibly be met by purchasing African slaves, which would have required a huge initial cash outlay, followed by maintenance expenses. Thus hacendados began hiring Indian wage laborers directly, circumventing the repartimiento.

From roughly 1580 to 1630, private and repartimiento labor systems often clashed, because Indian wage laborers (*gañanes*) were still subject to the repartimiento, which would assign them temporarily to other employers or put them to work on public construction projects. Not surprisingly, hacendados came to regard the repartimiento system, which could meet only a fraction of their labor requirements, as an economic obstacle. Whereas hacendados had opposed the Spanish Crown's attempt to abolish the repartimiento in 1601, they did not oppose the 1632 abolition order (Gibson 1964: 248).

The Indians certainly did not mourn the passing of the repartimiento system, which had arbitrarily assigned them to employers or public works projects at week-long intervals that disrupted their domestic, ritual, and economic routines. Wage-laborer status had the additional advantage of exempting Indians from labor service for public works within their own communities after 1586, and by 1600 or so, in some cases it also exempted them from appointment to community offices (Gibson 1964: 247–248). Furthermore, many hacendados paid the tribute (tax) owed by their gañanes (296–297), an act that registered them not only as free Indians who were stricken from the tax rolls of their places of origin but also as "assigned workers" (*trabajadores adscripticios*). Whether advantageous or inconsequential at the time, the latter practice came to have serious implications for the gañanes, whose "assignment" to the hacienda was thereafter enforced by colonial authorities (Nickel 1987: 32–40).

The recruitment of wage laborers was not always free of coercion, of course. As hacendados increasingly preempted Indian lands through purchase (often from persons lacking clear titles) and seizure—or by forcing sale or abandonment by repeatedly turning their livestock onto Indian fields—many Indians had little choice but to become wage laborers (Gibson 1964: 274–299; Henao 1980: 57–84). As Couturier (1976: 75) reports for central Hidalgo and Warman (1980: 52) for eastern Morelos, hacendados sometimes annexed adjoining lands solely to force peasants to become part-time wage workers. Wherever possible, these hacendados aimed to leave the surrounding villagers sufficient land to provide some part of their own livelihood, so that they would be eager to work for wages whenever the hacienda needed them but could survive on their own at no expense to the hacienda for the rest of the year (Avila S. 2002: 59–64; Couturier 1976: 28–30; Warman 1980: 52). Also, hacendados often relied on political or religious intimidation, paying Indian community governors or Spanish priests to recruit laborers on demand (Konrad 1980: 227). Another coercive means of recruitment was to threaten to cancel permission for Indians to rent hacienda pasturage—often on lands these Indians had lost through seizure or dubious sale—unless their communities sent laborers to the hacienda on demand (Konrad 1980: 227; also see Nickel 1987: 92–96; Nickel 1996: 82–89).

Debt created through advances against eventual wages was a mechanism of labor recruitment and retention for haciendas, but it does not appear to have resulted in debt bondage or other forms of oppression in Central Mexico during the colonial period. In fact, Gibson (1964) points to an official report of 1788 concerning a hacienda labor shortage that was having the effect of increasing Indian indebtedness, because it allowed Indians to negotiate sign-on advances of forty to eighty pesos, when the legal limit was five pesos. If an employer refused the higher amount, "the Indian would desert and move to another hacienda" where his demand was met. In other words, contrary to the usual view of debt labor, the worker's objective at this time "was not to escape but to enlarge the indebtedness," and its size was a proxy "measure of the bargaining power of the worker" (Gibson 1964: 255). This part of the 1788 report seems to have applied to regions less densely populated than the Valley of Mexico, but even there the records of the Jesuit hacienda Santa Lucía "suggest that the Jesuits had less interest in having workers in debt than workers had in being in debt" (Konrad 1980: 232).

At least in the Valley of Mexico, the fertile hinterlands of Mexico City, worker indebtedness usually did not exceed an amount that could be paid off with three weeks' labor. Even the legal limit of five pesos could have been liquidated with only twenty days' work at the going rate of two reales (one-fourth peso) per day during most of the colonial period (Gibson 1964: 251). For instance, fewer than half of the forty-two resident wage laborers (*gañanes radicados*) on Hacienda Santa Ana Aragón in 1771–1772 were in debt to the enterprise, and only four of them owed more than one peso each (254). On the much larger Hacienda Los Portales, about one hundred permanent or semipermanent wage workers owed a total of 367 pesos in 1778, "with individual debts ranging from a few reales to 28 pesos" (254). At Hacienda Santa Lucía in 1732, while it was still in Jesuit hands, the average debt was four pesos, mostly representing advances for marriages or funerals (Konrad 1980: 232), and the stated policy was to minimize indebtedness. "Only workers who proved themselves reliable were allowed to accumulate debts," and then only in amounts "that could be recouped within the period of the next accounting" (232).

Case Study: Hacienda Santa Lucía, 1576–1767

We are fortunate to have Herman Konrad's (1980, 1990) meticulous study of Hacienda Santa Lucía, in the northern Valley of Mexico, some thirty-five to forty kilometers (about twenty to twenty-nine miles) north of Mexico City, for the period 1576 to 1767. Except for being owned by the Jesuit order, Santa Lucía seems representative of highland Central Mexican haciendas during this period (see Konrad 1980: 332–349; Gibson 1964: 220–299).

Santa Lucía proper was the 70-square-kilometer (7000-hectare [ha], or 17,290-acre) ranch acquired by the Jesuits in 1576, but the name was later extended to a huge complex of scattered ranching and farming lands (*estancias*) in the valley. In 1681, the complex owned over 110,000 sheep, over 53,000 goats, 4,000 cattle, 2,000 horses, 40 donkeys, 25 mules, and 60 hogs. That same year, its crops included barley (180 ha), wheat (120 ha), maize (50 ha), chickpeas (20 ha), and haba beans (12 ha). The hacienda also owned and operated two slaughterhouses and a textile mill.

Its workforce was heterogeneous in two senses: it included both slaves and free workers, and it was finely graded according to skill and supervisory functions. Workers in the different branches of agrarian production also were known by different terms: ranch workers were *sirvientes*, workers who tended fields near the hacienda's residential center (*casco*) were gañanes, and agricultural field-workers on outlying lands were peones (Konrad 1980: 222–225). In 1740 Santa Lucía employed 433 sirvientes, 440 gañanes, and up to 400 peones (but an average of only 40, spread over the year) to meet seasonal needs (Konrad 1990: 131). Judging from Santa Lucía, it can be said that "occupational specialization was one of the dominating characteristics of [hacienda] labor organization" in colonial Central Mexico (Konrad 1990: 131; Konrad 1980: 217).

On its acquisition by the Jesuits in 1576, Santa Lucía proper had only 8 African/Afro-Mexican slaves, but their numbers grew greatly through both purchase and natural reproduction—to 108 in 1684, 291 in 1722, and 312 (including 160 adults) in 1743 (Konrad 1980: 246 ff.; Konrad 1990: 131). Most of the female slaves worked in the textile mill, although most of the weavers were male; apparently, the mill was mainly a slave domain. Slave women and children also worked as field hands and in household positions. Male slaves performed many different jobs, from herders (sometimes as supervisors) and field hands to artisans (carpenters, blacksmiths, muleteers) and trusted employees (couriers, secretaries). None of these jobs was the exclusive domain of slaves, however. There were free mestizos and mulattoes "employed . . . as carpenters, masons, muleteers, shepherds, and cowboys" (Konrad 1980: 251), and hundreds of Indian wage workers were employed for varying periods throughout the year. Most permanent positions were filled by Afro-Mexican slaves, mestizos, and Spaniards; few of the Indians worked on the hacienda for more than six weeks per year (336).

In the mid-eighteenth century, livestock production entailed four job levels (Konrad 1980: 218–225):

Level I: three or four grades of year-round employees who worked directly under the owners. They were paid annual salaries. In the top grade were the stewards (*mayordomos*), who kept accounts, doled out rations and advances, and oversaw the enterprise. Each had a "substitute" (*sobresaliente*) and an assistant (*ayudante*), who constituted the second and third grades. The fourth grade, where it existed, consisted of the steward's clerk (*escribano*), who helped to keep accounts.

Level II: the chief herdsmen and chief cowboys who supervised the shepherds and cowboys who tended specific flocks and herds. They were paid by the month, though they held supervisory positions, because their numbers were adjusted throughout the year to reflect fluctuating numbers of animals (and thus of shepherds and cowboys in need of supervision).

Level III: workers with "special skills required at important periods in the annual livestock cycles"—lambing, roundup, branding—and workers "responsible for special tasks," such as stable grooms, pack train drivers, ox drivers, and guards (Konrad 1980:

219). Some were employed seasonally and others year-round, but all were paid by the month. Although Level III employees were nonsupervisory, their pay scale overlapped that of the Level II supervisors, and both were well paid. In other words, the high skill requirements of Level III often commanded as much pay as the supervisory responsibilities of Level II.

Level IV: the most numerous and the lowest paid workers on the livestock ranches. Konrad (1980: 200) explains, "These were the shepherds, goatherds, and cowboys who cared for livestock under the direct supervision of others." They included boys—often the sons, younger brothers, or nephews of Level II and III workers—who received half an adult's pay. Everyone in Level IV was paid monthly.

The free gañanes who worked at or near the casco were similarly graded into four levels, generally comparable to the levels for the livestock workers (Konrad 1980: 222–225). Only two differences need to be mentioned. First, Level IV casco workers included many women who labored as field hands, tortilla makers (employed mostly to feed slaves), and domestics. Second, casco workers were paid by the day or, if skilled tradesmen, by the piece or task accomplished.

The peones who worked distant from the casco were also graded into four levels (Konrad 1980: 225–228). Levels III and IV required "more workers for shorter periods than any other hacienda activity" (225). They were engaged mainly for cultivation and weeding (about six weeks), as well as harvesting (about three weeks). Because these were all clearly defined seasonal tasks, "very few worked more than a hundred days in any year," and "only in exceptional circumstances were more than 100 workers employed at once" (225–226) on any hacienda division, or estancia. These seasonal workers lived in their own Indian communities, which were nearby but outside the hacienda boundaries. For some (probably most) of them, wage work on Santa Lucía or its divisions would have merely supplemented their basically peasant livelihood. We are less certain about the overall livelihood of the residents of such Indian towns as Tolcayuca, near the San Xavier division, who had lost their own lands to the hacienda (226); they probably made the rest of their living by sharecropping, perhaps on hacienda land that was previously theirs (see Gibson 1964: 274; Konrad 1980: 337).

Obviously, the hacienda was complex in terms of social classes from the start. Generally, employees comprised two social classes: a small middle class of salaried managers and a much larger working class. The former would have been a real class and the latter a nominal class, as defined in Chapter 1. The nominal working class comprised two real classes, though: full-time workers, most of whom resided on the hacienda, and part-time workers, who resided in Indian communities outside the hacienda. Present from the outset, this distinction grew in importance during the hacienda period.

Overlapping the hacienda social class distinctions was the increasingly complex array of estates and subestates discussed in Chapter 2. Spaniards, mestizos, and Afro-Mexican slaves held most of the permanent positions on the hacienda. Although the workforce was not perfectly hierarchized by race, Indians and Afro-Mexicans generally occupied the lowest occupational levels "and seldom the highest." In contrast, mixed-race workers usually "occupied the middle ranges . . . and seldom the highest or the lowest." Finally, "occupations of the middle range . . . were open to people of African, Indian, and Spanish origin" (Konrad 1980: 245).

The stratification system in Indian towns deserves some comment here as well. We have already noted that Indian "governors," mostly descendants of indigenous nobility, assisted hacendados in labor recruitment (Konrad 1980: 227). Furthermore, as Konrad notes for Hacienda Santa Lucía and its hinterland as early as the seventeenth century, Indians "holding well-paid jobs . . . or having access to hacienda resources (pasture, water, and land)" often "sided with the hacienda" to protect their personal advantages, even when these were contrary to community interests (347). Eventually, this mutuality of cross-estate interests became standard in Central Mexico (see Ouweneel 1995). In the eighteenth century, indigenous town rulers (caciques or *principales*) "were known as hacendados," and like their Spanish counterparts, they sold or rented land to outsiders "and disputed with Indian communities over possession" (Gibson 1964: 267). Furthermore, toward the end of the colonial period (late eighteenth/early nineteenth century), purportedly "Indian" caciques and "Spanish" hacendados "might both be mestizos, and their interests with respect to Indian communities might be much the same" (166).

The Heyday of the Hacienda: 1850–1910

Independence from Spain in 1821 did not result in great political or economic changes for most people, although it did bring almost immediate legal abolition of the racist casta system. In contrast, the political-economic reform legislation of the 1850s, known as La Reforma, touched the lives of all Mexicans. La Reforma made Mexico a secular state by stripping the Catholic Church of many of its privileges and monopolies. For instance, the 1855 Ley Juárez (Juárez's Law, named for Benito Juárez, then secretary of justice) removed the Church's judicial privilege (*fuero*), which had exempted it and all its personnel from civil and criminal prosecution in secular courts. It was followed by the 1857 Ley Iglesias (named for José María Iglesias, then secretary of justice), which forbade the Church's charging of high fees for administering the sacraments and specified that poor people should receive them free. Other reform laws established civil registries (births, adoptions, marriages, and deaths), civil administration of cemeteries, and secular primary and secondary education—all previously Church monopolies (see Meyer and Sherman 1991: 376–379).

The most important piece of economic reform legislation was the 1856 Ley Lerdo (Lerdo's Law, named for Miguel Lerdo de Tejada, then secretary of the treasury), which prohibited institutional ownership of property. Institutions (communities, governmental units, and religious bodies) were allowed to retain the resources that were essential to their expressed functions but only as trustees, not as owners. Thus the Catholic Church could retain, as trustee, "its church buildings, monasteries, and seminaries[,] and local and state units of governments their meeting halls, jails, and schools," but all other institutional property, including the Church's vast rural and urban landholdings, was to be sold at auction (Meyer and Sherman 1991: 378–379). Although the intended target of the Ley Lerdo was the Catholic Church, the law applied to *all* institutions, even the communally owned ejido lands of Indian communities.

The Ley Lerdo targeted the Catholic Church because it had accumulated vast, tax-free landholdings through donations and purchases. By the 1850s, the Church owned perhaps one-fifth of the country's nearly seven thousand haciendas and held mortgages against many more (de la Peña 1982: 73–74, 85–86, 119–121, 150). In part, the Ley Lerdo reflected the greed of Mexico's expanding upper-middle class, which coveted the Church's revenue-producing properties. It also reflected public resentment against the Church for its pro-Spanish stance during and after the wars of independence and for its inclination to use its great economic leverage to meddle in politics. At the same time, the liberals (free-market capitalists) who engineered La Reforma genuinely believed that putting the Church's vast lands under private ownership would be a powerful stimulus for the country's economic development.

But why were the Indian ejidos included under the Ley Lerdo? There are at least two answers. First, broadening the law to include all institutional property, not just that of the Church, was a "political tactic . . . to avoid the accusation of being an antireligious government" (de la Peña 1982: 126). Second, the reformers' liberal ideology held that communal ownership was an obstacle to the country's economic development, on grounds that it stifled economic initiative and investment. By extension, communal ownership of ejido lands was thought to be a principal cause of the Indians' poverty, because it sheltered them from personal responsibility and the supposedly invigorating competition and incentives of the market economy (124). Most of the reformers apparently believed sincerely that the parcelization of Indian ejidos, to give the cultivators pro rata shares in fee simple (clear title) ownership, coupled with the sale of the Church's rural lands, would generate an extensive farming middle class like that of the United States, their preferred model of economic development.

Within about six months of the passage of the Ley Lerdo, twenty-three million pesos worth of property (an astronomical sum in that economy) had changed hands. Church property accounted for twenty million pesos of this total. The remaining three million pesos represented properties of town governments and Indian communities, mostly the latter (de la Peña 1982: 128; Meyer and Sherman 1991: 378). Sadly, this massive transfer did not create the large middle class of rural capitalists projected by the reformers. To the contrary, it resulted in greater concentration of property in the hands of wealthy merchants and hacendados (de la Peña 1982: 127). Furthermore, over the next sixty years, the law contributed to Indian impoverishment, as the parcelization of ejidos facilitated both hardship sales by Indians during family crises and piecemeal encroachment (i.e., against one defenseless parcel at a time) by hacendados.

Economic liberalism remained the official political outlook from the 1850s until the Revolution of 1910–1920. During the Porfiriato, this philosophy was grounded in French positivism, which stressed the application of scientific principles to all social policy. For Mexico's ruling class of the period, positivism meant mainly economic rationality (capitalist maximization), the application of natural science to promote industrialization, and "scientific," or orderly, management of the country by its educated elites, all with the aim of promoting economic development and modernization. In practice, however, the philosophy was often more akin to British social Darwinism, which viewed differences in individual, class, and national wealth as the natural outcomes of the Darwinian survival (or financial success, in this case) of the fittest. As such, it was the perfect cover for racism and the maintenance of upper-class privilege (see Brading 1980b: 5–7; Meyer and Sherman 1991: 453–457; Zea 1968).

Of particular interest is the 1883 law that authorized the surveying of all public (*baldío*, or idle) lands, meaning all land without written legal title. Survey companies were reimbursed with one-third of all such land surveyed "and the privilege of purchasing the remaining two-thirds at bargain prices" (Meyer and Sherman 1991: 458). Often, these companies were able to run roughshod over the peasantry, few of whom had legal titles to their parcels. If they were able to produce ownership documents, they were told that these "had not been properly signed, or notarized, or stamped, or registered" (ibid.). By these means, the survey companies came to own "one-fifth of the total land mass of Mexico" by 1894, and by 1910 "over one-half of all rural Mexicans lived and worked on . . . haciendas" (458).

These processes did not operate uniformly throughout Mexico, however. First, the enormous tracts of land assembled by the survey companies were located mainly in the country's thinly populated and less productive regions, especially the northern deserts and southern mountains and jungles. Thus while a mere 110 haciendas—constituting only 0.75 percent of the country's 14,750 registered haciendas—owned about one-third of all Mexican hacienda lands shortly before the Revolution, these huge properties together were worth only 5.4 percent of the assessed value of Mexico's haciendas at the time (Brading 1980b: 14).

Second, while only about half of Mexico's rural population lived in independent peasant villages in 1910, the figure for major portions of Central Mexico exceeded 80 percent. Though many of these Central Mexican villagers had lost some or even most of their lands to hacienda encroachment, they did not necessarily all end up as half-starved or debt-bound servile laborers. Many of them rented or sharecropped hacienda lands that were typically readily available to them for this purpose because most Central Mexican hacendados cultivated only the irrigated or valley bottomland and let out the rest to peasants (Brading 1980b: 11–12; Sanderson 1984: 25–26). In this and other ways, the economic and social class structure of much of Central Mexico on the eve of the 1910–1920 Revolution shows great continuity with the colonial period, despite increasing land usurpation by haciendas during the late nineteenth century.

Important qualifications to the foregoing must be made with reference to the sugar-growing areas of Morelos and some portions of Puebla and Tlaxcala. The late nineteenth century saw an increased capitalization of sugarcane production and a concomitant squeeze on workers—longer workdays, reduced pay or rations, evictions from rented land—to pay for it, coupled with an increased pace of land seizures and swindles against peasants (see Avila S. 2002: 53–66; Brading 1980b: 13; Sanderson 1984: 25–27; Warman 1980: 40–65; Womack 1969: 41–51). Some other localized areas of Central Mexico doubtless experienced similar hardships and abuses during this period (see Herrera Feria 1990). More generally, the bargaining power of unskilled rural workers gradually declined over the whole region during the eighteenth and nineteenth centuries, as the rural population recovered from the demographic catastrophe of the early colonial period and as haciendas nibbled away more and more of the peasants' lands.

Case Study: Haciendas in Tlaxcala, 1910–1920

There are several excellent studies of haciendas in the state of Tlaxcala for the decades preceding and following the 1910–1920 revolution (Buve 1984b; Leal and Menegus 1995; Ramírez R. 1990; Rendón G. 1989). Like most haciendas in Central Mexico, Tlaxcala's were relatively small. The state's largest properties were about 10,000 hectares (24,700 acres, or about 39 sq. mi.), a fraction of the size of the great latifundia of North Mexico and more in the range of haciendas in Morelos (Meyer and Sherman 1991: 458–460; Womack 1969: 391–392).

Nevertheless, haciendas occupied a large area of Tlaxcala. In 1915 the state's 202 properties of 200 hectares or more covered 72 percent of its surface, and its 89 properties of more than 1000 hectares occupied 57 percent of the state's area. That same year, a mere 16 haciendas owned one-fourth of the state's surface (Ramírez R. 1990: 76–86). On the other hand, the great majority of its rural population lived in autonomous villages or towns, not on haciendas or farms; in 1910, only about one-fourth of its agricultural workers (roughly 9,400 of some 36,000) were peones acasillados, or resident workers.

FIGURE 3.1. Maguey plant (*Agave* spp.) with leaves up to two meters (6.5 ft.) long. Photo by Barry Isaac.

Although Tlaxcala is a small state—about 4000 square kilometers (compare Rhode Island's 3156 sq km)—it showed dramatic regional variation in terms of hacienda size and working arrangements on the eve of the Revolution. The northern part (roughly two-thirds of the state's area) was dominated by fully commercial haciendas of 1000 to 2000 hectares each (about 4 to 8 sq. mi.), many of which specialized in the production of *pulque*, a wine fermented from maguey sap (see Fig. 3.1). These haciendas employed many resident workers; in fact, almost all of this zone's population lived on the haciendas. In contrast, south-central Tlaxcala was typified by smallholder peasant agriculture and artisanry in independent villages with farming lands as well as pastures and commons. Its haciendas were medium-sized, about 500 to 1000 hectares (roughly 2 to 4 sq. mi.), and had some resident workers but also relied heavily on hired laborers from the nearby villages. Finally, southeastern Tlaxcala had many small haciendas of 250 to 500 hectares each (some 1 to 2 sq. mi.) that employed workers from the surrounding peasant villages to supplement their small force of residents. These villagers had lost most of their best land to hacienda encroachment, but they retained hillside parcels from which to make a partial living (Buve 1984b: 215–218; Leal and Menegus 1995: 74–75; Ramírez R. 1990: 41–42). As we shall see later, these regional differences had great implications for the 1910–1920 Revolution and its aftermath (Leal and Menegus 1995).

Leal and Menegus (1995) and Rendón G. (1989) provide detailed descriptions of Mazaquiahuac and El Rosario, large pulque-producing haciendas (4620 and 4158 hectares—roughly 18 and 16 sq. mi.—respectively) in northern Tlaxcala, both owned by the Solórzano family before and during the Revolution. In 1910, these haciendas employed four types of workers: trusted employees (*dependientes*), gang laborers (*peones de cuadrilla*), sap collectors (*tlachiqueros*), and weekly workers (*semaneros*). Dependientes were empleados de confianza who worked directly for the owner and, in effect, represented him or her to the rest of the workforce. They included the administrator, the brew master (*mayordomo del tinacal*), the supply master (*trojero*), and the foremen (*mayorales*). The haciendas' registers also included in this category all other workers "who carried out some domestic task"—accountants (*escribanos*), watchmen (*veladores*), porters and doormen (*porteros*), and janitors (*barrenderos*)—even though they would not usually have been regarded as such (Leal and Menegus 1995: 36). The dependientes received the highest pay, as well as food rations, "and could ask the haciendas for loans in cash or kind" (36). Such loans were regarded as a privilege, a point to which we shall return.

Peones de cuadrilla were the most numerous of the permanent employees. They performed general agricultural work in the cultivation of both cereals and maguey. They were paid a small wage, but their main recompense consisted of maize rations, shanties, and small plots of land on which to produce part of their livelihood. "They also . . . obtained loans in cash or kind" (Leal and Menegus 1995: 37).

Tlachiqueros were specialists who collected the maguey sap and brought it to the brewing vats, where it was fermented to make pulque (see Guerrero 1985; Ruvalcaba 1983). They were piece workers, paid according to the amount of sap they harvested. They "were not authorized to receive food rations nor could they request advances in kind or cash" (Leal and Menegus 1995: 37).

Semaneros were the most numerous of all, but they were hired as casual laborers (*eventuales*), that is, only as needed. They were employed in large numbers for the planting and harvesting seasons but were largely unemployed during the growing season. Although hired by the week, they were piece workers, paid according to the number of tasks finished during the week. They were paid in cash and "did not have the right to food rations or to advances in kind or cash" (Leal and Menegus 1995: 37).

There is more than one way to analyze these data in terms of social classes. Leal and Menegus (1995: 41–42) initially suggest two nominal classes, based on the type of remuneration received: workers who were paid primarily in cash (trusted employees, sap collectors, and weekly workers) and gang laborers who were paid mainly in kind (food, housing, land). They quickly reject this approach, however, in favor of distinguishing only the two real classes that became evident in the episodes of labor unrest that occurred during the 1910–1920 Revolution: hacendados and workers. We also prefer this alternative, for the following reason. Despite the clear differences among the four types of hacienda workers—pay basis (mainly cash vs. mainly kind), employment term (permanent vs. casual), and autonomy (supervisory vs. nonsupervisory)—they all made the same kinds of demands, typical of wage workers, during the period of local revolutionary turbulence (1910–1915): higher pay, shorter hours, task reduction, more steady employment, and forgiveness of debt. None of them, not even the administrators, demanded to be given land.

The *agrarista* (agrarianist) slogan "Land to the Tiller," which attracted revolutionary recruits in many parts of the country, simply had no resonance in this part of Tlaxcala (Leal and Menegus 1995: 22–31, 42, 48). As Warman (1980: 110) similarly observed in Morelos, these workers' peasant past was simply too distant for that; they had acquired different skills and formed new identities, even new class identities. In short, despite the obvious differences among them, the resident hacienda employees of all types in northern Tlaxcala and Morelos saw themselves as present and future wage workers, as hired help, not as potential yeoman farmers.

Regionally, hacendados also recognized a mutual class interest. In response to worker unrest and the country's revolutionary climate, the region's hacendados formed the Farmers' League (Liga de Agricultores) in 1912. The league slightly raised the wages of weekly workers, abolished maize rations (until terrible hardship among workers in 1916–1917 resulted in their partial restoration), and forgave the debts of gang laborers. This last provision carried the implication that no further debts could be incurred; even the trusted employees were to be denied their traditional draw against their annual salaries. In short, the hacendados regarded worker debt as burdensome and were at pains to avoid reinstituting it (Leal and Menegus 1995: 42–47, 113–114). "By standardizing pay and the other forms of remuneration over the whole region, the League eliminated competition for manpower among the hacendados themselves" (43), so that workers could no longer play one hacienda off against another in search of better wages or working conditions or larger advances. The league also succeeded in electing favorable candidates to state and national legislatures in 1912–1913. In fact, so successful was the league in Tlaxcala that it was widely imitated, resulting in the National Farmers' Congress (Congreso Nacional de Agricultores) in 1913 (45).

An alternative approach to the social class structure of northern Tlaxcala would separate trusted employees (dependientes) from the other three kinds of workers, as well as from the hacendados, yielding a tripartite division of real classes: hacendados (owners), managers and supervisors (dependientes), and laborers (all other employees). The trusted employees, after all, were overseers and specialists who supervised the laborers and reported directly to the owner. Although they had been demoralized by their loss of privileges under the labor reforms of the Farmers' League (Leal and Menegus 1995: 114)—which denied them their traditional advances against annual salaries—on Mazaquiahuac and El Rosario they remained loyal to the owner until about 1917–1918, when working conditions deteriorated drastically from guerrilla raids and general economic ruin. That they had held the line against the other workers under tough conditions is reflected in the fact that, by 1916, the administrators had become so frightened of the laborers that they no longer spent the night on the hacienda (118). Turnover now became a problem, as administrators who customarily "had remained all their life at their jobs succeeded one another over the course of a few months"; some left voluntarily, but others were fired for engaging in the pilfering—even in cahoots with guerrillas—that became common during the revolutionary chaos (115–121).

In south-central and southeastern Tlaxcala, the case for regarding dependientes as belonging to a social class distinct from that of the other hacienda workers is even stronger. Here, the clear majority of all other hacienda workers resided in independent peasant villages and had class interests that were in sharp contrast to those of both hacendados and their trusted administrators and supervisors. Although these laborers experienced much occupational and geographic mobility—moving "from country to city, from farmland to workshop or factory, from family mini-farm to the haciendas to be employed as seasonal agricultural workers" (Leal and Menegus 1995: 79)—they remained emotionally and socially independent, "tied to the political-religious traditions of [their] towns" and to their neighborhood reciprocity networks (79). They responded enthusiastically to the revolutionary agraristas who promised them a reward of land in return for their loyalty. In short, these workers continued to see themselves as peasants, even though their landed resources were so reduced that they had to supplement their village livelihood with outside wage labor.

At the regional level, the rural stratification picture is somewhat more complex. We would distinguish a real class of hacendados at the top, of course. Below them would be, first, a nominal middle class (or set of middle classes) consisting of the hacienda dependientes (in the broad sense of supervisors and skilled specialists) and *rancheros* (independent owners of middle-sized farms, or ranchos). At the bottom would be a nominal lower class (or set of lower classes) comprising both hacienda laborers and village peasants or artisans.

We must say a few words about the rancheros, the middle-sized farmers who occupied the interstices between the great hacendados and the peasant villagers in much of Central Mexico. In some areas, they date mainly to the Porfiriato, when the construction of railroads made medium-scale cash cropping profitable and attracted investment in farming lands by middle-class merchants (see Couturier 1976: 101–102). In other areas, they were present as early as 1580; some were non-Spanish immigrants (especially Portuguese), but many were the poor kinsmen or former employees of wealthy Spaniards (see Lockhart 1991: 55–70). In the state of Tlaxcala, ranchos became nearly as numerous as haciendas: 134 ranchos to 153 haciendas in 1824 and 110 to 117 in 1910 (Ramírez R. 1990: 26).

The distinction between hacienda and rancho has been problematic for historians, who often take 1000 hectares as the dividing line, but this criterion clearly would not apply to Tlaxcala, where many of the agrarian units classed officially as haciendas were well below this mark. Effectively, the distinction was not one of land size but of management culture. In contrast to hacendados, rancheros usually lived year-round on or very near their farms and participated in the actual work, in addition to supervising employees. Furthermore, rancheros and their employees dressed alike, talked and bantered alike, and shared many cultural values (Buve 1984b: 208–209; Lomnitz-Adler 1992: 169–178).

The ranchero class has not been well studied with reference to the 1910–1920 Revolution, but we are able to say that their participation and their fate varied substantially (Buve 1984b: 208–210, 256–261). In some areas they were overrun early in the conflict and/or were the first to be expropriated under agrarian reform, because they lacked the hacendados' fighting force and political connections (Couturier 1976: 176–181); in other areas, they survived relatively intact. Although most rancheros surely opposed the Revolution, at least in Guerrero state they endorsed it enthusiastically—politically, to restore the local autonomy that had been eroded during the Porfiriato; economically, to reduce taxes and dismantle the business monopolies enjoyed by the dictator's friends and patrons (Jacobs 1980: 83). In the end, though, rancheros and hacendados were subject to the agrarian reform laws, which generally divested them of all but 200 hectares (495 acres) of rainfall cropland or 100 hectares (248 acres) of irrigated land, although more generous allowances were granted in livestock areas (see below).

After the Haciendas: 1940–2000

The 1910–1920 Revolution and the subsequent agrarian reform overthrew the hacendados as a political and economic class. While long remaining the prestige class in the eyes of the rising plutocracy (see Chaps. 4, 8), the old hacendado aristocracy quickly became a scorned, even demonized social segment among the middle and lower classes. The rural lower stratum of peasants and agricultural wage workers was also strongly affected by the Revolution and its aftermath, but it was not as fundamentally transformed as the aristocracy.

The Revolution mobilized millions of village peasants, many of whom were part-time wage workers, who had lost lands to haciendas or even to royal land grants going back to the early colonial period. Many haciendas, especially the smaller ones that were not defended by armed force or that were abandoned in panic, were overrun and effectively appropriated by agrarista revolutionary forces. Although conservative President Venustiano Carranza (1915–1920) rolled back many of the agrarista victories, the hacendados' respite was temporary. Agrarian reform—a program of land expropriation and redistribution—was written into Article 27 of the 1917 Constitution and was a major policy focus under President Lázaro Cárdenas, who distributed millions of hectares of good land to rural villagers in the form of ejidos (inalienable land grants to communities). The *ejidatarios* (grantees) had to use the land themselves and could not sell, rent out, or mortgage their allotments.

The presidents who succeeded Lázaro Cárdenas after 1940 varied in their enthusiasm for agrarian reform, but until 1992 none dared to halt it. In that year, President Carlos Salinas (1988–1994) persuaded the legislature to amend Article 27 of the Constitution in accordance with his neoliberal (market-driven) reforms. The three most important changes were as follows: the government was no longer obligated to distribute land to petitioning villagers; ejidatarios could henceforth rent out, collateralize, or mortgage their parcels; and ejido communities could completely privatize their land, giving each ejidatario full title to his respective parcel, if half or more of the village ejidatarios voted to do so (see Collier 1994).

The proponents of these changes argued that agrarian reform had stymied agricultural production in Mexico by creating millions of tiny farms that were too small to absorb modern technology; in Central Mexico, for instance, the average holding per ejidatario had long been two hectares or less (Sanderson 1984: 98). Proponents further argued that the amendment would do no more than legalize existing arrangements, because many ejidatarios already (illegally) rented out their tiny parcels to large farmers, who had managed thereby to consolidate holdings that could support mechanized farming (see Medellín 1988: 63 ff.; Restrepo and Sánchez 1972: 103–121). Opponents of the amendment recalled the devastating alienation of peasant lands that had followed the liberal reforms of the 1850s and predicted that the 1992 neoliberal reform would likewise impoverish the peasantry. The outcome is still uncertain.

Under the agrarian reform policy (1917–1992), all large landholdings were subject to government expropriation. The legal provision for reimbursement was ignored in practice. Landowners were permitted to retain a portion equivalent to "small property," the size of which varied through time, by state or region, and by land quality and use. Generally, small property was defined as 100 to 150 hectares (247–370 acres) of irrigated land, 200 hectares (494 acres) of rain-fed land, and 500 hectares (1,235 acres, or slightly less than 2 sq. mi.) of pasture. The major exception was ranchland; beginning in 1937, ranchers who owned at least five hundred beef cattle or three hundred sheep could petition for twenty-five-year exemptions from expropriation, many of which were granted, so as not to disrupt these important economic activities.

Despite these limitations and exemptions, about half of Mexico's total land surface had been redistributed by 1970. In that year, ejidatarios held half or more of all land under cultivation in the seven states of Central Mexico: Morelos, 78 percent; Guerrero, 72 percent; Hidalgo, 68 percent; Mexico, 64 percent; Tlaxcala, 54 percent; Veracruz, 52 percent; and Puebla, 51 percent (Sanderson 1984: 3, 100–102).

Although massive in comparison to similar efforts elsewhere (Tuma 1965), Mexico's agrarian reform was only partially successful in meeting its goals. As a humanitarian gesture, it restored land to the descendants of the original indigenous owners, many of whom had been victims of land seizures or swindles. It also rewarded the rural people in whose name the Revolution of 1910 had been launched and who suffered most of its casualties. Politically, the reform succeeded in drawing the agrarian sector more tightly into the orbit of the central government (see Sanderson 1984: 51–63).

As a social welfare program, though, agrarian reform was both a short-term success and a long-term failure (see Restrepo and Sánchez 1972). For about twenty-five years (roughly 1940–1965), it succeeded in fortifying the livelihood of millions of peasants and, by that means, greatly slowed rural-to-urban migration, which otherwise might have created overwhelming urban hardship or political unrest. By the mid-1960s, however, the reform's long-term failure had become fully evident (see Arizpe 1985: 16–25).

Four factors stand out in the agrarian reform's failure to create long-term rural prosperity:

1. The typical ejido allocation was too small to absorb modern machinery efficiently.
2. The reform spawned massive bureaucratic corruption, often resulting in failure to deliver promised agricultural inputs (e.g., fertilizer, pesticides, herbicides), and also gave rise to a new breed of oppressive and self-serving local political bosses, or caciques, who inserted themselves between the national bureaucracy and local ejidatarios (see Bartra 1975b: 23–30; Knight 1991: 96–100; Paré 1975: 47–58; Restrepo and Sánchez 1972).
3. The reform's initial benefits to the peasantry were overwhelmed by population growth. Mexico's population quadru-

pled between 1900 and 1970; it doubled again by 2000, from 48.2 to 97.5 million (Sanderson 1984: 3; INEGI 2003: 3). As a result, many children of ejidatarios either did not inherit land rights at all or had to share the income of an ejido allotment that had been intended for only a single household.

4. The combination of rural modernization and national industrialization subtly but massively eroded most of the supplemental occupations that had rounded out the village economy (see Arizpe 1985: 21–23, 77–78). Almost all of the objects that the peasant household traditionally made for sale in regional markets to supplement its agricultural income—such as cloth, capes, sandals, baskets, mats, rope, implement handles, bags, pots and dishes, furniture, toys—are now made in distant factories. Even pulque, the quintessential Central Mexican fermented drink made from maguey sap, has been largely replaced by bottled soft drinks and brand-name beers; these bottled drinks were promoted by national industrial interests through a "propaganda war against pulque" intended to give it "a repulsive image" (Medellín 1988: 94–95), to the detriment of the rural economies of the semiarid maguey-growing areas of Central Mexico. Finally, even the traditional village service providers—musicians, curers, midwives, embroiderers, pack train muleteers, and so on—have been largely or entirely displaced by modern services that originate in the cities but today almost instantly reach the countryside.

By the mid-1960s, the foregoing factors had effectively erased the initial improvement in livelihood that many peasant households had achieved under the agrarian reform. Fewer and fewer of their children were able to make an adequate and satisfying living at farming. They had returned to square one. At best, they are once again part-time peasants who supplement their farming incomes with seasonal wage labor (see Aldana 1994; Paré 1977). Arguably worse off are the millions of unskilled rural-to-urban migrants who fled rural poverty only to end up in the slums of Mexico City and the state capitals, where they are at the mercy of a quixotic labor market and far removed from direct production of food and shelter (see Chap. 6).

PART TWO

The Postrevolutionary Period (1920–2000)

four: THE UPPER CLASSES

Aristocracy, Plutocracy, Political Class, and Prestige Upper-Middle Class

The main classes of Central Mexico's upper stratum are the traditional aristocracy and the plutocracy that displaced it as Mexico's ruling class during the late twentieth century (see Nutini 1995, 2004). Although many aristocratic families had urban as well as rural investments, the "main source of wealth for aristocrats everywhere has always been the land" (Nutini 2004: 153). In fact, the Mexican aristocracy was so heavily invested in and identified with the country's great haciendas that it quickly lost its ruling-class standing when most of its farm- and ranchlands were expropriated by the agrarian reform program in the three decades following the Revolution. The same decades saw the emergence of the present-day plutocracy, whose principal investments are in large-scale financial, manufacturing, and commercial enterprises.

The aristocracy and plutocracy often interact with the other two classes of Central Mexico's upper stratum: the political class and the top tier of the upper-middle class. The latter, which we call the prestige-UMC, comprises a thin veneer of elite families who provided social support to the aristocracy—principally by swelling attendance at their social functions—before the Revolution and who assimilated a large portion of the aristocratic expressive array. Following the Revolution, the aristocracy fled the provincial cities, leaving the prestige-UMC as the local upper class and the model of expressive emulation for the upwardly mobile, including the emerging provincial plutocracy.

The political class comprises present and former high office holders at the federal, state, and, less often, local levels—past presidents, cabinet members, state governors, large-city mayors, ambassadors, and members of official commissions. At the national level, the most influential members of this class have held high federal offices in Mexico City, frequently a source of enrichment, and many of these people became plutocrats on retiring from politics. In contrast, retired politicians whose highest offices were at the local or provincial level usually have not become plutocrats and, indeed, have tended to avoid further prominence.

The political class has always been small, at no time having more than about fifteen hundred members (Nutini 2004, 2005). From 1929 to 2000, virtually all members of the political class were affiliated with the so-called official party, the PRI. Few were highborn; most, in fact, originated in the lower-middle or solid-middle class (see Chap. 5). In contrast, the new members of the political class swept into office by the Partido de Acción Nacional (PAN; National Action Party) presidential victory in 2000 are mostly from the solid-middle and upper-middle classes.

The Aristocracy

IDEOLOGICAL SELF-IDENTIFICATION AND STRUCTURAL REALITY

Perhaps the most salient diagnostic trait of both the European aristocracy and its New World offshoots is their self-awareness as a distinctive estate or, after the late eighteenth century, social class. This self-consciousness was enhanced in the New World, where fresh conquest resulted in readily observable ethnic/racial distinctions between the superordinate and subordinate sectors. The ensuing centuries of colonialism, with its inherent ideology of discrete social estates, reinforced aristocratic self-consciousness. From this standpoint, being an aristocrat in the European and New World tradition entails both a set of structural attributes (social, economic, and material considerations) and a state of being (mostly expressive considerations) that define the aristocratic estate or class vis-à-vis all other social segments. Thus Mexican aristocrats have a very clear sense of themselves and their position in society, which quite often does not correspond to present structural reality but which nonetheless conditions much of their behavior. Although today's aristocrats acknowledge the reality of their class's loss of power and wealth, they feel that their lineage and role as carriers of a long expressive tradition entitle them to a privileged position in the social structure. Upwardly mobile plutocrats accept these aristocratic self-perceptions, which are rejected by those plutocrats and members of the political class who are not upwardly mobile.

The Mexican aristocracy is a real social class as defined in Chapter 1. Most important, it is a real class in the subjective, ideological sense (Laurin-Frenette 1976: 252–257), since it is a historical reality, has a collective consciousness, and has a definite view of itself in relation to the global society. Its unusually acute consciousness of kind is reflected in endogamy, which has remained important for maintaining its boundaries and integrity even during its long decline. Probably more important than any other factor in sustaining the aristocracy's sense of identity is the deep conviction that its ancestors were the true architects and rulers of Mexico for nearly four hundred years, a view not shaken by its political and economic downfall during the twentieth century. In fact, today the Mexican aristocracy is largely an anachronism and a testament to the persistence of social institutions long after the demise of the forces that gave rise to them.

In addition to self-identification, a superordinate real class must be recognized as such by other classes if it is to be a significant social entity. By this standard, the Mexican aristocracy exists only minimally today, for it is doubtful that more than a few percent of the total Mexican population is even aware of its continued existence, and even fewer accord it the high status that its members attribute to themselves. Of course, this is the inevitable result of the overall democratization of Mexican society since the 1910 Revolution, the aristocracy's post-Revolution residential and social self-segregation within the great urban sprawl of Mexico City, and the country's enormous population growth in the second half of the twentieth century.

While the plutocracy generally grants the aristocracy the highest degree of social recognition, the same cannot be said of other social classes or strata today. The lower classes recognize degrees of status but strictly on the basis of wealth and political power, not on the basis of lineage or exclusive refinements, and sheer wealth is definitely the more important in their eyes. For them, the aristocracy effectively no longer exists. The same is true of the middle classes, except for the upper-middle class and especially the small group at its apex, the prestige-UMC. The latter was closely associated with the aristocracy before the Revolution and retained most of its luster thereafter. During the last three decades of the twentieth century, the prestige-UMC significantly increased its ranks by incorporating foreign businessmen and professionals with whom the aristocracy had established a fairly active network of social relations. Thus the upper-middle class is still aware of the aristocracy and its historical role and can recognize aristocrats by surname association.

The aristocrats' ideological self-conception and the worldview that shapes their behavior constitute the model that upwardly mobile plutocrats have now largely acquired. The model is, of course, an idealized construct cultivated by aristocrats, based on historical facts and interpretations that are implicitly validated in every aspect of aristocratic behavior. At the same time, the model is designed to enhance a formerly exalted position and to bolster the aristocracy's vanishing bargaining power in the superordinate stratum, which is now dominated by the plutocracy. Thus aristocratic pride, refinement, and many kinds of behaviors are expressive reactions intended to increase beneficial interaction with plutocrats without causing offense through haughtiness or condescension. Plutocrats, for their part, are attracted to this collusion because it permits them to acquire and internalize aristocratic traits that will socially validate their own power and wealth, without unduly giving up the world wise attributes that made them wealthy and powerful in the first place.

CONCENTRATION AND REALIGNMENT IN MEXICO CITY

Since early colonial times, every aspect of Mexico's political, economic, religious, and social systems has gravitated toward the capital, Mexico City. This was especially the case with the superordinate stratum, even after the great changes ushered in by the revolution. Since its inception in the sixteenth century, the Mexican aristocracy has been closely associated with Mexico City, though its economic and power bases were provincial before the Revolution. Although landed wealth predominated, the aristocracy had diversified it financial holdings at the outset of the Revolution, and many provincial aristocrats had secondary residences in Mexico City, where they spent weeks or months each year (see, e.g., Leal and Menegus 1995: 60–61).

In 1910, on the eve of the Revolution, Mexico's hacendado cities par excellence were Puebla, Guadalajara, Querétaro, Oaxaca, Morelia, Guanajuato, Mérida, Chihuahua, Jalapa, Durango, San Luis Potosí, Zacatecas, and Tampico (Map 3). There were perhaps another four or five smaller cities that had a few aristocratic families each. Altogether, these cities harbored about two-thirds of the aristocracy; the remaining third lived in Mexico City (Nutini 1995). The average hacendado city had roughly 40 to

50 aristocratic households, but cities such as Puebla and Guadalajara had perhaps twice as many. The provincial households totaled about 700 to 750; those fully based in Mexico City numbered about 350.

The Revolution and especially the land expropriations under President Lázaro Cárdenas changed this situation. From the early 1920s onward, aristocrats fled the countryside for Mexico City in great numbers, and by the late 1950s, the overwhelming majority of provincial aristocrats had their principal or only residence there. By the early 1990s, there were probably fewer than 70 aristocratic households remaining in provincial cities, mainly Guadalajara, Querétaro, Morelia, and San Luis Potosí. Perhaps another 70 families who had remained in provincial cities after the exodus had lost their aristocratic affiliation and recognition by the 1990s; in that sense, they experienced downward mobility, although they now belong to the provincial plutocracy.

The aristocracy weathered the armed phase of the Revolution and its aftermath. Although some aristocrats were killed by local revolutionaries or by mob action, mostly between 1914 and 1917, the Revolution brought no political trials, organized persecution, or even official ostracism of the aristocracy. Nonetheless, it was extremely damaging to the aristocracy, and its effects were felt most strongly at the local and provincial levels.

The first decade after the fall of Porfirio Díaz in 1910 witnessed the demise of the traditional hacienda system: the destruction of most of the grand manors, the disintegration of the landed labor force, the erosion of income, and, above all, the end of the seigneurial system that had been the hallmark of the landed estate and its environs. The aristocratic emigration to Mexico City that began in the early 1920s primarily involved two kinds of families: (1) those whose haciendas had suffered the greatest destruction and whose land had either been given legally to peasants or had been overrun illegally; and (2) those who had been steadily losing their lands throughout the Porfiriato and whose financial base was by then mainly urban, that is, commercial and industrial.

From the outset of the Revolution in 1910, the provincial aristocrats were socially and economically more vulnerable than the financially more diversified aristocracy based in Mexico City. The former experienced more directly the destruction of the manors, banditry, and armed seizure of land. With their less diversified economy, provincial aristocrats were greatly affected by the loss of hacienda income almost immediately, and those who had no other source of income fell into dire straits. Those who owned urban properties often ended up selling them. These were fearsome times for the provincial aristocracy, who, unable to counteract the increasing political power of self-proclaimed revolutionaries and others who profited from the turmoil, felt their ancestral cities slipping from their control. Mexico City's aristocracy, in contrast, was relatively undisturbed by the revolution until the mid-1930s, when the federal government's agrarian reform program bore down on their rural properties.

Surprisingly, it took the provincial aristocracy nearly four decades (roughly 1920–1960) to migrate permanently to Mexico City, where most of them found a more favorable social and economic environment. The massive land reform program carried out by Lázaro Cárdenas greatly accelerated this emigration, because the confiscation of most of their lands forced provincial aristocrats to recognize that the hacienda system was finished. By the mid-1940s, in fact, all aristocratic families of such faraway cities as Mérida, Chihuahua, Durango, and Tampico had immigrated to Mexico City, and by the mid-1950s, no aristocratic families remained in such formerly prominent hacendado cities as Oaxaca and Jalapa. By 1950 about 80 percent of the provincial aristocracy had made the transition to Mexico City, and by 1960 perhaps as few as 70 aristocratic households still had their principal or only residence in provincial cities.

Concentration in Mexico City meant a degree of downward mobility for some of the immigrants, and during the 1950s, a significant number of them no longer had the wealth necessary to maintain their aristocratic status. On the other hand, many aristocratic families found a favorable environment in Mexico City, where opportunities opened up for them in business and the liberal professions, especially law and medicine, and where the resident aristocracy fully recognized them by virtue of old genealogical ties, their pedigrees as hacendados, and, most important, past marital alliances that even peripheral provincial aristocrats had maintained to some extent with the core. In fact, the blending of the provincial and national aristocrats took place surprisingly quickly and smoothly, beginning with the early arrivals of the 1920s and continuing through the massive immigration from the late 1930s to the late 1940s, resulting in a united superordinate social class.

Indeed, during the period between the massive land expropriations of 1934–1940 and the early 1950s, the aristocracy experienced a veritable renaissance in Mexico City. This period and the 1960s were a time of intensive expressive acculturation, during which the aristocracy served as the model of manners, behavior, and aspirations for the emerging, upwardly mobile plutocracy that was eventually to displace it. This terminal period of the aristocracy's social prominence, despite its gradually waning economic dominance, was triggered not only by its concentration in Mexico City but also by the emerging plutocracy's inexperience with elite refinements and its groping for social recognition.

THE ARISTOCRACY AT CENTURY'S END (1970–2000)

Although the Mexican aristocracy is not a fixed community, its boundaries are fairly well defined. In 1910, at the beginning of the great Revolution, the country's aristocracy numbered about 1,100 families, or 12,000 adults and children (Nutini 2005). By the mid-1950s, it had been reduced to about 900 households. This reduction mainly reflects declining aristocratic economic fortunes, especially among families who remained in provincial cities after the massive land reform. By 1975, the national aristocracy had been further reduced to some 800 households, or about 5,500 adults and children. In 2000, it comprised around 750 households, about 20 of them consisting of extended families. They bear roughly 150 surnames that are recognized as aristocratic by the overwhelming majority of aristocrats, although most of these surnames are shared by thousands—some of them, by tens of thousands—of Mexicans of all social classes.

Antiquity and Ancestry

Today's aristocrats can be divided into four categories according to antiquity and ancestry. These categories are recognized by at least the more traditional members of the aristocracy today, and they have genealogical, social, and expressive implications for both the aristocratic class's survival and its relationship with the plutocracy (Nutini 2004). The first category dates to the Spanish Conquest (1521) or shortly thereafter; the others have roots in aristocratic renewals—dating to 1630, 1730–1810, and 1850–1910—during which rich and powerful plutocrats joined the ranks of the aristocracy by acquiring its exclusive expressive array. The four categories are as follows:

1. Descendants of Spanish conquistadors, encomenderos, and early settlers, who together formed the original nucleus of the Mexican aristocracy (see Chap. 2). Numerically, this is the smallest category, as only about 10 percent of today's aristocratic families can document a genealogical claim to it. Most

of these families were always based in Mexico City, although several resided in important colonial cities, such as Puebla and Guadalajara, before immigrating to Mexico City in the 1920s and 1930s.

2. Descendants of plutocrats who achieved aristocratic rank by the end of the first renewal (1630), most of whom by then or shortly thereafter had become great hacendados, along with their interests in mining and commerce. By 1910, these families were located in Mexico City and in most of the provincial hacendado cities mentioned above, especially those within a radius of 500 kilometers (310 mi.) of the capital (see Map 3). Perhaps 25 percent of today's aristocratic families can substantiate this claim, and they are among the most prominent.
3. Descendants of plutocrats who achieved aristocratic status during the second renewal (1730–1810), that is, the great hacendado, mining, and commercial plutocracy that dominated New Spain from roughly 1750 until soon after independence in 1821. By 1910 they were found in Mexico City and all the provincial hacendado cities. Slightly over half of today's aristocratic families fall into this category.
4. Descendants of plutocrats who achieved aristocratic status mainly during the third renewal (1850–1910), although a fair number of families in this category did not achieve this status until the late 1940s. They were mainly bankers, manufacturers, and assorted businessmen of either domestic or foreign extraction who amassed great fortunes during the second half of the nineteenth century. Before the great aristocratic exodus to Mexico City (1920s–1950s), they were found both there and in the largest provincial cities. Perhaps 15 percent of today's aristocratic families fall into this category.

Obviously, antiquity of lineage is an important attribute of aristocratic standing, perhaps the most important, but it is tempered by more recently acquired power and wealth. Thus at the top are those families who are recognized as descendants of conquistadors or encomenderos and who are also wealthy. The wealthiest among them rank higher than those who can boast of nothing but a proven ancient lineage.

At the same time, the aristocracy is typically perceived as a homogeneous group in the wider context of today's superordinate stratum, within which social and expressive relations with the plutocracy have unfolded during the terminal renewal (1940–2000). In fact, concentration in Mexico City has somewhat homogenized the class, increasing its cohesion. In the process, self-identification and in-group recognition—an inherent aspect of the seigneurial system before the Revolution—have increased in importance as mechanisms of maintaining social boundaries. In today's rapidly changing world, those devices are losing their effectiveness, but most aristocrats continue to invoke them in an increasingly vain effort to maintain the aristocratic worldview.

In-Group Recognition

By the early 1950s, the Mexico City aristocracy included individuals and families from at least twelve provincial cities. While most of these provincial aristocrats had long-standing and extensive networks of friendship and intermarriage with the aristocrats who were permanent residents of Mexico City, they had few such intercity ties among themselves, especially before about 1940. Thus when large numbers of them immigrated to Mexico City, establishing their credentials and being recognized as bona fide aristocrats were matters of primary importance. Because Mexico at this time had no titles of nobility, registers of *hidalguía* (gentry), or other recorded means of establishing aristocratic status, different mechanisms had to be brought into play. Four mechanisms were crucial in this aristocratic realignment from the beginning of large-scale relocation to the capital in the 1920s until the new plutocracy began to assert itself forcefully in the 1970s.

The first step toward aristocratic recognition was establishing the aristocratic roots of the family surname. Although a few highly distinguished families were so well known that name recognition alone could establish their aristocratic affiliation, this was not the case for most provincial aristocrats, whose surnames were widely shared among people of all social classes. For them, rather, it was surname in conjunction with physical type—features that connoted either total European ancestry or the least non-European mixture—that set the stage for further aristocratic claims.

Second in importance was establishing city of origin and urban or regional connections. Basically, this meant confirming past social relationships with locally well known aristocratic families. This exercise was important to the extent that it helped to position aristocratic families of long standing in relation to those of more recent origin, that is, local plutocrats who had achieved aristocratic status within a generation or so.

The third and perhaps most important step toward aristocratic recognition was establishing the name of the hacienda(s) formerly in a family's hands. This step was not so much a question of validating a family's aristocratic identity as establishing the antiquity of its aristocratic lineage. Though there was a low degree of continuity of ownership of most landed estates throughout the colonial and early republican periods, the largest haciendas in several provinces had generally been in the hands of distinguished aristocratic families.

Fourth, and nearly as important as the preceding attribute, were genealogical links between aristocratic families of the capital and those from the provinces, as well as among the latter. Quite frequently, genealogical and matrimonial ties had long been dormant, sometimes for more than a century, but on being recognized, they immediately established social bonds and were included in the network of the receiving aristocratic family.

Present Perceptions

Since the early 1950s, the plutocracy, the political class, and the upper-middle class have regarded the aristocracy as a seamless unit, a view that does not take into account the fragmentation that the aristocracy has undergone in recent decades. Again, the exception is the dozen or so oldest or most distinguished aristocratic family groups that are known to most people in the upper stratum. Family names such as Rincón Gallardo, Romero de Terreros, Cervantes, Cortina, de Ovando, Icaza, Pérez de Salazar, Sánchez Navarro, Villar Villamil, Martínez del Río, and another score or so are well known throughout the upper classes and to some extent collectively denote the aristocracy as a class. Until roughly the early 1970s, a wider spectrum of educated Mexicans recognized these surnames as aristocratic markers, but this recognition is fading fast outside of the superordinate stratum itself.

More significantly, the superordinate stratum and the highly educated sector in general are aware of the aristocracy's former status as the country's ruling class or as the historical hacendado class with diversified financial interests. Especially among the highly educated members of the solid-middle class, the aristocracy is remembered as the exploiters of pre-Revolution times and, in more recent contexts, as *la sociedad* (high society). Alternatively, they disparage aristocrats in terms that can be paraphrased as "those decadent people who caused Mexico so much harm" or "those who believe they are a divine caste but who no longer count for much." Such statements reflect the fact that Mexico's middle classes make social distinctions almost entirely on the basis of power and wealth, to the exclusion of lineage and elite refinements that are of such great importance to the aristocracy.

The case is different with regard to the plutocracy. Since it began to emerge in the late 1920s, Mexico's plutocracy has been in close social contact with the aristocracy. The plutocracy was increasingly in a position of economic superiority but socially still under the guidance of the aristocracy until the early 1970s, when it began to assert its independence and create its own social life. Even today, though, for plutocrats as well as for aristocrats, previous hacienda ownership, the country-city axis, and lineage and genealogy are part of the aristocratic allure and the means by which to identify and relate to aristocrats.

The aristocracy's fragmentation in the second half of the twentieth century requires further comment. By 2000 it was no longer the united and organic social group that it had been in the late 1950s. Rather it was composed of perhaps a dozen segments each possessing six to ten family groups. These segments have a degree of organic unity that the aristocracy as a whole exhibited more than a generation ago. Fragmentation has been the result of occupational differentiation, physical distance within the Mexico City megalopolis, and preemigration kinship and genealogical relationships. Nevertheless, fragmentation has not diminished the aristocracy's self-image as a social class or its position (albeit residual) in Mexico City's stratification system.

The Plutocracy

ORIGIN AND DEVELOPMENT

The Mexican plutocracy—the late-twentieth-century ruling class that became wealthy primarily from industry, commerce, and finance rather than haciendas—is not easy to demarcate or analyze. It has neither the Mexican aristocracy's unitary configuration and organic worldview nor the European industrial and banking tradition dating to the seventeenth century. Yet since the end of the Revolution the plutocracy has carved out a distinct and powerful niche in the country's upper stratum. This kind of social mobility is peculiar to the New World, where it occurs in both Anglo-Saxon and Latin countries. Nevertheless, given the effects of diffusion and the fact that the economic world-system has readily transcended national boundaries for the past two generations, the Mexican plutocracy today is not significantly different, socially or economically, from the plutocracies of many other countries, including the United States.

As Mexico's ruling class and the dominant component of the country's superordinate stratum, the plutocracy dates to the late twentieth century (roughly from the early 1970s onward). Furthermore, its roots can be traced only to the 1920s, as there was little plutocratic continuity from the Porfiriato. The revolution not only terminated the traditional landed system that had been central to the aristocracy's economy and identity but also significantly transformed the country's banking, industrial, and commercial establishments. As owners of the most visible sources of urban wealth, the Porfirian plutocrats suffered the rapacity of revolutionaries, and when the armed stage subsided, most of their economic enterprises in both Mexico City and the provincial cities were diminished. It is rare to find a descendant of the Porfirian plutocracy in the ranks of today's ruling class; rather most of them have achieved aristocratic status, while the rest have sunk into the middle classes.

On the other hand, many members of the pre-Revolution aristocratic hacendado class were also businessmen engaged in a variety of nonagrarian enterprises, which typically were less affected by the Revolution than were their lands. Some of these aristocrats survived the turmoil of those times with sufficient capital to become members of the plutocracy that began to emerge in the 1920s. Today their descendants are generally among the richest plutocrats who can claim aristocratic standing, but they are far less wealthy or powerful than the leading plutocrats, whose fortunes originated after the Revolution.

The 1920s were the gestation period of the new plutocracy, during which a new breed of businessmen-entrepreneurs—engaged in all aspects of modern banking, industry, manufacturing, and trade—began to create the present economic foundation of Mexico. Almost all members of this incipient plutocracy were Mexican nationals from Mexico City and several large provincial cities. Although many foreign investors were operating in the country during the 1920s and 1930s, they did not become part of the national plutocracy. From the 1940s onward, though, many other foreign businessmen-entrepreneurs entered the ranks of the rising new plutocracy.

With few exceptions, the wealth generated by the incipient plutocracy during the 1920s was modest. Furthermore, until the presidency of Plutarco Elías Calles (1924–1928), the economy and infrastructure were still in turmoil from the Revolution, and we cannot speak of a plutocracy exercising ruling functions independently of the political class then. Beginning in the early 1930s, though, the incipient plutocracy entered a period of uninterrupted prosperity that resulted in truly great fortunes during the Miguel Alemán presidency (1946–1952).

By the mid-1940s, some of the new plutocrats had become part of the national ruling class. Among them were a number of politicians of revolutionary extraction who became plutocrats after a term in high office. More important, however, was a burst of new entrepreneurial activity that resulted in large modern businesses each employing thousands of people. Although the great state-owned enterprises (railroads, petroleum industry, postal system, and a few others) were still the country's economic backbone, the private sector was now generating huge new sources of employment and wealth.

Not surprisingly, the plutocratic magnates who increasingly controlled this dynamic private sector began to assume more and more ruling-class functions. During the 1940s, a tacit understanding of mutual economic goals, procedures, and modus operandi began to shape their relationship with the political class. In its new capacity, the plutocracy asserted a strong influence over national economic policy in general and the central government's labor policies in particular.

Officially, of course, Mexico was controlled by the PRI, which kept a tight rein on the country for seventy-one years (1929–2000), all the while voicing pseudorevolutionary rhetoric intended to make Mexico appear a socialist state. In fact, during this time Mexico was a tightly centralized, semidemocratic country with a mixed economy that was far more capitalist than socialist in orientation, despite the massive land expropriation and redistribution in 1934–1940, the expropriation of the petroleum industry in 1938, and large expenditures on public welfare. Indeed, one can make a good case that post-Revolution Mexico was governed largely through the same kind of tacit alliance of ruling and political classes that had predominated during the nineteenth century.

Perhaps a decade later than the massive emigration of aristocrats to Mexico City (1920s–1950s), the provincial plutocracy began a similar movement, largely as the result of Mexico's increasing centralization. Until the early 1940s, many plutocratic fortunes apparently were still being made in the largest provincial cities, particularly Monterrey, Guadalajara, Puebla, and perhaps two or three others (see Map 3). By the early 1960s, though, most provincial plutocrats had relocated to Mexico City.

From roughly 1945 to the early 1970s, the plutocracy reached maturity as a ruling class and thereafter began to differentiate along lines of power and wealth, on the one hand, and an inclination or disinclination toward upward mobility by acquiring aristocratic expressive trappings, on the other. The least and most wealthy plutocrats have shown the lowest tendency for such striving; those in the middle range of wealth and power have been the most upwardly mobile. Of course, there are exceptions to this generalization, mostly reflecting individual idiosyncrasies or prior contacts with the aristocratic milieu before the new plutocracy's concentration in Mexico City.

Throughout its developmental stage (late 1940s to early 1970s), Mexico's plutocracy had diversified investments in banking, manufacturing, and commerce, but most of its wealth derived from large investments in major banks and in a wide range of manufacturing enterprises (Nutini 2004, 2005). From these portfolios, the least wealthy of the plutocratic magnates accumulated fortunes of U.S.$30–40 million (in 2000 dollars); fortunes of U.S.$50–100 million were common. Roughly twenty-five to thirty individuals surpassed U.S.$200 million, and five or six exceeded U.S.$500 million. All told, these wealth categories encompassed about 500 plutocrats based in Mexico City, of whom perhaps 300 were upwardly mobile and about 600 in the U.S.$30–40 million range still resident in provincial cities.

Finally, during this developmental stage the plutocracy expanded by incorporating two or three dozen capitalists of foreign extraction, mostly from Europe and the Near East, plus a few from the United States. With few exceptions, the latter two groups have not become upwardly mobile, in the sense of striving to become aristocratized, whereas almost all the Europeans have done so. These upwardly mobile Europeans are mostly Spanish, Italian, and French, and almost all have settled in Mexico City. The French and Italians had a good class position to begin with, several of them being aristocrats (some titled), and they quickly developed extensive social networks among Mexican aristocrats.

To summarize, by the early 1970s we can no longer speak of the Mexican plutocracy as "new," because they had now become the country's ruling class. Among them were plutocrats who made their fortunes while holding high office as well as those who had made fortunes in business. By virtue of their economic power, they had begun to exercise significant and increasing influence in the country's political affairs, and during the 1990s they became the undisputed ruling class.

Several political shifts are important in this plutocratic upsurge, as both cause and effect. First, during the 1990s the central government largely dropped the pseudorevolutionary rhetoric that had been de rigueur while the Revolution was still part of living memory. At the same time, the PRI moved increasingly toward the neoliberal (deregulated, market-driven) model of economic development, beginning with the administration of President Miguel de la Madrid (1982–1988). He and the two succeeding presidents, Carlos Salinas (1988–1994) and Ernesto Zedillo (1994–2000), significantly "privatized" the economy by selling many of the parastatial enterprises in which the central government was invested—most famously, the telephone system, mining companies, major portions of the food processing and distribution system, and airlines (see Ochoa 2000: 208 ff.; Puga 1993: 181–204; Teichman 1995: 130–193). The acquisition of these enterprises, often at bargain prices, significantly increased the wealth of certain plutocrats, raising the net worth of some of them to the billions of dollars.

Finally, the 1990s witnessed much greater participation of plutocrats of political origin in the economic direction of the country. Although political plutocrats have been a feature of post-Revolution Mexico since at least the 1940s (Aguilar 1983: 92–140; Carrión and Aguilar 1972: 159–184), they have been much more public, even about the origin of their fortunes, since the 1980s. For instance, the journalist Andrés Oppenheimer (1996: 180) reports a revealing statement by one of them: "When he was asked . . . how he had risen from penniless rural teacher to a multimillionaire, he had smiled and quipped, *'Un político pobre es un pobre político'*—'A politician who is poor is a poor politician.'"

Be that as it may, there is now little functional difference between financial and political plutocrats. Furthermore, most of today's plutocrats can no longer be spoken of as nouveaux riches, because they or their families have been rich and powerful for nearly two generations. In the meantime, the great majority of plutocrats, who had no prior aristocratic background, have learned sufficient expressive refinement from the national aristocracy and from international business contacts to erase or at least hide their formerly nouveau riche manners.

Few aristocrats would consider even the more socially active plutocrats as members of their own group. In most respects, however, aristocrats increasingly recognize, even admiringly, that many upwardly mobile plutocrats have come to display behaviors and lifestyles that are not different from the aristocratic ideal. At the same time, aristocrats uniformly continue to regard many other plutocrats, whether from Mexico City or the larger industrial cities, as coarse and "new rich." This condescending attitude is not one-sided, for most plutocrats look down on aristocrats as lacking in power and wealth and as being unable to compete at their own traditional game.

In absolute terms, the plutocracy's wealth has increased greatly in recent decades, especially the largest fortunes. By 1994, according to *Forbes* magazine, there were more billionaires (in U.S. dollars) in Mexico, twenty-four, than in any other Latin American country, placing Mexico fourth in the world in terms of private fortunes, after the United States, Germany, and Japan (*Forbes* 1994a). The richest Mexican was worth U.S.$6.6 billion, five other individuals or families had U.S.$2.5–5.5 billion each, and the remaining eighteen were in the U.S.$1.1–2.4 billion range. Devaluation of the Mexican peso had cut the number of billionaires from twenty-four to ten by the following year's report (*Forbes* 1995); the number rose to fifteen in 1996 but then declined to thirteen in 2000, eleven in 2004, and ten in 2005, where it remained through 2007 (*Forbes* 1996–2007). But even these reduced figures are impressive for a country that is still in the process of industrializing. It is worth noting that these great fortunes are directly or indirectly the product of the government's intensive privatization program that was initiated in 1988. Indeed, there was only one billionaire in Mexico in 1987, on the eve of privatization (*Forbes* 1994b).

Most of this great surge of plutocratic wealth has been centered in Mexico City, but a similar concentration of wealth has been taking place elsewhere in the country, although less spectacularly. Several of the larger cities have recently seen tremendous growth in private wealth, and there are many more provincial plutocrats today than there were in the 1970s. Even such medium-sized cities as Jalapa, Córdoba, and Querétaro may now have local plutocrats worth U.S.$100 million or more.

Some of the more interesting cases of wealth expansion in recent decades have occurred at the billionaire level and have involved new wealth that has not much affected the long-term interaction of aristocrats and plutocrats. For instance, the richest family in Mexico appearing in *Forbes* (1994a) is of provincial extraction and has not, to our knowledge, undergone aristocratization derived from the national scene; rather, whatever social and expressive changes the family has undergone are due to involvement in the international business scene. Pretty much the same can be said about the country's richest individual; compared to plutocrats of long standing (i.e., more than two generations), this man is on the periphery of aristocratic-plutocratic interaction. On the whole, however, aristocratization and increasing superordinate class consciousness have accompanied the increased concentration of wealth among the Mexican plutocracy in recent decades.

THE NATIONAL PLUTOCRACY

Original Class Position

Today's plutocrats appear to fall into four groups with regard to class origins. First, the rags-to-riches pattern probably accounts for about one-third of them. These are individuals of modest beginnings, usually lower-middle class, with little or no formal education, and almost invariably of provincial origin. So far as we know, none of the country's richest plutocrats are in this group; rather, most of the members of this group occupy the lowest wealth niche, U.S.$50–75 million. The category includes individuals of both domestic and foreign extraction. The former are mostly from cities that became large manufacturing and commercial centers after the 1930s, especially Guadalajara, Monterrey, Puebla, and Ciudad Juárez. The foreign plutocrats are mostly from Spain and the Near East (especially Lebanese and Palestinian Christians). A few have accumulated medium-sized to large fortunes, but only during the 1990s did they become socially and economically prominent. The Spaniards among them are most illustrative of the rags-to-riches pattern, having become multimillionaires in a single generation.

The second group consists of individuals of solid-middle-class origin who typically attained a university education, usually in law, engineering, or finance. This is the largest category, and its members are the backbone of the plutocracy as a ruling class. It includes most of the plutocrats and especially the great majority of politicians-turned-plutocrats. In terms of wealth, the majority of plutocrats with medium-sized to large fortunes—the latter typically exceeding U.S.$300 million—fall in this category. They are all based in Mexico City and are the most visible on the national scene.

Partially excluding the political plutocrats, the members of this second category who are of provincial origin usually gravitated to Mexico

City while young, as the capital's Universidad Nacional Autónoma de México has always been a magnet for ambitious middle-class students from all over the country. Some members of this category have no formal higher education at all, but they are the distinct exceptions, as are those who have studied abroad. Generally, this is the best formally educated plutocratic segment, as well as the most professional from the finance, manufacturing, and business standpoint. It is also the most innovative and upwardly mobile plutocratic segment, and by 2000 most of its members had exhibited the expressive equivalent of the aristocracy for nearly two generations (see Chap. 8). This last statement excludes the political plutocrats in this category, as they have been reluctant to engage in this form of social climbing until quite recently.

The third category includes individuals with the best original class position, many of them upper-middle class and a few of Porfirian extraction. A considerable number had solid ties to the aristocracy before the onset of their plutocratic careers, and many of them immigrated to Mexico City at the time of the aristocratic exodus. This group is also the best educated in terms of classical high culture, and it is the most socially and expressively active segment of the plutocracy. Families in this category are the most aristocratized, generally having had the longest relationship to the aristocracy, and are now the leaders of the superordinate stratum. From the standpoint of class formation, this is the group to emulate, and its outstanding members are the leaders who have done the most, and the most creatively, to blend plutocratic power and wealth with aristocratic values and expressive achievements.

Fourth are foreign-born plutocrats, mostly French and Italian, of high social origin. They quickly became important in the ongoing formation of the plutocratic class in Mexico and also were readily absorbed into the Mexican aristocracy, by virtue of having brought with them an aristocratic expressive array virtually identical to the local model. Indeed, a significant degree of the expressive acculturation undergone by the Mexican plutocracy originated from this foreign infusion, independently of the national aristocracy. In terms of wealth, this elite foreign group falls in the middle of the local range; economically, they are not among the most influential plutocrats, but this factor is counterbalanced by their expressive and social prominence.

Aristocratization and Upward Mobility

Although there is considerable individual variation, the entire range of Mexico's plutocracy can be encompassed in three categories. First, more than one-third of all plutocrats are opposed or indifferent to expressive acculturation; they are not striving for upward mobility in terms of either aristocratization or other models presented to them in national or international business circles. While enjoying the power and wealth that come with plutocratic status, they do not engage in any of the expressive activities that are so much a part of superordinate stratification: participating in or sponsoring Mexico City's artistic/literary life, socializing in aristocratic-plutocratic circles, intermarrying with aristocrats, making philanthropic donations, and so on. Aristocrats and upwardly mobile plutocrats alike regard these individuals as nouveaux riches (in the worst sense) and as inimical to the interests of the plutocracy as a prestige class. Analytically, this is a difficult group to categorize. Given their power and wealth, these individuals are in the top tier of the superordinate stratum, but they are not even upper-middle class by expressive criteria. Although they are part of the ruling class, they keep a low profile and are in fact the least visible sector of the plutocracy. They are the newest sector, having achieved this status within the past twenty-five years or so. They had the lowest original class position, and most of them are still in the low ranges of plutocratic wealth.

Second, perhaps another one-third of the plutocracy is composed of individuals who are both upwardly mobile and seeking social recognition from aristocrats. Although not as recent in origin as the first group, the plutocratic careers of these individuals go back no farther than the mid-1940s, and the majority acquired plutocratic status no earlier than 1960. Furthermore, they were latecomers to the game of upward mobility. Until roughly the early 1970s, many of them were reluctant to acquire aristocratic-plutocratic expressive trappings. Since then, however, they have become upwardly mobile, establishing solid social ties to the aristocracy, including intermarriage in some cases, and to the more aristocratized segment of the plutocracy. They have played the game well, and there are probably no expressive domains that they have not attempted in their drive to achieve parity with the older plutocratic sector, although they have not yet acquired its full expressive array. In terms of wealth, they had acquired medium to large fortunes by 2000. They include most politicians-turned-plutocrats, for whom recent national political changes have made it easier to shed their once-fashionable pseudorevolutionary stance. Their original class position ranges from solid-middle to upper-middle class. This category includes most of the Spanish and Near Eastern plutocrats discussed earlier.

Third, slightly less than one-third of the plutocracy has been vigorously upwardly mobile since the 1920s or 1930s. Today they are the structural and expressive core of the Mexican plutocracy, its social leaders and most influential members and the most expressively innovative superordinate sector. Their worldview and expressive array are the closest to those of aristocrats, from whom they are almost indistinguishable in terms of manners and other behavior in most social domains. Most of them are in the upper reaches of plutocratic wealth. As a group, they had the best original class position, coming primarily from the upper-middle class and including a few Porfirian plutocrats. Most of the French and Italian immigrant plutocrats belong to this category as well.

National Profile

The plutocracy is Mexico's present ruling class. Its countrywide strength is difficult to estimate, but it is probably no larger than two thousand households (Nutini 2004). About two-thirds of them are based in Mexico City; while their varied enterprises may be located in many places throughout the country, they reside permanently in the capital, and their social life is exclusively centered there. Leaving aside the non–upwardly mobile sector, there are roughly 850 plutocratic families in the capital who are, and have been for two generations, in a relationship of expressive acculturation vis-à-vis the aristocracy. Basically the second and third mobility categories discussed above, they present the model to emulate by the rich and powerful. This group is in the eviable position of being able to dictate its own expressive terms but still appreciate what the dying aristocracy represents socially and expressively, and their appreciative attitude prolongs the aristocracy's demise as Mexico's prestige class.

For their part, the aristocrats, especially the more conservative among them, know that their exalted position is coming to an inevitable end. They are sadly aware that they could have become ruling plutocrats if their expressive concerns had not prevented their immersion in manufacturing and commerce. As things stand, many conservative aristocrats feel that the last card has been played in their own game, although they still hope that their children stand a chance of becoming part of the new superordinate stratum.

THE PROVINCIAL PLUTOCRACY

Background

Today's provincial plutocrats reside in Central Mexico's large and medium-sized cities (Nutini 2004, 2005). Their inception as a class dates from the late 1920s to the early 1940s, when the medium-sized cities—such as Acapulco (Guerrero), Cuernavaca (Morelos), Toluca (México), Pachuca (Hidalgo), and Jalapa, Orizaba, and Córdoba (Veracruz)—had populations in the 50,000 to 100,000 range. Central Mexico's two large provincial cities, Puebla and Veracruz, both had populations of less than 200,000 at that time. (By 2000 Veracruz had grown to about 535,000 and Puebla to nearly 1.3 million.)

The provincial plutocracy emerged first in the largest of these cities. In Puebla, for example, the plutocracy was well established and influential by the early 1930s, with some continuity from the Porfiriato. This was to be expected, because Puebla was then Mexico's second most important city and had been home to a large Spanish and Spanish-Mexican population continuously since the early colonial period. In contrast, the plutocracy of medium-sized Córdoba did not begin to coalesce until the early 1940s, while its counterparts in other medium-sized cities date from the late 1920s to the early 1940s. Regardless of their respective founding dates, though, Central Mexico's provincial plutocracies were all thriving by the late 1950s.

While Puebla and Veracruz, historically large and economically important centers, have plutocratic traditions going back to Porfirian times, the plutocracy of practically all of the medium-sized cities postdates the demise of the hacienda system in the wake of the Revolution. The emigration of most of the provincial aristocracy to Mexico City left a local vacuum that was soon filled by a fledgling plutocracy.

Most Central Mexican cities experienced unprecedented growth during the presidency of Miguel Alemán (1946–1952). From market towns for the surrounding hinterlands, they developed into thriving commercial and small-scale industrial centers. By the late 1950s, most medium-sized cities were bustling hubs of all kinds of business activities, most commonly cement plants, metallurgical and automotive-parts factories, sugar mills, large livestock and agribusiness concerns, processing plants (coffee, rice, wheat), large retail and wholesale stores, and the like. Up to this point, plutocratic fortunes were in the U.S.$10–30 million range. By the early 1970s, other sources of wealth had appeared: transportation, real estate, and hotel and supermarket chains. At this stage, many plutocratic fortunes surpassed U.S.$100 million and a few were in the U.S.$200–300 million range.

Toward the end of the López Portillo administration (1976–1982), diversification of business and industry in provincial cities became even greater, and so did the fortunes of plutocratic magnates. Medium-sized and large factories of all kinds were established but primarily in automotive and electronic parts, beer and soft drinks, textiles, chemicals and fertilizers, animal feeds, and food processing. Today every medium-sized city in Central Mexico has twenty-five to fifty plutocratic magnates with fortunes in the U.S.$300–500 million range. In Puebla and Veracruz, in contrast, such fortunes were relatively large as far back as the mid-1930s, and today these two cities have plutocrats who are approaching billionaire status.

Most of the richest plutocrats have combined financial strategies that include several of the foregoing enterprises. The only major source of wealth in which provincial plutocrats have not invested is banking, simply because there are no regional banks; rather all business is conducted through branches of the main national banks operating out of Mexico City. This circumstance placed banking outside the orbit of provincial plutocrats, whose wealth was entirely generated in the cities in which they resided, though most of them probably are not natives of these regions and many are not native-born Mexicans.

Social and Cultural Characteristics

To a great extent, the provincial plutocracy is similar to the national plutocracy that is largely headquartered in Mexico City. In fact, their organization and general functions are based on the same model. Nevertheless, there are some important differences, most notably the provincial plutocracy's lesser degree of wealth, its less complex demographic and social setting, and the absence of a local aristocratic model to emulate. As we discuss below, these differences translate into a significantly different expressive culture, compared to that of the longtime national plutocrats of Mexico City.

Whereas the national plutocracy in the megalopolis of Mexico City is difficult to identify, the plutocracy in provincial cities is not. The twenty-five to fifty plutocrats in each of the medium-sized cities, as well as the larger numbers based in Puebla and Veracruz, are highly visible and are generally well known to the people at large, who like to guess—seldom accurately—at the size of their individual and family fortunes. Upper-middle-class people, for whom the local plutocrats serve as a model, are especially prone to greatly exaggerate plutocratic wealth. Solid-middle- and working-class people, for their part, are aware of the various enterprises that the plutocracy owns and almost invariably attribute dishonest means to their acquisition; at the same time, they generally have a grudging admiration for the plutocrats' achievements, which they regard as beyond their own reasonable aspirations.

We have already covered the historical rise of provincial plutocrats, but we need to say a bit more about their career development. Although there were a few moderately rich individuals before the mid-1940s in the medium-sized cities—members of prominent families with roots in pre-Porfirian times—none of today's largest provincial fortunes originated before 1950. In fact, most of the largest fortunes have been amassed since 1970; a few of them, as recently as the mid-1980s. While some of the rich families of the pre-1950 era had made it into the second rank of the rich by century's end, none of them have fortunes of more than U.S.$40 million.

Provincial fortunes of the first rank in 2000 have basically two beginnings. On the one hand are the individual or family owners of one or two very large enterprises dating to the late 1960s, which attained plutocratic dimensions (putatively worth more than U.S.$100 million) between the early 1980s and the mid-1990s. Their financial bases combined wholesale commerce and agriculture—in Veracruz and Puebla states, mostly sugar, rice, and coffee; in the other states, livestock, wheat, and various other crops—or else rested on vast real estate holdings or medium-sized industries. On the other hand we find provincial fortunes of the first rank that were amassed entirely from 1980 to 1995, mostly by individuals of non-Mexican origin. At century's end, these individuals owned the provincial cities' largest industrial plants, transportation companies, and supermarket chains.

Though small, local provincial plutocracies are not in any sense integrated groups, nor do they exhibit an effective class consciousness. These characteristics probably reflect diversity of original class position (and the accompanying educational differences) and diversity of ethnicity or nationality. Of course, local plutocrats are aware of one another as being rich and influential, and they share an elite self-identification with the two other superordinate sectors of provincial society, the political class and the prestige-UMC. Nevertheless, this awareness does not result in collective action by plutocrats, either alone or with these other two classes.

Ethnically, provincial plutocrats are quite varied, but more of them are of recent foreign extraction (first or second generation in Mexico) than of long-term Mexican nationality. Indeed, almost two-thirds of the plutocrats in the average provincial city are of recent foreign extraction. About half of them are Spaniards; most of the others are Lebanese, Syrians, and Palestinians, as well as a few French. The predominance of these "foreigners" elicits much resentment from the middle classes, especially merchants and entrepreneurs. Their reaction is psychologically complicated, however: while resenting the foreigners' success, they nonetheless admire their hard work, dedication, and sense of purpose in amassing their fortunes. Not surprisingly, given the persisting rancor of many Mexicans about the colonial past, the Spaniards are the most severely resented.

Notably absent among provincial plutocrats are the individuals of political extraction, with fortunes made during or as the result of a term in political office (especially in the 1960s and 1970s), who exist in significant numbers among the national plutocrats of Mexico City. The politicians of provincial origin who amassed fortunes while serving in national office apparently remained in Mexico City or its environs after leaving political life. Furthermore, the opportunities for enrichment through political service in provincial cities and their hinterlands are insufficient—with the possible exception of Veracruz state—to amass the immense fortunes of today's plutocracy.

In terms of their original class position, most of today's provincial plutocrats had rather modest beginnings (Nutini 2005: 48–62). About 35 percent of the average provincial city's plutocrats, in fact, originated in the lower-middle class and were from families who made their livings as clerical workers or the lowest-paid professionals. These rags-to-riches plutocrats made their fortunes in less than a generation and are now of the second rank in terms of wealth, worth U.S.$20–50 million (in 2000 dollars). Another 50 percent of the average provincial city's plutocrats are of solid-middle-class origin, and they are all in the first rank today in terms of wealth. Typically, they are university educated, mostly at such elite institutions as the Universidad Nacional Autónoma de México and Universidad Iberoamericana (both in Mexico City), the Instituto Technológico de Monterrey (in Nuevo León state), or the leading universities of the United States or Britain. This young generation (ages twenty-five to thirty-five in 2000) is regarded as the most professional and innovative of the provincial plutocracy and as the example to emulate. Ethnically, they include both Mexicans of deep roots and recent immigrant families (roughly 70 percent and 30 percent, respectively). Finally, about 15 percent of the average provincial city's plutocrats originated from good class positions, almost invariably upper-middle-class families with deep local roots, some going back to colonial times. Although their fortunes are in the lowest range of plutocratic wealth (U.S.$50–75 million), they are of high social standing and are much sought after socially by the richest and most powerful plutocrats.

In terms of residence, the plutocratic families invariably live in the choicest residential areas of their cities, together with upper-middle-class families. Some of the richest plutocrats have primary residences that could be called mansions—typically, a one- or two-story house of twenty to twenty-five rooms in the midst of one or two city blocks of luxuriously landscaped grounds. The average plutocratic residence is more modest in size, though, and not nearly as ostentatious. Most plutocratic families also have country retreats, usually within ten to twenty kilometers of their urban residences, and many also own houses in California, Arizona, or Texas, which they inhabit for a month or more each year.

Elite Behavior and Expression

For all its obvious wealth, the provincial plutocracy has never enjoyed the extent of local influence that the now-vanished provincial aristocracy continued to exert for nearly a generation after the onset of the Revolution of 1910, despite the great changes that had taken place. Socially, the provincial plutocracy maintains a rather low profile, both individually and collectively. For instance, there are no clubs that the plutocracy exclusively patronizes. The only public fanfare generated by individual plutocrats is an occasional philanthropic donation of money or property to public institutions (e.g., the Red Cross, theater groups, literary groups) or sponsorship of cultural and educational activities. Generally, the household is the hub of their social life, and celebrations of the yearly and life cycles almost invariably take place there. These celebrations are elaborate affairs to which politicians and upper-middle-class people are also invited. The latter constitute the plutocratic families' social support group.

Politically, the provincial plutocracy exerts considerable influence. Its political sway, together with its control of the regional economy, justifies terming it a local ruling class. It is not a political class, however, as very few of its members have ever held political office, and they generally view politicians with distaste. Rather, they cultivate local and regional officeholders as a strategy to safeguard and advance their economic interests, especially to secure the relaxation of city and state regulations and to obtain choice locations for their enterprises. Social contact with politicians is carefully limited and usually takes place in the home. While the relationship is characteristically polite and low-key, plutocrats would not hesitate to coerce politicians if necessary to exert their will, at the same time soothing hurt feelings by paying the traditional *mordida* (bribe).

Economically, the provincial plutocracy is highly visible, as its wealth is much more concentrated in their relatively small cities than is the case with the national plutocracy in Mexico City. Plutocrats are the only large provincial employers, and they control the manufacture of the most important commodities, the distribution of the major consumption items, the transportation network, and regional agriculture. As individuals, though, provincial plutocrats strive to maintain low personal profiles. They exercise their economic power and political influence, even their limited philanthropy, discreetly. In this aspect, they differ from the national plutocracy, which operates in the much more diversified and sophisticated ambiance of Mexico City, where the public ostentation characteristically associated with the rich and powerful does not generate the active resentment and censure that it almost certainly would in the provincial plutocracy's smaller social setting.

Also significant for the expressive development of provincial plutocracies is the fact that by the time they began their ascent, the aristocratic hacendados had relocated to Mexico City. Thus provincial plutocrats lacked a local model of traditional upper-class culture. They had to improvise an elite expressive culture. They adopted many elements of Mexican aristocratic culture, mostly by emulating what they read about or saw in the mass media, especially magazines and newspapers. They also emulated foreign plutocrats whom they observed through business contacts or while traveling abroad. The result is an elite but clearly "provincial" expressive culture when compared to the expressive array of the sophisticated national plutocracy (see Chap. 8).

five: THE MIDDLE CLASSES

Central Mexico's middle classes span a wide social spectrum, the top and the bottom of which overlap with the upper and lower social strata. At the same time, they constitute a much smaller proportion of the total social system than is the case in more industrialized societies such as the United States or Western Europe. In this chapter, we distinguish the upper-middle, solid-middle, and lower-middle classes.

Until the 1910–1920 Revolution, Mexico had a basically two-class system: the superordinate sector and the masses, mediated by a small middle class of merchants and professionals (Granato and Mostkoff 1990; Stern 1994). The Revolution most famously brought dramatic changes in the composition of the superordinate stratum, but it also generated a degree of upward social mobility that significantly expanded the middle classes. This has been especially the case since about 1950, owing to increased formal education opportunities and industrial growth (Careaga 1974; Contreras S. 1978; González C. 1976).

The middle stratum is hard to conceptualize in provincial cities and regions precisely because of this recent surge in upward mobility, which has taken two major forms: a rapid rise from the ranks of the dispossessed into the lower-middle and working classes; and generational mobility from the lower-middle to the solid-middle class (Nutini 2005). The picture is further complicated by the geographic mobility of the rural dispossessed, almost entirely to the dominant regional cities, where they enter the marginal class (see Chap. 6). In fact, the great majority of the urban marginal class consists of displaced rural folk, few of whom were in the working class in their natal communities. This is another way of saying that provincial cities do not themselves breed a marginal class; rather, this stratum originates as dispossessed labor migrants from rural communities. Furthermore, once settled in the provincial cities, they seldom move to Mexico City or other large cities, which instead receive almost all their marginal components directly from rural communities. Thus for those at the bottom of the system, upward mobility (if it occurs) is almost always local.

The migrants' entry into the working class is a matter of securing at least an urban survival income from one or more jobs, serially or simultaneously. Upward mobility to the solid-middle class, though, is more complicated. It is achieved primarily by lower-middle- and working-class young people whose parents (and sometimes other family members) work long hours and sacrifice some of their own consumption desires to secure their children a university education. Mostly, these young people study law, medicine, engineering, chemistry, veterinary medicine, economics, business administration, accounting, and primary or secondary education.

One significant consequence of this considerable mobility by the working and lower-middle classes is their lack of verbalized class consciousness, in contrast to the three main classes of the superordinate stratum who have a clear conception of who they are and can articulate their position in society. When pressed to state their class position, almost all identify themselves as middle class, regardless of occupation or social function. This situation became abundantly clear in Nutini's (2005) study of the Córdoba-Orizaba area of Veracruz state, where more than six hundred questionnaire respondents were asked, "To what social class do you belong?" Although the project's field-workers hoped to elicit differentiation among middle-stratum components, the invariable answer was a stark "clase media" (middle class). As we will see in Chapter 6, the lower and middle classes of Mexico City are similarly inclined to report themselves as "middle class."

The foregoing does not mean, however, that working- and middle-class people truly see themselves as an undifferentiated stratum, only that they cannot readily make distinctions using the sociologist's terminology. There is, in fact, a pronounced ideological and expressive distinction, drawn almost universally in Mexico, between what U.S. sociologists would call blue-collar and white-collar workers, roughly corresponding to the working class and the lower-middle class, respectively. The distinction is underlain by differences in formal education and earning power but is more significantly determined by the traditional Mexican view that those who do manual work command less respect and rank lower on the social scale than those who do not work with their hands. In general, this distinction is more important than either ethnicity (Indian vs. mestizo) or putative race (especially, lighter vs. darker skin color) in people's perception of stratification in the middle sector.

The Upper-Middle Class

The upper-middle class is the most difficult middle-stratum component to conceptualize, in Mexico City and in the provincial cities. It cannot be adequately delineated by the objective tradition of conventional sociology (i.e., wealth, education, place of residence, and the like). Nor is it precisely equivalent to the upper-middle class of the United States.

In Central Mexico, an elite group at its apex is also a prestige class (after Aron 1966: 205) with a socially significant expressive component and a distinguished lineage and tradition dating to the Porfiriato. In terms of its social interactions, the prestige-UMC is part of the superordinate stratum and thus is closely related to the plutocracy in Mexico City and provincial cities, as well as to the aristocracy in Mexico City. In these provincial cities today, the prestige-UMC serves as the social support group for the resident plutocracy and also provides the expressive model for upward mobility (see Chap. 8). In Mexico City, in contrast, the prestige-UMC is simply a support group for the aristocracy and plutocracy, because the aristocracy still serves as the major expressive model there.

Even in highly industrialized countries, the upper-middle class is always small, probably never exceeding more than about 7 percent of the total population. In Mexico, it is even smaller, constituting no more than about 1.5 to 2.0 percent of the population of either Mexico City or the provincial cities (and their hinterlands) of Central Mexico. In the provincial cities, the great majority of upper-middle-class households have achieved this status since 1960, especially during the period 1975–2000, when the class grew by more than 50 percent. The prestige-UMC is much smaller, of course, never exceeding about one-third of the total upper-middle class in either the provincial cities or Mexico City (Nutini 2004, 2005).

In terms of social derivation, the upper-middle class has the following components. At the top is a small group—about 5 to 8 percent of this class in provincial cities and about 10 percent in Mexico City—of

Porfirian extraction or even with roots extending to the colonial period. On the whole, they are the least affluent but the most socially prestigious. Roughly another 35 percent of upper-middle-class families, mostly of more recent extraction, but some going as far back as 1900, fall into the middle range of economic affluence but also have significant social prestige. The oldest families among them are also part of the local prestige-UMC. Finally, the majority (some 55 to 60 percent) of upper-middle-class families today acquired this status during the past generation and, accordingly, rank lowest in prestige within their class. They had the lowest original class position but are now the most affluent. Most often, they own important retail outlets or small- to medium-sized factories, or they are the most notable professionals. They are also the most socially active and the most visible middle-class segment in their provincial cities. In Mexico City, upper-middle-class families in this category are the most likely to seek inclusion in the social section of the capital's daily newspapers.

Economically, the upper-middle class of provincial cities and their hinterlands includes nuclear families with annual disposable incomes in the range of U.S.$100,000–200,000 (in 2000 dollars). In Mexico City, with its larger and more diversified economy, the upper-middle class is more affluent, having disposable incomes as high as U.S.$300,000. In both settings, their income is derived from manifold sources. Prominent among them are large retail stores, small factories, clinics (*sanatorios*), automobile dealerships, and real estate. In provincial cities, many upper-middle-class families engage in farming as well. Also in this class—constituting about 5 to 10 percent in provincial cities and about 10 percent in Mexico City—are many of the top practicing professionals, primarily lawyers, physicians, accountants, and engineers. Some of them also own related businesses, such as notary public, accounting, and consulting firms. In short, the upper-middle class is clearly affluent, by both Mexican and U.S. standards, and its worldview is centered on making money and maintaining a high standard of living.

At the same time, this class does not have significant political influence, compared to the plutocracy and the political class, nor does it significantly control specific sectors of social and economic life. Indeed, the upper-middle class is the most apolitical sector of the stratification system, beyond the folk-Indian environment (see Chap. 7), in the sense that only a few have been elected to public office. But they are everywhere the most vocal critics of the political establishment, as their economic ambitions inevitably draw them into the political and bureaucratic web of bribery, extortion, and graft.

With the exception of the professionals among them, upper-middle-class individuals are generally viewed as very educated (*instruidos, cultos*), a characteristic they share with much of the plutocracy. They are the best read and the best informed, and they generally have a passable grasp of history, literature, philosophy, and the arts. Education in this sense is ordinarily acquired at home, as part of a family tradition, as attested by the extensive libraries found in many upper-middle-class (and plutocratic) homes. Or it may be the product of the international travel that characterizes the leisure life of these two classes, especially the plutocrats. On the other hand, neither the upper-middle class nor the plutocracy, on the whole, is among the best-trained sectors of the population, as relatively few of them have professional degrees. This situation has been changing during the past generation, however, and most people (both males and females) over the age of thirty in both classes have attended universities in Mexico or in the United States, England, or France.

In terms of residence, there is nothing exclusive about the upper-middle class that we have not already discussed with reference to the plutocracy. Both classes reside in the upscale sections of provincial cities and Mexico City, and their residences are likely to be pretentious and kitschy. Two exceptions to the latter generalization are, first, the few provincial upper-middle-class families who still reside in *casas porfirianas* (houses built between 1876 and 1910, during the Porfirio Díaz dictatorship), and second, the plutocratic and upper-middle-class families in Mexico City whose homes were built by Mexico's leading architects.

Together with the minuscule plutocracy, the upper-middle class is the most phenotypically homogeneous of the urban and regional population components of Central Mexico (Nutini 2004, 2005). Most of its members are predominantly or entirely of European or Near Eastern origin and are considered "white," although there are some light mestizo phenotypes (showing some Indian ancestry) and about 5 percent with dark mestizo/Indian features. In this sense, the upper-middle class is representative of the ruling classes of Central Mexico.

Generally, the higher the social class, the more predominant is the European phenotype. The only exception is the upper stratum's political class, which has a strong representation of mestizo/Indian phenotypes. As a rule, though, the more European an individual appears, the more likely he or she is to rise socially and the greater the possibility of success in business and professional activities. This situation is a colonial legacy that has saddled an essentially mestizo/Indian society with standards of appearance, beauty, and behavior that are not its own.

The upper-middle class and the plutocracy are very conscious of their European extraction and collectively consider themselves "white." This outlook is underlain by a "whitening syndrome" designed to minimize the mestizo/Indian phenotypic traits exhibited by a minority of the members of these classes (see Chap. 8). Collectively, both classes are unquestionably racist, although seldom overtly so in public. Privately, many such individuals not only explain their own economic success racially, attributing it to their European ancestry, but also consider laziness, improvidence, and lack of persistence racial traits of most other Mexicans (usually lumping together mestizo and Indian populations). The same private racism occurs among solid-middle-class individuals of "white" phenotype, who must then rationalize their own failure to achieve greater wealth or better positions by appealing to political corruption or other unrealistic constructions.

As a social entity, the upper-middle class everywhere is the most visible sector of the stratification system, especially in provincial cities, and the prestige-UMC is the most identifiable component of the upper stratum, given that the provincial plutocracy keeps a low profile. In fact, the prestige-UMC is what the other provincial middle classes call *la sociedad*—the socially prominent, those who are in the limelight and whose comings and goings are routinely reported in the press. Moreover, public activities such as sponsoring fairs, drawing in well-known musicians, organizing art exhibitions, and promoting other "cultural" affairs are mostly associated with upper-middle-class individuals who take a public interest in enhancing the prestige of their cities or who participate in these activities as a way to advertise their businesses. In Mexico City, in contrast, the aristocracy formerly played this role, which today is carried out almost exclusively by the plutocracy.

Upper-middle-class families in provincial cities are the most accessible models of upward mobility for middle- and working-class families. Their wealth and social standing are perceived as attainable goals for those who are willing to sacrifice and work hard, whereas the huge fortunes (by local standards) of the plutocracy are considered unattainable. The plutocracy's wealth and power are also generally viewed as ill gained, whereas most people regard the affluence of the upper-middle class as having been earned honestly, through hard work. Moreover, most middle- and working-class people still quietly admire the "good" lineage and tradition of the old families who constitute the local prestige-UMC, and they regard its members as the social leaders of the upper-middle class. The provincial plutocracy, in turn, cultivates prestige-UMC friendships as a validating symbol of its own, recently acquired wealth and power. As we pointed out earlier, the aristocracy serves this function in Mexico City.

Finally, we want to highlight two cultural aspects—religion and kinship/household organization—in which the upper-middle class is similar to the main classes of the superordinate stratum. In terms of religion, these classes are the most conservative sector in the stratification system. Except for a few Muslim and Jewish families, even in the provincial cities, they are all Catholics; we are not aware of any Protestants among them. Furthermore, their Catholicism is very conventional, with few of the folk beliefs and practices that characterize the religiosity of everyone else—such as the cult of the dead, elaborate service to the saints, emphasis on life-cycle celebrations, and inclusion of magical elements (see Chap. 7).

The religious conventionality of these classes is not total, however. For the most part, they are not strict churchgoers. In fact, a few of them (mostly politicians) are agnostic, and others are anticlerical, complaining that the church and its priests are doing a poor job of counteracting the inroads made by Protestant evangelism among the lower classes. The more pious members of the upper-middle class, particularly, suggest that Evangelical Protestants have no right to proselytize in a traditionally Catholic country, despite the official lifting of this ban in 1992. As a rule, upper-middle-class families celebrate the manifold events of the annual religious and life cycles, but they are not nearly as ritualistic as the rest of the middle stratum and the lower classes. Finally, the religiosity of all the superordinate sectors is significantly less traditionally orthodox in Mexico City, except among the aristocracy.

Kinship and household organization are also basically the same throughout the superordinate classes and the upper-middle class as a whole. As in all of Mexico (and the United States)—except in some Indian communities—kinship is reckoned bilaterally, that is, with equal weight ideally given to mother's and father's kin; furthermore, the only operational unit beyond the household is the loosely organized nonresidential extended family, which may include from five to nine lineally and collaterally related households (Nutini 1968a, 1968b). The extended family here lacks the organic cohesion that it has in rural villages and mainly functions as a support group for the celebration of the annual and life cycles. The patrilocal extended-family household, formed when a son brings his wife to live in his parental home, occurs but is always of short duration, seldom longer than three or four years, while the young married couple is accumulating the wherewithal to establish their own household. Rather, the nuclear-family household (parents and unmarried children) is the norm. It is always small, seldom including more than three children. The ideal today is a total of two or three children, whereas six or seven children per marriage was common two generations ago. Family size is treated almost entirely as a practical matter, and religious considerations seldom if ever are a significant factor. In closing, we should note that kinship is much more important to Mexico City's aristocracy, which emphasizes lineage and family tradition, than it is to the other upper classes there or in provincial cities.

The Solid-Middle Class

The solid-middle class (SMC) is small, probably less than 15 percent of the total population of Central Mexico's provincial cities and their hinterlands and about 10 percent of Mexico City (Nutini 2005). It comprises professionals (physicians, lawyers, engineers, architects, dentists, accountants, and agronomists), owners of medium-sized businesses (retail stores, specialty shops, laboratories, small clinics, local construction firms, and service providers), medium-sized farmers, middle-level bank officials, and government bureaucrats (local, state, and federal). Most of the business and professional families have been SMC since the 1970s, some since the 1950s.

The SMC is affluent, but there is considerable internal variation (Nutini 2005). Business owners and farmers earn the highest incomes, which we estimate at U.S.$75,000–150,000 gross annually (in 2000 dollars), putting some of them (business owners) in the same income range as the upper-middle class (U.S.$100,000–200,000). Thus the wealthier SMC families can afford well-appointed homes with three or four bedrooms, quite often in their city's elite residential sections. They also typically employ one or two maids, own two or three late-model cars, and send their children to the best prep schools and universities in Mexico City and the provincial capitals. In fact, outwardly they are difficult to distinguish from the upper-middle-class families in their communities, and the two classes frequently interact socially and occasionally intermarry.

The difference between them is further blurred by the fact that some SMC families also have country retreats. Finally, we should note that the SMC generally enjoys a higher standard of living than its "middle-middle-class" counterpart in the United States. The comparison loses some of its importance, however, when we take into account that the SMC constitutes a much smaller percentage of the population.

Professional families are less affluent than the business owners and farmers but enjoy higher prestige. The most prestigious professionals are graduates of the Universidad Nacional Autónoma de México or the Universidad Iberoamericana in Mexico City, the Tecnológico de Monterrey in the state of Nuevo León, and a few other elite schools. A few have pursued postgraduate studies in the United States, but most professionals are graduates of local or state universities in Mexico. All other things being equal, the more prestigious the university from which they graduated, the greater their income. The professions themselves are rank-ordered as follows in terms of prestige: medicine, architecture, engineering, agronomy, accounting, law, and dentistry. In terms of earning power, though, lawyers are at the top, followed in order by physicians, accountants, dentists, engineers, architects, and agronomists.

While lawyers generally earn the highest incomes among the professionals, they also have the greatest range of income variation. The lowest earners among them—grossing less than U.S.$25,000 per year—are those who hold degrees from local or state universities and either have small private practices or hold jobs in private businesses or government agencies. At the opposite extreme are lawyers with degrees from the Universidad Nacional Autónoma de México or other prestigious universities in Mexico City; they may earn more than U.S.$150,000 annually, especially if they own a public notary office (*notaria*), a necessary stop in any formal or bureaucratic transaction. Pretty much the same obtains with physicians, except that their income range is smaller, an estimated U.S.$30,000–120,000 per year, depending on specialty and duration in practice. All other professionals have considerably less income. They seldom make more than U.S.$80,000 per year, and about a third earn less than U.S.$30,000. The least well paid of the SMC are middle-level bank personnel and government bureaucrats, whose annual salaries are in the U.S.$15,000–40,000 range.

Calculating SMC disposable income is complicated by rampant tax evasion. Among professionals, the most common means of evasion is neglecting to provide receipts for services or to enter the transactions in accounting logs. Business owners also sometimes falsify their records, and they must frequently pay off-the-books bribes, even to tax officials, that can either erode their visible income or enhance future revenue or both. Farmers, especially sugar and coffee growers, can evade taxes by underreporting production or by selling portions of the crop without receipts. These and many other means of tax evasion may exempt over 60 percent of gross earnings, thereby nearly doubling disposable income.

That all practicing professionals have university degrees does not necessarily mean that they are the best educated—in the liberal arts sense of the term—members of their class. Rather, businessmen and bureaucrats are often the most educated (*más cultos*, lit., "most cultured"); as a group, they are probably the best read and best informed. At the same time, their formal education credentials may not be impressive, perhaps no more than high school (*preparatoria*) or a year or two of college, although some have received degrees in economics or business administration (relatively low-prestige credentials). Ethnically and phenotypically, the majority of the SMC is of mestizo extraction, although mostly light skinned, but this class also includes many individuals who display a wide range of Indian-Negroid and European phenotypes. While racial considerations cannot play a determinant role in interclass relations because the gradations of genetic mixture are impossible to categorize on the basis of phenotype, "race" does play a small role in SMC self-perception. The majority of its members commonly think of themselves as *criollos* in the term's everyday meaning, light-skinned mestizos. Also, SMC individuals often engage in the cultural whitening syndrome—manipulating cultural and phenotypic traits in order to be perceived as more European and thus of a better social class position—to maximize economic and social ends when the occasion demands it.

In terms of verbalized class consciousness, the SMC stands in contrast to both the lower-middle class and the lower classes, who do not express a collective perception of occupying a well-defined niche in society or a sense of belonging to a clearly defined social or economic group. SMC people readily verbalize their standing and role in society, emphasizing that they are the cogs that make the social machinery work—through their own efforts and without the dishonesty and illegalities of the rich and powerful. Their claim to being the social movers is largely empty, however, because the SMC has never formed voluntary civic associations to promote the general welfare or to fight the political corruption they decry, and they seldom (and never as organized groups) engage in charity work. Indeed, of all the social classes of Central Mexico, the SMC is the most socially, politically, and ideologically isolated from the majority of the people. This is surprising, because the whole SMC, by the very nature of its economic and professional activities, is in intimate physical contact with the rest of the society.

The SMC is probably the least religious of all the classes of Central Mexico. Its members are the least likely to attend church, are not much involved in parish affairs, and are the least traditional in celebrations of most of the religious events in the annual cycle. Regarding religious identity, the SMC is overwhelmingly Catholic; in the average provincial city, there are no SMC Protestants and only a few Muslim and Jewish families. In fact, we are not personally aware of any SMC individuals who have converted to Protestantism, despite more than sixty years of intense proselytism (Dow 2001a). The explanation is twofold. First, as the least religious sector of the population, the SMC is not likely to convert, especially since Evangelical Protestantism is identified with the lower and lower-middle classes. Second, members of the SMC do not need the social and economic support that Evangelical Protestant sects provide.

The SMC kinship system and household organization are essentially the same as those of the upper-middle class, except in three respects. First, the SMC has a higher incidence of bifocal extended-family households, in which newlyweds are residing with the parents of either one while accumulating the wherewithal to establish a separate home. Second, the SMC has closer ties among the households of sliding kindreds. That is, the bilateral kindred (kin on both father's and mother's side) is structured by nonkinship variables, such as the relative affluence or social renown of certain households, and the wealthier and more prestigious households attract larger numbers of younger households to their social orbits.

Third, the SMC has significantly larger *compadrazgo* (ritual kinship) networks. In fact, SMC couples contract more than twice as many types of compadrazgo as the three main classes of the national superordinate stratum. Furthermore, superordinate compadrazgo is confined to the sacramental types (baptism, confirmation, first communion, and marriage) and is symmetrically structured, except when politicians or, occasionally, plutocrats engage in public-collective forms, such as when they sponsor an entire graduating high school class. SMC families, in contrast, contract all sacramental types plus several others, such as graduation (from grammar school, high school, college, etc.), silver wedding anniversary, *quince años* (celebration of a girl's fifteenth birthday), and *primera piedra* (setting the foundation of a house). The resulting compadrazgo networks have considerable social and economic importance for the SMC. In contrast, superordinate stratum compadrazgo is confined to the immediate rites and ceremonies and seldom has social and economic consequences.

There is a significant degree of mobility from the SMC to the upper-middle class, especially by the more distinguished professionals and agricultural entrepreneurs. Successful upward mobility begins with casual interaction (usually business contacts), proceeds to exchanges of invitations to household events (e.g., cocktail parties), and may culminate in intermarriage. The whole sequence requires from five to ten years. The major changes undergone by the SMC family are expressive, and thus they are described in Chapter 8.

The Lower-Middle Class

Structurally, the lower-middle and working classes have much in common. Their differences are more expressive than structural. Also significant are the deep-rooted distinctions between white- and blue-collar employment and between the self-employed and salaried workers. Given these circumstances, we adopt a mixed strategy here. We emphasize what the lower-middle and working classes share, both structurally and expressively; in Chapter 6 we treat the working class structurally and as a component of the urban lower stratum.

It is difficult to assess the size of these two classes. Official statistics are only indirectly useful, as they are organized by either income or occupation, considered separately from one another and from such other class criteria as neighborhood, education, and lifestyle. Our estimate is that the lower-middle class constitutes around 20 to 25 percent of Central Mexico's population, and the working class accounts for at least another 30 to 35 percent. In short, these two classes constitute 50 to 60 percent of the area's population.

There is also a large marginal class whose precise size is very difficult to estimate because its employment is sporadic and often in the informal (unlicensed, untaxed, or illegal) economy. Poverty measurements provide some indirect insight here: they show that a clear majority of the population—from 54 to 75 percent, depending on the measuring device (see Damián and Boltvinik 2003)—was living in either extreme or moderate poverty in 2000. Their ranks would include the working class, the marginal class, and the bottom one-third or so of the lower-middle class. These figures are for the entire national population, but there is no reason to believe that Central Mexico is exceptional in this regard (see Chap. 6).

Let us now briefly address the white-collar/blue-collar and self-employed/salaried distinctions. Although both distinctions also occur in the United States and elsewhere, they have somewhat different meanings or implications in each country. As it is played out in Mexico, the white-collar/blue-collar distinction is probably rooted in the Spanish attitude that those who do manual labor automatically rank lower than those who do not. Of course, this is an ideological distinction that fits poorly with the modern, industrialized world, in which a white-collar office worker often earns considerably less than a blue-collar factory worker or mechanic. Also, as we shall see, the lower-middle class includes a mixture of white- and blue-collar households. Yet the white-collar preference still prevails in Mexico and strongly influences the strategies of upward mobility for lower-middle and working-class people, who almost always prefer that their children become poorly paid bank clerks and secretaries rather than better-paid factory workers, for example.

The self-employed sector is complex in Central Mexico. It includes not only the service businesses that are still present in highly industrialized countries (e.g., barbershops, beauty parlors, dry cleaners) but many other kinds of small shops and service providers as well. The precise nature of self-employment in Central Mexico will become clear in a moment, when we contrast lower-middle- and working-class occupations.

The lower-middle class consists primarily of white-collar workers but also contains some blue-collar workers. The latter are manual laborers who may also own a small business, such as an electrical or automotive repair shop. In contrast, all manual wage earners and piece-/task-workers belong to the working class, whether they work independently or in factories or lower-middle-class shops. To clarify, some carpenters, masons, electricians, seamstresses, beauticians, and so on, work independently and may be called to private residences to perform their trades, whereas a larger number of them work for shops to which clients come to have the work done or from which they are dispatched to residences to do specific jobs. All of them belong to the working class. The shop owner, in contrast, ranks higher on the social scale (i.e., in the lower-middle class) because he owns the business, even if he does some of the manual work himself.

More specifically, the lower-middle class is composed of the following kinds of individuals and their nuclear families:

- Schoolteachers (grammar, middle, and high school)
- Instructors in technical schools (secretarial, practical nursing, accounting, etc.)
- Middle- and lower-level bureaucrats (local, state, and federal), including secretarial personnel
- Banking personnel (middle and lower levels)
- Registered nurses, hospital technical personnel, independent lab operators
- Secretaries and receptionists in professional offices
- Clerks employed by large stores
- Owners of small retail businesses—eateries, bars, bakeries, butcher shops, and other food outlets (for tortillas, sandwiches, tacos, pastries, pizza, fish); convenience stores (popularly known as *misceláneas* or *changarros*) selling a narrow range of canned foods, soda pop, fruits, vegetables, and miscellaneous other items of frequent household consumption; shops specializing in hardware, books, notions (*mercerías*), flowers, jewelry, curios, saddles and other leather goods, medicines (*boticas*), and so on; service providers (beauty shops and barbershops, dry cleaners, locksmiths, glass cutters, upholstery, etc.), and several other types of businesses, such as tanneries and cigar makers
- Owners of small automotive shops specializing in mechanical repairs, body work, spare parts, wheel alignment, tire repair, and the like
- Owners of other repair shops—primarily for electrical appliances, radios and television sets, bicycles, motorcycles, agricultural equipment, and hydraulic equipment
- Owners of video and Internet kiosks

The working class is composed of the following types of individuals and their nuclear families:

- Workers in manufacturing and processing establishments—factories producing a diverse range of goods (automotive parts, agricultural machinery, other metallurgical products, textiles, paper, cement, chemicals, fertilizers, etc.) and food-producing

or food-processing plants (poultry, sugar, coffee, rice, cooking oil, sodas and alcoholic beverages, etc.)
- Taxi drivers, bus drivers (both local and long-distance), and agricultural machinery operators
- Cooks, bartenders, and waiters
- Railroad and road workers
- Handymen, craftsmen, and specialized workers employed by city governments
- Craftsmen (carpenters, masons, electricians, plumbers, mechanics, cabinetmakers, furniture makers) working independently or employed by the kinds of shops specified earlier with reference to the lower-middle class
- Traditional midwives (*parteras*), curers, and herbalists

In terms of income, there is considerable variation within the lower-middle and working classes, but we can make the following generalizations (adapted from Nutini 2005). First, most blue-collar and white-collar workers make at least three "minimum wages" (*salarios mínimos*) per day. The minimum wage rate is set by the federal government at the beginning of each year and varies according to the country's three cost-of-living "zones" (A, B, C). For 2005, the rates were set at 46.80 pesos for Zone A, 45.35 pesos for Zone B, and 44.05 pesos for Zone C. At the official monetary exchange rate, these amounts translate to U.S.$4.20, $4.07, and $3.96 per day. Thus the three "minimum wages" earned by most workers in the lower-middle and working classes would amount to U.S.$12.60, $12.21, and $11.88 per day, respectively. There are, however, anywhere from 780,000 to 918,000 such workers employed in "good" jobs, meaning those with social security benefits through the Instituto Mexicano de Seguro Social (IMSS), who earn only one minimum wage per day (F. Martínez 2004a, 2004b), and doubtless there are as many others earning only two.

Second, blue-collar workers (especially factory workers) are almost always better paid than lower-middle-class white-collar workers (especially store clerks, most banking personnel, secretaries, and receptionists). Third, primary and middle school (*secundaria*) teachers are paid about the same as factory workers, while high school (*preparatoria*) teachers receive a bit more. Fourth, the self-employed among specialized craftsmen (mechanics, carpenters, electricians, plumbers, etc.) have higher incomes than those who work for neighborhood retail stores, repair shops, or other small establishments. Fifth, the owners of small businesses (e.g., restaurants, retail stores, repair shops) are by far the most affluent in the class. While they are extremely reluctant to provide precise information on their incomes, it is evident from their lifestyles that at least a few of them have disposable annual incomes of tens of thousands of dollars. (The earnings of most employed workers are a matter of public record, but not so the incomes of the self-employed. Also, the greater their affluence, the less willing people are to talk about the money they earn or have acquired.)

A representative sample of monthly earnings of lower-middle and working-class people in and around Córdoba, Veracruz, in 2002 (Nutini 2005) is illuminating. These figures are in Mexican pesos (MXP) (U.S.$1 = MXP9.1530 on January 1, 2002, and MXP10.4237 on December 31, 2002). For the reasons stated above, we are confident of the figures for the first five categories; those for the sixth and seventh are rough estimates.

1. Primary and middle school teachers, 1,900 to 2,900; high school and technical school teachers, 3,000 to 4,200
2. bank clerks, 2,000 to 4,000; office receptionists, 1,500 to 3,000; office secretaries, 1,000 to 2,000
3. store clerks, 900 to 1,500
4. Factory workers (including sugar mills), 3,200 to 6,000
5. Self-employed mechanics, carpenters, electricians, plumbers, masons, and other specialized workers, 3,500 to 5,500
6. Owners of small retail stores and repair shops, 6,500 to 10,000
7. Owners of restaurants, commercial-zone stores, and many other small businesses, 12,500 to 30,000

This earnings picture translates into a varied standard of living for the lower-middle and working classes, but we can say the following about housing, household equipment, and car ownership. While there is great variation in house construction and elaboration, most of the seven categories of workers listed above are home owners or occupants of government-sponsored housing; very few live in rented apartments, fewer still in rented houses. The lower-middle and working classes live outside the upscale sections inhabited by the rich and the solid-middle class, but otherwise their residences are scattered throughout the urban area, in the periphery as well as in the midst of the commercial center. Usually, the homes of both classes are equipped with gas stoves, refrigerators, radios, and television sets, regardless of what other equipment and appliances they may or may not possess (also see Chap. 8). Approximately 20 percent of working-class households own a car, often fifteen to twenty years old. A much larger proportion of lower-middle-class households own cars, often of more recent vintage, and the more affluent business owners have the largest and most expensive models.

Ethnically, the lower-middle and working classes are overwhelmingly mestizo, including many with quite evident Indian and/or Negroid features. There are also a few "criollos" and a sprinkling of fully European phenotypes, but together they make up no more than about 2 percent of the lower-middle and working classes combined. Their more affluent look-alikes in the SMC and upper-middle class often regard them as "losers," especially those doing manual work—a form of racism that implies that light-skinned individuals should not have such a low social status.

Complicating the depiction of Central Mexico's racial-ethnic composition is the pronounced Afro-Mexican admixture that occurs almost exclusively in the coastal states. For example, the population of the Córdoba-Orizaba region of Veracruz is significantly darker than that of the average community in the interior highlands (the states of Puebla, Tlaxcala, Mexico, and Morelos, plus the Federal District). There are no entirely Afro-Mexican communities in the two-city region, but many people have noticeably Negroid features, especially in lowland communities (below 600 m elev.). As we pointed out in Chapter 2, these phenotypical differences elicit a mild degree of racism but are not reliable social class indicators, because it has long been impossible to sort the gradations of Indian, African, and European admixtures into consistent or replicable categories.

The whitening syndrome occurs rarely among the lower-middle and working classes. It can be found mainly among the most upwardly mobile families. To enhance their European appearance, women might leave their legs unshaven, avoid wearing garments reminiscent of Indian clothing, and cease braiding their hair. To take another example, parents often favor their more European-appearing offspring, and men may avoid marrying women who appear "Indian," in order to enhance their progeny's phenotypes, and both parents may encourage their children to do likewise.

In the lower-middle class, the upwardly mobile are mainly the more successful small business owners and ambitious office personnel, in both the government and the private sector, on their way upward to managerial positions. By the very nature of their occupations, they interact closely with SMC individuals and families, which is the immediate stimulus for upward mobility. If this strictly job-related interaction develops into further socializing, the next step is emulation (see Chap. 8). In the working class, the cases of this nature are mainly specialized artisans (e.g., cabinetmakers, upholsterers, and hydraulic mechanics) and factory workers (who are, generally, the best-paid people in their class). Through sacrifice in the form of extra work and forgone consumption, some of these blue-collar families manage to put one or more of their children through college, greatly enhancing their chances of upward mobility. Such generational mobility may eventually result in greatly different expressive styles within the households of parents and their married children, and they may even be perceived as belonging to different classes.

Working-class people almost invariably have finished primary school, and perhaps a third have completed middle school, while about 10 percent have some technical school education. Lower-middle-class people are generally better educated; many have completed *preparatoria*, and a few have finished college or technical school. Self-made men with little formal education—a common phenomenon throughout the stratification system—are found here among the most affluent small- to medium-sized merchants. Nevertheless, even the lower-middle- and working-class individuals with little formal education invariably value education as an instrument of upward mobility and strive to secure it for their children, sometimes at considerable personal cost.

Kinship is very important in building social and economic ties, even among urbanites, and working-class people retain some of the attributes of rural village kinship. As we noted earlier, kinship is reckoned bilaterally in most of Mexico (as in the United States), with equal weight ideally given to matrilateral and patrilateral kin. Very often, though, there is a patrilateral bias, and this is the case for most of Central Mexico's working class, especially in families with a recent village past. This set of kin, or kindred, also has the same "sliding" aspect here that we noted for the solid-middle class: "closeness" is affected by nonkinship variables, so that the wealthier or more prestigious households are the most sought after. The patrilaterally biased sliding kindred has a significant role in organizing working-class social life, sometimes almost as effectively as in the village situation. This is especially the case among families who are only one generation or less removed from the rural context. Although the nonresidential extended family tends to be more scattered in the cities than in rural communities, it continues to play a significant role in urban working-class celebrations of the life and yearly cycles.

In the working class, compadrazgo is nearly as complex as in the rural village system. It includes all the types carried out by the solid-middle class, in addition to several others (e.g., the blessing of a new house, a saint's picture, or a vehicle), for a total of more than fifteen (Nutini and Bell 1980; Nutini and Isaac 1977). Working-class compadrazgo is always symmetrical, which means that return requests for sponsorship are expected (i.e., the person who is asked now becomes the one who asks later). As in the rural village context, the compadrazgo relationship extends beyond the immediate rites and ceremonies, rivaling ordinary kinship in generating social, economic, and religious/ceremonial resources.

Lower-middle- and working-class people are the most overtly Catholic in the entire stratification spectrum. At the same time, their Catholicism is the least orthodox of all urbanites, as their practices are quite close to village "folk" Catholicism, and they are not especially strict about regular confession or taking communion. Traditional village customs also permeate many of the events in the annual religious calendar and the life cycle, which do not necessarily include going to confession or taking communion. Furthermore, lower-middle- and working-class people (especially the latter) are the most dissatisfied with the Catholic Church's social and economic support, rendering them the most vulnerable to Evangelical Protestantism.

Throughout Central Mexico, Evangelical Protestants have been highly successful in attracting dissatisfied Catholics since about 1970, converting perhaps as much as 20 percent of the lower-middle and working classes. For example, there was only one Evangelical Protestant congregation in the city of Fortín, Veracruz, in 1980; by 1995 the city had seven such congregations, even though the population had remained steady at about twenty-five thousand, and local Catholic authorities had come to regard the much larger neighboring city of Córdoba as a hotbed of evangelism. The most active sects are Jehovah's Witness, Pentecostal, Seventh Day Adventist, and Mormon. By 2000, they had over 350 rural and urban congregations in the Córdoba-Orizaba region, all converts from Catholicism and all from the lower-middle and working classes, especially the latter.

An interesting development since about 1985 has been the proliferation of native evangelical sects—locally generated dissident (anti-Catholic) movements that are both doctrinally and organizationally derived from U.S. Evangelical Protestantism (Nutini 2000). Their most common models are the Pentecostal and Jehovah's Witness denominations. Basically, they arise in two different ways. One or more members of a Protestant congregation become dissatisfied with some organizational or doctrinal aspect, whereupon they secede and launch a new movement. Or a divinely inspired leader initiates a native sect on hearing the word of God, who—in the time-honored Christian tradition—reveals the one true doctrinal path of worship and provides the blueprint for a new congregation. In reality, the new sect is an amalgam of beliefs and practices of Evangelical Protestant origin. Native evangelist congregations generally view themselves as a distinctly Mexican movement away from Catholicism, however, and this nationalistic aspect is likely to grow, making these new religions even stronger competitors of both Catholicism and established Protestantism.

Finally, the lower-middle and the working classes both exhibit far less class consciousness than does the SMC. The successful merchants who are the more affluent members of the lower-middle class quite often identify with the SMC as the first step toward upward mobility, but the class itself does not engage in characteristic social or economic action. The working class is similarly lacking in class consciousness. The fact that its members are all manual workers does not translate into communal social or economic action, as there is not a sufficient basis for solidarity between, for instance, factory workers and independent craftsmen.

The foregoing account of the lower-middle and working classes applies to all the provincial cities and regions of Central Mexico, as well as to Mexico City. The main difference between the megalopolis and the provincial cities is the lower proportion of these classes in the total population of the latter. The smaller cities and towns that serve the rural hinterlands have their own class structures, of course, sometimes including local elites with considerable wealth and sophistication. In terms of regional stratification, however, the bulk of these populations—apart from wealthy elites, the associated peasantry and part-time wage workers, and the economically dispossessed—are either lower-middle or working class.

six: THE URBAN LOWER CLASSES

In 1900 Mexico's population was about 90 percent rural, that is, living in communities of fewer than 2,500 inhabitants. The urban and rural populations became roughly equal sometime during the 1950s, and the urban component became a majority during the 1960s (Stern 1994: 423). By 1970 the urban population (i.e., settlements of 2,500 or more) constituted 58.7 percent of the national total; it reached 71.3 percent by 1990 and 74.6 percent by 2000 (INEGI 2003: 15). And by 2000, 13.6 percent of Mexico's population lived in cities of one million or more inhabitants, 47.3 percent in cities of 100,000 or more, and 60.9 percent in cities of 15,000 or more (INEGI 2003: 13).

Central Mexico reflects this pattern of urbanization (INEGI 2003: 18). Of the seven states and the Federal District, only Hidalgo has less than 50 percent of its population in settlements of over 2,500 inhabitants. Hidalgo (49.3 percent) is followed by Guerrero (55.3 percent), Veracruz (59.1 percent), Puebla (68.3 percent), Tlaxcala (78.5 percent), Morelos (85.4 percent), México (86.3 percent), and the Federal District (99.8 percent). Most of this population is poor and forms the bulk of Mexico's lower-stratum majority.

The urban lower classes can be conceived initially as comprising two large divisions: the working class, whose members hold steady jobs in the formal economy, and the marginal class, for whom employment is sporadic and often in the informal (unlicensed, untaxed) economy. Many of the latter are periodically self-employed service providers (plumbers, carpenters, masons, and the like) or street vendors, while others (especially women) are home-based pieceworkers for the garment, toy, plastics, electronics, and other industries (Alba Vega and Kruijt 1995; Benería and Roldán 1987). Nevertheless, there is so much occupational fluidity that even these generalizations are tentative. As Selby and colleagues (1990: 6) point out, "Today's factory worker is tomorrow's Kleenex salesman [on the street], often perforce but other times by desire" (also see Cross 1998; González de la Rocha 1994: 8–9).

Economic Change: The Rise of the Service Sector

Mexico's economic structure changed commensurately as its population became predominantly urban during the twentieth century (Stern 1994: 423). In 1900 some 65 percent of the country's workforce was engaged in primary economic activities (almost entirely farming and ranching), and only 20 percent was in the tertiary sector (commerce and services). Soon after 1910, the primary and tertiary sectors embarked on opposing trajectories, the former declining and the latter rising, and they intersected during the mid-1970s, at around 35 percent each. The secondary sector (extractive industries, manufacturing, energy production, construction) was at about 15 percent in 1910 and did not exceed 20 percent until the 1960s.

By 2000 Mexico had a predominantly service economy, with 55.7 percent of the entire workforce engaged in the tertiary sector—including nearly one-half (47.6 percent) of all working men and just under three-fourths (71.6 percent) of all working women (Table 6.1). The secondary sector comprised 26 percent of the workforce, with much less disparity between men (28.0 percent) and women (22.0 percent). The primary sector had dipped to 18.3 percent, with an apparently great disparity between men (23.9 percent) and women (6.2 percent); women are almost certainly undercounted, however; rural women often do not report their agrarian contributions because they consider them "an extension of their domestic duties" (INEGI 2003: 383). Even allowing for underrepresentation, we can say that by 2000 slightly over half of Mexico's workforce was in the tertiary sector, with the other half split between the primary and secondary sectors, perhaps more evenly than the available quantifiable data would indicate. It is worth noting that Central Mexico is quite similar to the country as a whole in this regard (see Table 6.1).

Tables 6.2 and 6.3 provide additional views of the present-day workforce. Of the occupational groups shown in Table 6.2, all but "Agricultural"

TABLE 6.1

Central Mexican and National Workforce in 2001, by Economic Sector and Gender, in Percentages[a]

Economic Sector	Male (%)	Female (%)	Both (%)
Primary[b]			
Central Mexico	28.5	6.4	
excluding Federal District	32.5	7.2	
National	23.9	6.2	18.3
Secondary[c]			
Central Mexico	25.9	19.2	
excluding Federal District	25.9	19.2	
National	28.0	22.0	26.0
Tertiary[d]			
Central Mexico	45.6	74.5	
excluding Federal District	41.6	73.3	
National	47.6	71.6	55.7

Source: Compiled from INEGI 2003: 383–385.

[a] As elsewhere in this book, Central Mexico includes the states of Guerrero, México, Morelos, Puebla, Tlaxcala, Hidalgo, and Veracruz, as well as the Federal District (which includes Mexico City).

[b] The primary sector comprises "economic activities related to agriculture, animal husbandry, forestry, hunting, and fishing" (INEGI 2003: 383).

[c] The secondary sector comprises "all the activities related to the extractive industry, manufacturing, electricity, water, gas, and construction" (INEGI 2003: 384).

[d] The tertiary sector "is also known as the commerce and services sector" (INEGI 2003: 385).

TABLE 6.2

Mexican Workforce in 2001, by Major Occupational Groups and Gender, in Percentages

Major Occupational Groups	Total (%) (N 39,385,505)	Males (%) (N 25,992,774)	Females (%) (N 13,392,731)
Artisanal and blue-collar[a]	25.4	28.6	19.1
Professional, managerial, and white-collar[b]	21.1	17.1	28.8
Agricultural	17.3	23.2	5.9
Commercial[c]	16.6	12.3	24.9
Subtotal	80.4	81.2	78.7
All others[d]	19.6	18.8	21.3
Total	100.0	100.0	100.0

Source: Derived from INEGI 2003: 375.

[a] Artisans, blue-collar workers (*obreros*), and workers' helpers (*ayudantes de obreros*).

[b] Professionals, technicians and specialized personnel, teachers and related, art workers, public officials and private sector managers, agricultural and ranching administrators, and office workers.

[c] Merchants, salespeople, shop assistants (*dependientes*), and street vendors (*vendedores ambulantes*).

[d] Services (M = 6.0%, F = 8.6%), domestics (M = 0.8%, F = 11.1%), transport operators (M = 6.5%, F = 0.1), protection/guarding (M = 2.8%, F = 0.3%), agricultural/ranching overseers (M = 0.2%, F = 0.0%), agricultural machinery operators (M = 0.3%, F = 0.0%), and industrial supervisors and foremen (M = 2.2%, F = 1.2%).

(17.3 percent) are predominantly urban, and all but the patently middle-class "Professional, Managerial, and White-Collar" workers (21.1 percent) belong mainly to the lower classes. "Artisanal and Blue-Collar," a quintessentially working-class grouping, has the highest representation overall (25.4 percent) and among males (28.6 percent). Female workers, in contrast, are heavily concentrated in office jobs (28.8 percent) and commerce (24.9 percent). Table 6.3 analyzes the workforce by work position rather than occupational group and shows that "Salaried/Waged Workers" comprise over half of all workers (56.8 percent), whether male (55.7

TABLE 6.3
Mexican Workforce in 2001, by Work Position and Gender, in Percentages

Work Positions	Total (%) (N 39,385,505)	Males (%) (N 25,992,774)	Females (%) (N 13,392,731)
Salaried/waged workers	56.8	55.7	59.2
Self-employed	24.1	25.1	22.0
Unpaid workers[a]	8.7	6.7	12.5
Piece–task workers	6.0	6.8	4.5
Employers	4.4	5.7	1.8
Total	100.0	100.0	100.0

Source: Adapted from INEGI 2003: 377.
[a] Mainly working in family businesses (i.e., in the self-employed sector).

percent) or female (59.2 percent). Most of these positions are available in towns and cities, of course. Roughly one quarter (24.1 percent) of all workers are officially classed as self-employed, mainly in agriculture and commerce, but this figure includes only persons who are earning money directly from the enterprises; in reality, most of the "Unpaid Workers" (8.7 percent), who comprise 12.5 percent of the female and 6.7 percent of the male workforce, are also working in these same enterprises. Thus about 30 percent of the total workforce is employed by private enterprises, most of which are small, family-owned, and urban. In the Federal District (which includes Mexico City) alone, self-employed street vending absorbed nearly 200,000 workers in the mid-1990s (Cross 1998: 18) and possibly as many as 500,000 by 2007 (Notimex 2007) (Fig. 6.1).

Poverty among the Urban Lower Classes

The hallmark of Mexico's lower classes is their relative poverty. Although this condition is readily visible and often remarked on by both Mexicans and foreigners, there is no single definition or measure of poverty that

FIGURE 6.1. Street vendors completely blocking the sidewalk in downtown Mexico City, forcing pedestrians to walk in the street. Photo by Barry Isaac.

is agreed on by all social scientists. Accordingly, there is considerable variation in the proportion of the Mexican population that is considered poor and thus included in the lower classes (Pardinas 2004). Nevertheless, most scholars would agree to a distinction between *extreme* poverty, in which life's most basic needs (food, clothing, shelter, transportation) cannot be met consistently (or at all), and *moderate* poverty, in which the household or person regularly meets minimal basic needs but can afford few of the comforts and conveniences enjoyed by people who may have only slightly higher incomes. We shall return to such definitional matters after looking at Mexico's general income structure.

A common way of depicting the poverty of the lower classes relative to the rest of the society is to compare their share of national income with that of the richer segments. Table 6.4 presents this contrast for Mexico (in 2000) and the United States (in 1999). In both countries, the bottom (poorest) 20 percent of households earn less than 5 percent of all income, and the bottom 40 percent of households earn less than 15 percent. In contrast, the top (richest) 20 percent of households earn over half of all income in Mexico (58.6 percent) and nearly half (47.2 percent) in the United States, while the top 40 percent take in about three-fourths of all income (77.7 percent in Mexico; 70.2 percent in the United States).

TABLE 6.4
Household Income as Percentage of National Income in Mexico (2003) and the United States (1999)[a]

Households' Percentage of National Income, by Country			
Households	Mexico	USA	Mexico vs. USA
Top 20%	58.6	47.2	+ 11.4
Top 40%	77.7	70.2	+ 7.5
Bottom 40%	10.4	14.2	- 3.8
Bottom 20%	3.2	4.3	- 1.1

[a] Data for Mexico are from Cortés 2000: 142. The United States figures are from Perrucci and Wysong 2003: 53.

Given the striking similarity in household income distribution in Mexico and the United States, why is poverty both more evident and more severe in the former? The answer lies in the two countries' relative economic size. In 2003 Mexico's gross domestic product (GDP) fell short of $1 trillion ($934.5 billion), while the U.S. GDP was $10.87 trillion, or 11.6 times larger. Thus Mexico's poor receive a small slice of a small pie, whereas the U.S. poor get a relatively small—but much larger in absolute terms—slice of a big pie.

The bottom two quintiles (lowest 40 percent) of Mexican households are by definition poor, as they receive only 10.4 percent of all household income (see Table 6.4). The Mexican economist Teresa Bracho (2000: 252–253) identifies the bottom quintile (one-fifth, or 20 percent), which receives 3.2 percent of national income, as extremely poor; and the second quintile, which earns 7.2 percent, as moderately poor. On the other hand, the economist Julio Boltvinik (2000: 193–195 passim), Mexico's foremost poverty expert, argues for a much higher poverty rate. He assesses poverty by the Integrated Poverty Measurement Method (IPMM), which takes into account not only per capita income in relation to the cost of basic necessities but also such indicators of life quality as housing conditions, equipment for housekeeping and personal care, and access to

TABLE 6.5
Percentage of Poverty among Urban and Rural Individuals, Mexico 1989

Poverty Groupings	Urban(%)	Rural (%)	National (%)
Extremely poor	34.1	61.8	44.7
Indigent	19.3	45.7	29.4
Very poor	14.8	16.1	15.3
Moderately poor	27.6	23.2	25.9
Total poor	61.7	85.0	70.6
Total nonpoor	38.3	15.0	29.4

Source: After Boltvinik 1999: cuadro 5.2.

public education and health care (Boltvinik 2000, 2002, 2003: 439–443; Damián and Boltvinik 2003). In his best-known analysis, which uses data from 1989, Boltvinik (2000: 193–195 passim) classified about two-thirds of the country's households as poor and nearly one-fourth as "indigent"; taking individuals rather than households as the units of analysis resulted in even higher poverty rates: 70.6 percent poor, including 29.4 percent indigent (see Table 6.5). The rural areas showed not only a much greater total household incidence of poverty (85.0 percent rural vs. 61.7 percent urban) but also a greater intensity of it, as indicated by a much higher percentage of "indigents" (45.7 percent rural vs. 19.3 percent urban). As we shall see later, these 1989 poverty figures are actually lower than those for the year 2000.

Boltvinik (2000: 229–233) describes the living conditions of both rural and urban "indigent" and "moderately poor" households in 1989. The former are below the poverty line, which means that their incomes are too small to afford basic necessities consistently, often resulting in malnutrition. The moderately poor, on the other hand, typically do not fall below the poverty line and "do not present serious problems in terms of necessities" (233).

Boltvinik (2000: 229–231) depicts the *indigent rural household* (45.7 percent) thus:

House: Adobe or plank walls, palm thatch (or similar) roof, dirt floor; 1.5 bedroom equivalents for 5 persons; shared kitchen; piped water outside but not inside the house; no drain or sewer connection.
Goods: Electric radio and television, petroleum (oil) stove, and iron; lacking bicycle, tape player, refrigerator, washing machine, blender (for making juice), fan (desirable for hot climates), telephone, automobile.
Education: Children and young people are below the educational norm; adults are far below it.
Health Care: No Social Security (IMSS) or other governmental health coverage; household income is inadequate for private health services.

The *moderately poor rural household* (23.2 percent) is characterized as follows (Boltvinik 2000: 232):

House: Cement block (*tabique*) walls, asbestos sheet or palm thatch roof, cement floor (untiled); 2.5 bedroom equivalents for 5 persons; private kitchen; piped water in kitchen and bath but no drain or sewer connection.
Goods: Electric radio and television, petroleum (oil) stove, iron, bicycle, refrigerator, and *lavadora* (washing machine; more likely, in our experience, a *lavadero* [laundry place with built-in scrub ridges]); no telephone or automobile.
Education: Children and young people are nearly at the educational norm; adults attain about half of the norm (with four years of schooling).
Health Care: No Social Security (IMSS) coverage, but public health services (hospitals, clinics, rural nursing) are accessible, although medical treatment typically requires payment.

Conditions were somewhat better for the urban poor. Boltvinik (2000: 232–233) typifies the *indigent urban household* (19.4 percent) in Mexico City as follows:

House: Durable (e.g., cement block) walls, tiled or cement roof, cement floor (untiled); less crowded than indigent rural household; piped water inside the house; sink has a drain but "although [the house] has a toilet stool, it lacks connection to water" (and must be flushed by pouring water from a bucket into the basin).

Goods: Same appliances as in rural indigent household (but natural gas instead of oil stove), plus bicycle, blender, tape player, and lavadora (more likely, in our experience, a *lavadero* [washing place]); no telephone or automobile.

Education: Children are at or near the educational norm; adults, at three-fourths of the norm.

Health Care: Similar to the situation of the rural indigent household.

The *moderately poor urban household* (27.6 percent) in Mexico City is characterized thus (Boltvinik 2000: 233):

House: Durable (e.g., cement block, tile) walls and roof, cement floor (untiled); less crowded than indigent urban household; piped water inside the house; sewer connection "but some have a toilet stool without connection to water" (i.e., it must be flushed by pouring water from a bucket into the basin).

Goods: More appliances than rural equivalent household but typically no telephone or automobile.

Education: Only adults over the age of forty and "those with special problems" are below educational norms.

Health Care: About half of these households are covered by Social Security (IMSS) or other governmental health care assistance.

As indicated earlier, poverty actually increased between 1989, the base date for Boltvinik's (2000) analysis, and century's end. Using the same measure, the IPMM, Damián and Boltvinik (2003: 528) found that the national incidence of poverty climbed 4.7 percent between 1989 (70.6 percent) and 2000 (75.3 percent); urban poverty had increased from 61.7 to 69.1 percent and rural poverty from 85.0 to 93.5 percent. Even the measurement method preferred by the Mexican government—a poverty line variant that Boltvinik claims sorely underestimates poverty by excluding from analysis some important standard of living measures—classified 53.7 percent of the national population as poor in 2000, compared to 44.2 percent in 1992 (also see Pardinas 2004: 68–70; Griffin and Ickowitz 2003: 584–591). In fact, all major studies show that poverty increased appreciably between 1992 and 2000, regardless of the measurement criteria or method used. During the period 1968–2000, the poverty rate reached a dramatic low in 1981 (about 50 percent by IPMM) and a dramatic high in 1996 (about 82 percent by IPMM) and then fell again by 2000 to almost exactly the 1968 rate (about 75 percent) (Damián and Boltvinik 2003: 523–525; Hernández Laos and Velázquez Roa 2003: 143–152).

According to official figures (INEGI 2003), 37.1 percent of rural and 7.8 percent of urban dwellings still lacked piped water "within the dwelling or on the property" in 2000; two-thirds (66.7 percent) of rural and over one-tenth (11.5 percent) of urban dwellings had no water drainage connection (to sewer line or septic system) that year; and nearly one-third (31.9 percent) of rural and one-twelfth (7.8 percent) of urban dwellings lacked a toilet stool "with water or other type of connection" (INEGI 2003: 334). Chronic malnutrition caused by poverty was also readily evident in infants and young children. In 1999, 7.6 percent of Mexican infants aged 0 to 5 years were underweight and 17.8 percent were underheight (vs. 3 to 4 percent expected in a well-nourished population); these are serious deficiencies because "retarded growth in these age groups is not recovered later" (163–165). In the 5 to 11 years cohort, 4.5 percent were underweight in 1999, 15.9 percent were underheight, and 19.5 percent suffered anemia (167–170).

Migration: From Rural Poverty to Urban Poverty

As in other countries, Mexico's urban transformation occurred mainly through rural-to-urban migration. Both "push" and "pull" forces were at work in this regard. From the 1940s onward, some migrants were pulled toward the cities by the prospect of material improvement through employment in the expanding urban industrial and service sectors. Even larger numbers, though, were pushed toward the cities by rural impoverishment, especially after about 1960 (Arizpe 1985; Godínez and Martín 1991).

Two major poverty factors were at work. First, the improved rural standard of living that resulted from Mexico's agrarian reform of the late 1930s (see Chap. 3) was soon eroded by a rural population increase that pushed a large portion of succeeding generations out of the countryside. In communities with partible inheritance (division among all children or all sons), the rights to ejido parcels often became fragmented among the multiple heirs, most of whom eventually received less than a livable share. Where impartible (single-heir) inheritance obtained, noninheriting siblings who did not succeed in marrying an inheriting spouse also had to seek another livelihood. Once the countryside's capacity to absorb wage labor was reached, the main solution became that of migrating to towns and cities in search of either wage work or self-employment in petty commerce or artisanry.

Second, a series of federal government policies helped urban industrial and commercial interests at the expense of the peasantry. Beginning in the 1940s, the central government embarked on a vigorous program of industrialization, in the hope of transforming Mexico into a "developed" country. The reigning development model was import substitution. Through protective tariffs, tax incentives, and direct investment, the government encouraged the growth of industries that could produce substitutes for the imported consumer goods, especially clothing and household items, that were eagerly sought by the "modernizing" urban masses. If these industrial substitutes—which lacked the snob appeal of "genuine" imports—were to find a mass market, they had to sell relatively cheaply, and the avenue chosen to achieve this goal was to hold down production costs by holding down industrial wages, by means explained in the next section. In turn, low wages had to be accompanied by cheap basic foods, to forestall food riots and other forms of political unrest. Food prices (especially of rice, beans, wheat, and corn) were kept low through a combination of price controls and market manipulation by timely releases of stored grains purchased by government agencies at harvest, when prices hit their annual lows. These mechanisms depressed the prices that farmers received for their produce (see Ochoa 2000: 100 ff.).

We have here the link between the government's import substitution model of development and the impoverishment of the countryside: inflation gradually drove up the cost of the things that peasants had to purchase, including agricultural inputs, while the controlled or manipulated prices they received for their produce rose much more slowly. Furthermore, their small scale of operation and lack of access to investment capital prevented them from achieving economies of scale to overcome this dilemma. By the mid-1960s, millions of peasants were unable to make a living in the countryside. They and/or their children were forced to abandon the countryside for the towns and cities in desperate search of livelihood. The anguish of this massive migration is captured by the widely told joke about a child's prayer on the eve of departure: "Please,

God, take good care of Grandma and Grandpa after we leave. Also, please remember Papa and Mama and me, and that I was good. You won't be able to find us after today, because we're going to Mexico City."

Permanent migration to the unforgiving slums of Mexico's large cities usually was not the first stage in the migratory process, however. For several decades, many thousands of peasant-workers were commuters, working during the week in the towns and cities but returning to their rural homes most weekends, a pattern made possible by Mexico's large investment in roads and railroads, beginning during the Porfiriato. Others were revolving migrants who went to the cities for periods of months or years before returning to the countryside, often to repeat the pattern several times or to be replaced in the cycle by younger siblings (see Arizpe 1985: 46–66; Nutini and Isaac 1974: 402–427; Nutini and Murphy 1968: 91–95; Romero 2002). During these stints, most found low-skilled employment as construction laborers, factory employees, warehouse and shop laborers, gardeners, restaurant servers, housemaids, prostitutes, barbers and hairdressers, truck drivers, and the like. More fortunate were the village skilled workers (e.g., carpenters, masons, tailors), who found better-paying outlets for their talents in the cities. For instance, by the 1950s or earlier, the tailors who did alterations for the patrons of Mexico City's clothing stores were mainly migrants from rural Tlaxcala (Nutini and Isaac 1974: 425). To take a second example, one rural community in Tlaxcala still specializes in providing both housemaids and prostitutes to Mexico City; some of these women return to the countryside after several years in the city, whereas others become lifelong urban residents, even if they did not intend to do so when they first arrived (Romero 2002). Since about 1960, though, a larger and larger proportion of the migrants have arrived with the intention of establishing permanent residence there, for the reasons explained above.

Urban Wage Work and Unionism

Although the history of urban wage work in Central Mexico goes back to early colonial times, with the establishment of wool workshops during the 1530s, it is only since the late nineteenth century that urban wage workers have constituted a major component of Mexico's population. The factories of that period generally offered wretched working conditions and low pay (Anderson 1974; Rajchenberg 1995; Ramírez R. 1984), resulting in some two hundred fifty "declared strikes . . . of economic origin" between 1887 and 1904 (Olivares 1978: 58–59). The first labor union, the Gran Círculo de Obreros (Great Workers' Circle), was founded in 1872 and soon had 10,000 members, a testament to the depth of factory workers' dissatisfaction. Railroad workers also organized over the period 1887–1904 (58). In 1911 the Confederación de Sindicatos de Obreros de la República Mexicana (Confederation of Labor Unions of the Mexican Republic) was organized in Veracruz, a state with many textile factories, and 1912 saw the formation of the Casa del Obrero Mundial (House of the World's Workers), initially as an aggregation of nonfactory artisans—"tailors, cobblers, carpenters, typographers, and stone-cutters" (59–60).

This nonfactory artisans' union, rather than the organizations of factory workers, formed the basis of the supposedly "proletarian" Batallones Rojos (Red Brigades) who joined the Revolution in 1915. Revolutionary leaders, who were either agrarian or bourgeois (industrial-commercial) in outlook, distrusted the factory unions. The latter reciprocated the distrust and "contributed only a few comrades to the fighting; mainly they kept on working" (Anderson 1974: 112). The factory workers' distrust turned out to be well founded. President Venustiano Carranza (1915–1920) turned against even the Batallones Rojos once the armed phase had passed its zenith, and his successor, Alvarado Obregón (1920–1924), "launched an open repression against the labor movement" (69)—despite the many protections and guarantees, including the rights to organize and strike, included in Article 123 of the 1917 Constitution (see Delgado M. 2004: 277–294).

Under President Lázaro Cárdenas, wage workers got a much friendlier reception in national politics, although the long-term result was dismal. Both to promote national political integration and to solidify his own power against potentially rebellious factions, Cárdenas created a "sectorial government" consisting initially of four official "sectors": *militar* (military), *campesino* (peasant), *obrero* (wage worker), and *popular* (people's, or general). This last was a catchall sector that included government employees, small merchants, students, artisans, and other groups (but not large merchants, manufacturers, or other entrepreneurs) that were obviously neither peasants nor wage workers. The military sector was soon abolished, but the other three sectors were still intact at century's end (Anguiano 1975: 137–139; Rubio 1998: 10–13).

Each sector was to elect its own local, regional, and national leaders who would express and negotiate its demands. Thus sectorial representation ideally meant that both workers and peasants had a ready mechanism to express their needs and an open channel to the seat of power. In practice, however, the system quickly evolved from a bottom-up to a top-down apparatus (Anguiano 1975: 127–139), in accordance with Mexico's "presidentialist" government, in which the president made all the final decisions. As necessary, the president saw that his decisions were ratified by the legislature, both houses of which were controlled by his own party, the PRI.

Top-down leadership fell most heavily on the wage workers' sector (*sector obrero*), whose membership was more vulnerable to market forces (and thus more controllable) than were either the white-collar workers of the popular sector or the more self-reliant peasantry. Labor leaders became entrenched in office, most noticeably in the giant Confederación de Trabajadores de México (CTM; Mexican Workers' Confederation), which was ruled by the autocratic Fidel Velázquez from 1941 until 1997. Under his domination, the CTM came to include roughly 80 percent of all Mexico's unionized workers (Trejo D. and Woldenberg 1984: 234). By the time Fidel Velázquez died at age ninety-seven in 1997, still at the helm of the CTM, "Mexican workers typically earn[ed] between $3.00 and $10.00 U.S. dollars per day, the lowest paid industrial workers in the world," and their combined under- and unemployment rate was "estimate[d] . . . at 25 percent" (La Botz 1997: 6).

Membership in state-controlled unions, especially the CTM, was a condition of employment in government or parastatial jobs, as well as for most nonmanagerial jobs in large private enterprises. Union locals were threatened with "decertification"—and thus with denial of employment—in precincts where the "official party," the PRI, did not receive a majority of votes in local or national elections. The CTM colluded with private enterprise, as well as with the PRI government, negotiating "protection contracts" against labor unrest of any type, sometimes on behalf of "ghost unions" that existed in name only. The CTM also could call down police, army, and thug violence (beatings, killings, imprisonment, torture, "disappearance") on workers who threatened independence or even an unauthorized strike. Independent-minded union officers were replaced by "charros," an epithet that originated with a 1940s union boss who liked to dress up as a *charro* (Mexican cowboy), and *charrismo* became the popular term for union corruption and subservience to the one-party PRI state (see La Botz 1992: 185–190; La Botz 1997; Olivares 1978: 80–81; Rendón C. 2001; Samstad 2001).

Thus, despite a long history of organized labor and the ideals expressed in Article 123 of the 1917 Constitution (still in force today), the majority of Mexican wage workers were still poor at the end of the twentieth century. Accordingly, it is no surprise that the lower classes still constituted a majority of the Mexican population. While the death of the widely hated and feared Fidel Velázquez effectively ended CTM hegemony, it did not give rise to the genuine advancement of workers' interests that his many enemies had hoped for. Instead, the crushing economic changes of the 1990s generally reduced the bargaining position of organized labor, leading to loss of purchasing power and lower living standards for the working class.

"The Mexican Solution": Home and Family

We have adopted the phrase "the Mexican solution" from *The Mexican Urban Household* (Selby, Murphy, and Lorenzen 1990), which reports on a ten-city survey of 9,458 lower-class, urban Mexican households in 1977–1979 and a follow-up study of 604 such households in 1987. The phrase denotes a kin-based, household-centered strategy for weathering economic hardship. The strategy's two main elements are increasing household size, through either high fertility per conjugal pair or co-residence of related conjugal pairs, intended to increase the number of present or future income earners; and "a degree of income pooling that makes everybody better off," as well as both intra- and interhousehold reciprocity in times of increased need (52–53, 107 ff.; see also Lomnitz 1975: 141–170).

ORGANIZING FOR SELF-DEFENSE: THE PRIMACY OF HOUSING

"Organizing for self-defense," as Selby and colleagues (1990) aptly subtitle their book, begins with finding and securing adequate housing. The popular ideal is that each nuclear family (a conjugal pair and their children) will form its own household in a separate dwelling, usually after a period of residence in one of the parental households. For the urban lower classes, achieving household independence typically begins with purchasing a small lot from a land dealer (*fraccionista*) on the urban fringe or by squatting on an undefended property, even in the city center. In either case, securing legal title often involves a long struggle, typically waged through a neighborhood organization headed by a local political boss, or cacique (see Cornelius 1973; Díaz B. 1996). In the meantime, the house is built in stages over a year or more, often beginning with a shack made of scrap materials (Selby, Murphy, and Lorenzen 1990: 88–89). The finished product, preferably with cement block or brick walls, typically has a floor area of less than 100 square meters (1,075 sq. ft.). "Over 86 percent of the houses are one story, and 61 percent of them have three rooms or less" (89).

In 1977–1979 most urban Mexican households were based on the nuclear family (74 percent) and lived in "privately owned, detached houses" (73 percent), although Mexico City was the exception, with 43 percent of the study sample there consisting of "apartment dwellers and renters," compared with only 8 percent in the ten cities combined (Selby, Murphy, and Lorenzen 1990: 40). In 2000 Mexico was still predominantly a country of home owners: 78.3 percent of national, 88.0 percent of rural, and 75.2 percent of urban households owned their homes outright or were purchasing them by installments that year (INEGI 2003: 336). The renter fraction continues to be high in the Federal District (mainly Mexico City), though—20.3 percent in 2000 (590).

HOUSEHOLD SURVIVAL STRATEGY, I: PRE-1982

Large households have a survival advantage for the lower classes of urban Mexico, because they "have more members in the work force, and their dependency ratios, taken as the ratio of members not in the work force to those in, are lower" (Selby, Murphy, and Lorenzen 1990: 110). In 1977–1979, the poorest households (56 percent in their survey) averaged 5.0 members, 1.2 children in the workforce, and a dependency ratio of 3.1; the most prosperous households (10 percent in the survey), earning 2.7 times or more income, averaged 6.4 members, 2.0 children in the workforce, and a dependency ratio of 2.2 (109). Schooling, which was universally recognized as virtually the only avenue of social mobility, was also more easily attainable in the larger households, in which "the older kids can work and the younger kids can study," whereas all children in smaller households would have to work and study simultaneously (4). Finally, larger households were twice as likely as smaller ones (23 percent vs. 11 percent) to be able to send out migrant workers who would remit part of their earnings to help sustain the parental household (109), easing the work burden on younger siblings in the process.

Before 1982, when a general economic crisis devastated the lower stratum and even the lower-middle class (see below), poor households became larger, mainly through high fertility. At that time, almost all children aged twelve and older in the sample contributed significantly to household income (Selby, Murphy, and Lorenzen 1990: 107–108). Boys earned money by shining shoes, hawking newspapers, and helping other household members or neighbors in their work. Girls baby-sat, swept patios, sold small edibles (fruits, gelatin desserts, nuts, chewing gum, etc.) on the sidewalks or door-to-door, and did other small jobs. Both boys and girls ran errands for their neighbors. With the money earned, they were expected to pay some of their own expenses, either directly or by giving their earnings to their parents. For the most part, these children took pride in being able to contribute to their households, and many of them longed to drop out of school in order to work more, often against the strong opposition of their parents.

Additional children contributed relatively little to household expenses. Basic needs such as food, clothing, gas, electricity, and water made up 60 to 65 percent of lower-class households' monthly expenditures and did not change appreciably with the addition of another child. In fact, "there [was] little change in the household budget from the third to the seventh" child (Selby, Murphy, and Lorenzen 1990: 110). The dwelling simply became more crowded, clothing was handed down one more time, and cheaper dietary items were purchased and/or portions were made smaller. Potentially, medical expenses could increase, but they "are not an important part of the household budget, since they are forgone . . . except in emergencies, and then often subsidized or free medical help is available" (110–111). Clothing costs might eventually rise, "but by the time the child demands high-quality clothing and new clothes, he or she will be in a position to contribute to its cost if not defray the expense entirely" (111). Furthermore, primary school education was still free, and fees for neighborhood secondary schools were very low.

HOUSEHOLD SURVIVAL STRATEGY, II: POST-1982

The scenario changed considerably after 1982, when Mexico was plunged into a general economic crisis that reduced the value of working-class wages by 40 percent within six years (Selby, Murphy, and Lorenzen 1990: 163–177; Griffin and Ickowitz 2003: 585–589; Trejo and Jones 1998: 68–72) and by 1996 resulted in the highest poverty rate in decades. The seeds of this crisis can be traced to the mid-1960s or earlier, when the import substitution model of development resulted in massive migration of the rural poor to the cities, greatly increasing the government's administrative and service burden. Another turning point occurred in October 1968, when police and military forces killed a large number of unarmed student demonstrators (perhaps several hundred), costing the PRI government much of the legitimacy it had enjoyed during the previous thirty-five years (Poniatowska 1975). In an attempt to regain legitimacy, President Luis Echeverría (1970–1976) spent huge sums on education, food and agricultural subsidies, the creation of public sector jobs, and the like. These policies incorporated many disaffected elements but also strained governmental resources and caused enormous inflation that gobbled up much of the lower and middle classes' remaining purchasing power.

In the meantime, the import substitution policy was precipitating a crisis of its own. In the first place, economic growth through this approach, which concentrated on domestic manufacture of cheap products that would substitute for equivalent imports, had reached a ceiling; further expansion would have meant huge investments in research and development to produce costly goods and manufacturing inputs, an impracticality because these expensive products could be purchased more cheaply from the United States (Selby, Murphy, and Lorenzen 1990: 166). Furthermore, the protectionist (high-tariff) manufacturing environment, coupled with bureaucratic inefficiencies and corruption, meant that the import substitutes produced were often of such poor quality that they could not readily be exported as a means of creating new jobs and fueling economic growth. To the contrary, imported goods of all kinds acquired added snob appeal for the middle and upper classes, exacerbating the country's capital flight and negative balance of payments.

For a while, it seemed that Mexico's salvation lay in petroleum production, as prices of this commodity had risen sharply in the late 1970s. Accordingly, the government borrowed abroad with abandon, not only to develop its petroleum-producing capacity but also to sustain its legitimacy through public sector expansion. This dream largely ended when crude oil prices fell in 1982, sharply reducing government revenues both to fund its internal programs and to make payments on its huge foreign debt. The value of the country's imports also rose sharply again in relation to its exports, creating pressure to devalue the peso in order to make Mexican petroleum cheaper on the export market and increase its world market share.

Because devaluation would also make all imported goods and manufacturing components more expensive, thereby increasing inflation, President José López Portillo (1976–1982) initially resisted this move, proclaiming with much bravado that he would defend the peso "like a dog." When he nevertheless sharply devalued the currency shortly thereafter, the public greeted him with loud barking and howling for the rest of his term. As if all this were not enough, he unexpectedly nationalized all the banks in September 1982, at the tail end of his term, precipitating a financial crisis from which the country had still not recovered twenty years later. Inflation so devalued the currency that ordinary goods came to cost thousands of pesos, until the government issued new money in 1993 at the ratio of 1:1,000—or, as people commonly phrased it, "They cut three zeros off our money."

The December 1994 "peso crisis" turned the economic hardship experienced since 1982 into a "permanent crisis." In brief, the Mexican government had attempted to overcome the earlier crisis by liberalization in two directions: allowing massive foreign purchases of Mexican bonds, in order to attract new investment capital; and eliminating most monetary exchange controls. So long as Mexican bonds were paying higher interest rates than comparable investments in the United States, dollars were converted into pesos in order to take advantage of the investment opportunity. When the U.S. Federal Reserve Board raised domestic interest rates in early 1994, however, Mexico's investment attractiveness shrank. In the same year, a dramatic Indian rebellion in Chiapas and the assassination of the PRI's presidential candidate led many investors to conclude that Mexico was becoming politically unstable.

The result was a massive capital outflow as both Mexicans and foreigners rushed to convert their peso investments into dollars. Stopping the financial bleeding required making conversion less attractive through devaluation, so that more pesos would be required to purchase each dollar. Accordingly, the Mexican government allowed the peso to float freely, seeking its supply-demand level on world markets, where it quickly lost over half its previous value (Griffin and Ickowitz 2003: 586–587; Polaski 2003: 18–19). Once again, the poor bore the brunt of these policies, as devaluation always drives up the price of both imported goods and domestic manufactures with imported components.

The prolonged economic crisis was accompanied by several other factors that added to the cost of having children. After 1982, federal policy tilted sharply away from welfarism and toward a free market economy. Government subsidies for basic foodstuffs, electricity and other utilities, and transportation were withdrawn, reduced, or targeted to specific areas or population segments. The result was a painful belt-tightening in other areas or segments, including much of the working class and lower-middle class (Ochoa 2000: 199–220; also see Enríquez 2003; Griffin and Ickowitz 2003; Laurell 2003; Molina and Sánchez 1999; Trejo and Jones 1998). Housing costs rose along with inflation. School budgets declined, and some of the slack had to be taken up by parents; at the same time, credentialism increased, so that a secondary school certificate became necessary for jobs that previously required either basic literacy or a primary school certificate (Selby, Murphy, and Lorenzen 1990: 168–169).

On top of these household hardships, the general economic crisis resulted in fewer moneymaking opportunities for children, as most poor people had to reduce expenditures on the services and small retail items they offered (Selby, Murphy, and Lorenzen 1990: 169). Simultaneously, the legions of shoeshine boys who plied their trade in the streets and public squares found fewer and fewer takers because sneakers were replacing leather shoes for everyday wear.

Large household size continues to be advantageous for the urban lower classes, but the old strategy for achieving it—high fertility—is no longer the preferred mechanism, as children now cost more while contributing less toward their own and the household's expenses. In fact, fertility has declined dramatically, from an average completed fertility of 5.7 children per woman in 1976 to 3.8 in 1987, 3.2 in 1992, and 2.3 in 2002; Mexico City stands out in the national profile, at 2.0 (INEGI 2003: 67–69). Under these circumstances, according to Selby and colleagues (Selby, Murphy, and Lorenzen 1990: 171 ff.), "the most successful household now is a large household made up of multiple small [nuclear] families." Typically, this effect is achieved by prolonging the co-residence of parent(s) and newly married children or through the co-residence of married siblings (especially brothers); less often, aggregation involves other kin or even unrelated nuclear units (also see González de la Rocha 1994: 272–275).

Nevertheless, the ideal in all social classes, both urban and rural, remains the independent nuclear-family residence (Selby, Murphy, and Lorenzen 1990: 57–58; Nutini 1968a: 387–391), and most people eventually achieve this traditional ideal. In 2000, nearly identical percentages of urban (69.3 percent) and rural (70.0 percent) households were of the nuclear type, while just under one-fourth (24.3 percent urban, 23.9 percent rural) were extended-family households (INEGI 2003: 302). The official figures also reflect Mexicans' abhorrence of living alone, a condition that is also extremely disadvantageous to the poor: one-person households constituted only 6.4 percent of urban and 6.1 percent of rural households in 2000 (INEGI 2003: 302; also see González de la Rocha 1994: 213–228).

Another lower-class adjustment to the "permanent crisis" has been the massive entry of married women of childbearing age into the paid labor force (Selby, Murphy, and Lorenzen 1990: 174–175; Chant 1991; Enríquez R. 2003; González de la Rocha 1994). In 1970 only 22.2 percent of women aged 20 to 29 were in the national labor force, a figure that had risen to 44.7 percent in 2000. The disparity is even greater among women ages 30 to 39 (16.7 percent in 1970 vs. 46.8 percent in 2000), 40 to 49 (16.8 percent vs. 46.3 percent), and 50 to 59 (15.8 percent vs. 35.3 percent). In contrast, the male workforce participation rate increased much less over that period (INEGI 2003: 369).

SECURITY NETWORKS

Neither the extremely poor "marginals" famously studied by Larissa Lomnitz (1975) nor the urban lower classes generally (see González de la Rocha 1994: 128 ff.; Hirabayashi 1993) could survive in the cities without extensive social networks based on kinship, residence (household and neighborhood), and compadrazgo, a complex and variable institution in Mexico (see Nutini 1984; Nutini and Bell 1980; Nutini and Isaac 1977). Generally, compadrazgo entails both vertical and horizontal social ties. Vertically, it typically links a godchild to a set of godparents who must then make contributions at life transition points and even assume the parental role if a godchild becomes orphaned or destitute. This form of compadrazgo will be familiar to both U. S. and Mexican readers. For the latter, though, the vertical godparent-godchild tie is often less important than the horizontal tie established between *compadres* (lit., "co-parents"; parents and godparents), who should treat each other with respect and mutual assistance. Both kin and nonkin are chosen for this sacred relationship. For instance, in her 1969–1971 study of slum-dwellers in Mexico City, Lomnitz (1975: 180) found that 41 percent of all compadres were kin, most frequently siblings. Residential closeness is an important consideration, too, and Lomnitz (180) reported that 60 percent of all baptismal compadres were neighbors (including 25 percent who were also kin).

The mutual assistance provided through such social networks includes emergency loans and gifts of tangibles such as money, food, tools, clothing, and household items; gifts and social support for the celebration of life transitions (birthdays, school graduations, first communion, and the like); and services and information (Lomnitz 1975: 160 ff.). This last category includes housing and meals for arriving migrants from the countryside, news about job opportunities and other help in obtaining paid work, assistance in house construction, occasional child care, and assistance with shopping or water carrying. Except in cases of loans that are understood to require precise repayment (i.e., balanced reciprocity), assistance within the network is provided as needed in the spirit of *hoy por ti, mañana para mí* (today for you, tomorrow for me), without explicit reckoning of debits or credits (see Lomnitz 1975: 169–170, 205). This form of exchange, which anthropologists call generalized reciprocity, is possible because the members of the network are roughly equal in terms of economic wherewithal; in other words, they have not only similar access to and availability of resources but also similar liabilities and vulnerabilities. Such casual reciprocity rests on the *confianza* (confidence, trust) that grows out of interaction framed by mutual acknowledgment of a shared socioeconomic condition. Upward social mobility by any network member threatens this sense of trust, typically "to the point at which a tacit balance is sought between favors given and favors received" (170).

Most social interaction outside of the household occurs within these informal mutual aid networks. Participation in formal organizations is generally low, whether through the workplace (unions or sports teams), the school (parents' associations), or the church (confraternities). Voluntary political participation is also low and ad hoc, usually sparked by particular grievances or a specific local crisis or pressing need centered on living conditions (Lomnitz 1975: 189–202; González de la Rocha 1994: 253–254). As we discuss below, most recreational and leisure activities also revolve around the home, the family, and the informal security network.

Class Consciousness and Ideology

The urban lower classes exhibit very little class consciousness, beyond their identification with the equally poor and politically powerless individuals within their security networks. In their pioneering study of two hundred factory workers in Mexico City in 1960–1961, Julio César Olivé Negrete and Beatriz Barba de Piña Chan (1962) found not only a "great anarchy" of ideas about social stratification but also a near-lack of class consciousness, despite the fact that all their subjects belonged to an industrial labor union. While their union activities (meeting participation and voting) showed that the subjects recognized their specific interests and had developed "a collective conduct adequate to defend them," this perception did not result in class consciousness or a concrete ideology "with concepts, program and orientation rooted in a knowledge of the role that they, and those in their same condition, play within the society" (235).

In fact, these researchers classed 82.5 percent of their subjects as "without class consciousness." Not only did the subjects evidence "great confusion about the general panorama of classes," but only 8 percent identified themselves as "working class" (Olivé Negrete and Barba de Piña Chan 1962: 235–236, 256). Perhaps not surprisingly, given their imprecision about social class placement, 82 percent responded that they were "satisfied" with their class affiliation, "even in the cases in which workers classed themselves as among the poor, the downtrodden [*amolados*], the lowly [*los de abajo*], etc." (235, 255). At the same time, 73.5 percent reported that they did not wish to change their social situation (235, 256).

Other researchers have reported similar findings. For instance, Américo Saldívar's 1971 study of 206 manual and 335 white-collar workers in Mexico City found that 53 percent of the former, including a third of the lowest paid, identified themselves as "middle class"; furthermore, 45 percent of these workers agreed with the statement, "In Mexico every person has the same opportunities to live well and comfortably." Saldívar found the prevailing vision of Mexican society among both his working- and middle-class subjects one of "a society of middle classes, egalitarian and open, where . . . the same work opportunities exist for everyone, and where they can [all] enjoy decent life styles without anxieties of an economic nature" (Saldívar 1977: 198–201). In short, both classes studied showed "ample acceptance of the ideology of the dominant class and its justification of the system," which obscured or denied differential class rewards; this amounts to saying that the political and ruling classes had achieved a high degree of legitimacy, even hegemony, among both working and middle classes in Mexico City.

To a large extent, the foregoing reflects the effectiveness of the developmentalist, reformist (favoring gradual rather than abrupt change), and populist ideology disseminated by governmental agencies, political parties (both the PRI and its main rival, the bourgeois National Action Party), state-controlled labor unions, and the school system. It also doubtless reflects the genuine social mobility experienced by many of the impoverished migrants (or their children) who flooded the capital in the 1950s and early 1960s (Saldívar 1977: 210–211). Enrique Contreras S. (1978: 243–251) came to similar conclusions about the apparent lack of class consciousness among the 1,816 middle-class men he studied in Mexico City in 1965–1966. We have seen no evidence that the situation had changed in Mexico City by century's end.

Nor is the apparent lack of class consciousness confined to Mexico City. Nutini (2005: 81–86) reports highly similar findings from the Córdoba-Orizaba area of Veracruz state. It is important to remember that this is an area where factory work predates the Revolution of 1910 and by 1920 occupied at least 10 percent of the local workforce (Rajchenberg 1995: 398). Notwithstanding the appalling working conditions of the early factories, class consciousness was not very evident there either before or during the Revolution. Instead, the ideology that moved workers and fueled both their attempts to organize themselves and their frequent strikes was a xenophobic nationalism—more properly speaking, "Mexicanism"—against the predominantly foreign-born factory owners. In other words, the enemies perceived by the workers were foreign intruders who had appropriated Mexican patrimony, not the region's or country's ruling classes (Rajchenberg 1995: 403–406). More generally, Mexican factory workers at the time of the Revolution "viewed themselves as working Mexicans rather than Mexican workers," and the few who participated in the Revolution "were defining their outrage in terms of demands for social justice they believed lawfully due them as Mexicans, not in terms of a heightened class consciousness" (Anderson 1974: 113).

Recreation and Leisure Activities

Thus far we have concentrated on the structural factors that shape lower-class life. While that is the dominant approach to social stratification, it excludes much of the flavor of daily life. Chapter 8 largely redresses the imbalance through a comparative treatment of the expressive behavior of all the major social classes. Here, we want to restrict our coverage to some specific aspects of lower-class recreation and leisure activities.

Recreation and leisure activities among the urban lower classes follow the general pattern of being centered mainly on the home and the immediate social network. Fortunately, Olivé Negrete and Barba de Piña Chan's (1962: 230, 248) study of Mexico City in 1960–1961 allows us a detailed look at lower-class recreation before television became ubiquitous, as only five of the two hundred households in their sample had TV sets. As shown in Table 6.6, the favorite type of entertainment for both husbands (65 percent) and wives (44 percent) was attendance at public events (*espectáculos*) such as movies, shows (*teatro frívolo*), bullfights, cockfights, and sporting competitions. In second place for wives (31 percent) were *paseos* (walks or short trips on public conveyances), which were nearly tied (53.5 percent vs. 54.5 percent) with drinking in neighborhood bars and *pulquerías* (pubs serving fermented maguey sap) among husbands. (We assume that at least some readers will share our suspicion that many husbands gave high priority to paseos simply to please their wives during joint interviews.) Sports participation was fourth (30.5 percent) and reading a distant fifth (10.7 percent) among husbands (also see Lomnitz 1975: 198). Among wives, only the first two preferences (public events and paseos) scored higher than 10 percent, perhaps because over one-third (36.7 percent) of them said they had no recreational activities at all (compared to only 6 percent among men)!

That no wives enjoyed the bars and pubs that were popular among husbands is not surprising, because at the time (and for another twenty years or so) these establishments prominently posted signs disallowing entrance to minors, women, vendors, and, often, uniformed personnel. Thus public drunkenness and alcoholism occurred then and now mainly among men (see INEGI 2003: 199–203). In her 1969–1971 study of a Mexico City slum, Lomnitz (1975: 190–191) also noted the prominence of alcohol consumption among lower-class men, especially among the very close friends whom a man refers to as his *cuates* (figuratively, "twins"): "The act of getting drunk together is considered a mark of trust [*confianza*] . . . [that] entails . . . handing over to the *cuate* the key to all the secrets of the soul."

Television was becoming a popular source of entertainment by the late 1960s, and 39 percent of the Mexico City slum households in Lomnitz's (1975: 197) study had television, although "there was besides an ample consumption of entertainment literature (graphic novels, sports magazines, comic books)." These entertainment media, along with the public schools attended by 80 percent of children under age twelve in the survey households, "transmit the values, norms and aspirations of the national urban culture" to slum children (197). The 1977–1979 survey by Selby and colleagues (1990: 57) likewise reported that television had become a window to the world in Mexico City's poorer neighborhoods, where *The Dukes of Hazard* (dubbed into Spanish) was especially popular. By 2000 roughly 85 percent of all Mexican households had a TV set and nearly 40 percent had a VCR (INEGI 2003: 337).

TABLE 6.6
Favorite Recreational Activities of Husbands (N = 200) and Wives (N = 177) in 200 Working-Class Households in Mexico City, 1960–1961

Recreational Activities	Husbands (%)	Wives (%)
Public events (*espectáculos*)	65.2	44.1
Walks/outings (*paseos*)	53.5	31.1
Reading	10.7	2.8
Sports participation	30.5	1.7
Manual work	6.9	6.8
Bars and *pulquerías* (maguey wine pubs)	54.5	zero
Gatherings (*reuniones*)	6.9	1.1
None	6.0	36.7

Source: After Olivé Negrete and Barba de Piña Chan 1962: 248, cuadro 19.

Sports, especially soccer, provide a major leisure outlet for lower-stratum men. The ubiquity of television has greatly broadened the spectator base, but active participation also remains important. Groups of neighborhood male playmates aged about six through early adolescence form ad hoc teams to play soccer in the streets, parks, or nearby playing fields after school and on weekends. Young adult men with a modicum of talent can join neighborhood soccer clubs, and some also play on teams formed among workmates, sometimes organized informally and sometimes with employer sponsorship.

Consumerism and Personal Care

In closing, we want to highlight two other characteristics of the urban lower classes. The first is their relative lack of concern with social climbing. Of course, they are interested in improving their own economic lot and in enhancing their children's life chances through formal education.

Unlike much of the middle stratum, though, the lower classes generally do not strive to imitate other, more expensive lifestyles. One implication of this pattern is that industrial consumerism is much stronger in the middle than in the lower classes. At least as long ago as the 1950s, the husbands in urban lower-middle-class families often held multiple jobs or worked multiple shifts and their wives took formal employment—principally to be able to afford a modernized lifestyle based on industrial products, such as pressure cookers, TV sets, washing machines, refrigerators, and automobiles (Barba de Piña Chan 1960). In contrast, few working-class wife-mothers in Mexico City held formal employment outside the home in the 1950s, and the household's employed males each typically worked a single job or shift (Olivé Negrete and Barba de Piña Chan 1962: 227–228, 277). Although this lower-class employment pattern doubtless reflected the exhausting nature of manual work at the time, we think it also reflected a realistic rejection of expressive emulation through industrial consumerism.

The second aspect of the lower-class adjustment that we wish to highlight here is the great importance placed on personal care and good grooming. The rarity of offensive body odors on crowded buses and the subway in urban Mexico is one reflection of this emphasis. A second is the typical neatness and cleanliness of street clothing. A third is the generally pleasing appearance of hair, nails, whiskers, and—in a surprising proportion of cases—teeth. The lower classes share these traits with the middle and upper classes, but only the lower classes face a daily struggle to maintain them. The lower classes' crowded living conditions often make daily bathing and laundering a considerable individual challenge of scheduling and patience. Their low incomes also limit wardrobe options. Nevertheless, they typically manage to bathe often, attend to coiffure and other grooming details, and appear more than adequately dressed, often with just three sets of daily clothes—one "in the bucket" soaking, one on the clothesline drying, and one to wear today.

seven: THE INDIAN-MESTIZO TRANSITION

From Ethnic Estates to Social Classes

This chapter returns us to Central Mexico's small towns and villages, where a transition from Indian to mestizo cultural status has occurred widely during the past two hundred years and especially since about 1950. Structurally, this profound transition involves the final breakdown of vestigial estate stratification rooted in colonial-era ethnic relations and its replacement by class stratification along national lines. Culturally, it involves the loss of most of traditional Indian culture—that syncretic amalgam of Spanish, Indian, and African elements that emerged during the seventeenth century and then persisted, albeit evolving and adapting, through much of the twentieth century (Nutini and Bell 1980: 287–378; Nutini and Roberts 1993: 80–116). The Indian-mestizo transition also entails the reduction or loss of traditional Indian ethnicity at the community level, although Indian ethnicities may be revitalized in reconfigured form at a later date.

We will lay the foundation for understanding the transition by first comparing a few salient aspects of Indian and mestizo cultures and then depicting some distinctive features of traditional Indian religion as it has been described ethnographically. Next, we introduce the concepts of modernization, secularization, and mestizoization and show how these processes have transformed the community of Chignautla in northeastern Puebla state. To convey an idea of local and regional variation in the operation of these processes, as well as the time factor involved, we then contrast the Tlaxcala-Pueblan Valley (central Tlaxcala and Puebla states) and the Córdoba-Orizaba region (west-central Veracruz state). Finally, we discuss some of the implications of the completed transition to mestizo national culture, including the loss of the rich expressive culture that was integral to traditional Indian religion.

The terms *Indian* and *mestizo* require only brief comment here, as they were discussed at length in Chapter 2. The term *mestizo* has wide scholarly currency, especially in anthropology and history, to denote the bearers of modern national culture, and it also retains an official aura from the efforts to construct a new nation, a "Mestizo Mexico," following the 1910–1920 Revolution. But the term is seldom employed in the countryside. Indians use a variety of local terms to designate mestizos, such as *gente de razón* (people with reason, intelligent people), *gente decente* (proper people), *catrines* (city people, city slickers), *coyome* (coyotes, shady characters) or, less commonly today, *castellanos* and other terms that refer to Spanish identity. Mestizos typically refer to themselves with terms of regional or national identity—such as *mexicano* (Mexican), *jarocho* (from Veracruz city), *poblano* (from Puebla city or state), *guerrerense* (from Guerrero state), *chilango* (from Mexico City), *morelense* (from Morelos state), and *cuernavaquense* (from Cuernavaca).

The Spanish word *indio* long ago came to be considered derogatory in Mexico, owing to its deprecatory usage during the three centuries of Spanish colonial rule. Today, one occasionally hears its diminutive form, *indito*, the connotation of which varies from region to region; in a few places, it is a term of endearment, but generally its connotation is deprecatory or, at least, condescending. In Spanish, the term usually employed today is *indígena* (indigenous, indigene), both by the people themselves and in public discourse. Indeed, that is the term we would use if we were writing this book in Spanish, except for certain historical contexts. In English, however, the term *Indian* lacks the deprecatory connotations of its Spanish equivalent with regard to Mexico, and *indigene* would seem both eccentric and stilted.

Indians and Mestizos: General Observations

The Indian population under discussion consists, of course, of the descendants of the population conquered and colonized by the Spaniards in the sixteenth century. The mestizo population has its origins in the Spanish-Indian biological and cultural amalgamation that began with the Spanish conquest and continued through the colonial period. As we saw in Chapter 2, *mestizo*, or mixed, originated as a term of reference for the children produced by Spanish men with Indian women but eventually lost its biological referents and came to designate instead the amalgam of cultures (Indian, Spanish and, to a lesser extent, African) in New Spain.

Today, there are no consistent physical differences between mestizo and Indian populations, although there are individuals in *both* populations who show pronounced European or Indian physical traits. In other words, we could not reliably distinguish Indian and mestizo populations or individuals on the basis of physical traits alone, given the extent of genetic mixture over nearly five centuries. For instance, a genetic study in Tlaxcala state showed that "from 23 to 32 percent of the Mestizo gene pool is of Spanish and/or West African origin," while the remainder is of Indian origin (Crawford et al. 1976: 165).

The indigenous population of Central Mexico was ethnically heterogeneous at the time of the Spanish Conquest, in 1521. The Nahuas (Nahuatl or Nahuat speakers), though, constituted an overwhelming majority—up to 90 percent in much of the area—followed by Otomí, Totonac, and Mazahua speakers and fewer numbers of speakers of perhaps another dozen languages (see Carmack, Gasco, and Gossen 1996: 379–406; Harvey 1972: 314–315, Fig. 6; Rodríguez López 1988: 12–15; Valdés 1995: 94–99). Roughly 80 percent of the Indians of the regions to which we shall give special attention later in this chapter—the Tlaxcala-Pueblan Valley and the Córdoba-Orizaba region—were and are Nahuas. The only other significant ethnicities are Otomí and Totonac, each constituting about 10 percent of the present Indian population. These minority ethnic components share a high common cultural denominator with the Nahuas, however, and the casual observer today would not notice any difference except language.

On the other hand, the cultural differences between Indians and mestizos were historically highly visible and unmistakable. The most immediately obvious were the differences in clothing (see Figs. 7.1–7.4; also see Cordry and Cordry 1968: 222–253; Friedlander 1975: 92–96). Indian men dressed in the white cotton garments that the Spanish colonial administration mandated to replace the indigenous breechcloths and capes. The outfit had pajama-like pants secured at the waist by long string ties and/or a sash and with the legs tied at some location between the ankle and the upper calf, depending on local custom. The accompanying garments were a long-sleeved, collarless pullover shirt and a serape, straw hat, and sandals (formerly of maguey fiber, later replaced by car-tire soles and leather straps). Indian women wore a long wraparound skirt, made of cotton or wool, that reached the lower calf or ankle and was secured at the waist by a woven belt, accompanied by a pullover, square-cut, white cotton blouse and a dark shawl and sometimes maguey fiber sandals. In contrast, mestizo clothing was tailored in the European style and did not differ basically from that worn in similar occupational settings, economic levels, and time periods in Europe or the United States.

Indian and mestizo cultures also differ at levels so subtle that they are taken for granted within each group and are not ordinarily articulated as such. Drawing on his own research and that of Paul Jean Provost (1975), Alan Sandstrom (1991: 141–145) specifies five Nahua "cultural principles" that underlie social interaction and also form "a set of unspoken or rarely articulated guidelines for how a person should present himself or herself to others" (141). These principles are indirectness, attrition, informality, individuality, and reciprocity.

The first principle, indirectness, denotes a preference for avoiding direct confrontation. "Pointed questions, authoritative assertions, commands, or direct requests are considered rude and aggressive" (142). Attrition, the second principle, is an extension of the first and denotes a manner of persuasion that avoids direct argumentation and instead achieves the desired result "by wearing the listener down with subtle and persistent suggestion" (142). Informality, the third principle, refers to the relative lack of rigid rules and strict procedures in most areas of life. A notable exception is hospitality, about which Nahuas are typically punctilious: "A visitor is always provided with a special chair, food is prepared, and the guest is treated very cordially" (142). The fourth principle, individuality, is an extension of the third but also connotes a deep belief in personal dignity and the unique worth of each individual. The final principle, reciprocity, refers to more than the exchanges of gifts and labor that lubricate social relations and underlie economic relations; it also includes relations with the supernatural forces that are propitiated with ritual offerings in the hope of receiving health, wealth, fertility, or other favors.

Mestizos typically have a more direct mode of interaction, including a more confrontational and argumentative style of dispute articulation. To Nahuas, they seem to "lack proper reserve and are overly direct and blunt. Mestizos . . . appear rude, aggressive, demanding, and overbearing" (Sandstrom 1991: 142). In turn, many mestizos interpret Nahua modes of interaction as reflecting a lack of cooperation or even of intelligence. The reinforcement of negative stereotypes can begin at first meeting, when

FIGURE 7.1. Rural Nahua woman in Veracruz state wearing traditional *huipil* blouse, shawl, sash, and full skirt. Photo by Hugo Nutini.

FIGURE 7.2. Rural Nahua man in Veracruz state wearing traditional white *calzón* pants, serape, and straw hat. Photo by Hugo Nutini.

FIGURE 7.3. Rural Nahuas, showing the full spectrum of clothing, from Indian-traditional (left) to mestizoized (right). Photo by Hugo Nutini.

FIGURE 7.4. Rural Nahua men in Veracruz state: Indian-traditional father and mestizoized son. Photo by Hugo Nutini.

the Nahua utters a characteristically soft, nearly whispered greeting and offers his or her hand with the fingers fully extended, expecting to gently touch fingertips, and the mestizo grasps the whole hand, squeezes the fingers tightly together, and pumps arms.

Traditional Indian Religion and Worldview

The Indian and mestizo worldviews are fundamentally different. Spirituality permeates Indian life to an extent that distinguishes it markedly from the mestizo outlook, and Indian worldview is highly sacred. Sandstrom (1991: 319) singles out pantheism—"the idea that the universe and everything in it partakes of a living spiritual essence" that provides spiritual unity to everyone and everything—as the foremost principle of Nahua religion. "In Nahua thought, human beings are part of the sacred universe, and each of us contains within our bodies a spark of the divine energy that makes the world live. This energy ultimately derives from the sun" (246–247).

The earth itself is "a powerful spiritual presence" that is acknowledged in all of daily life. For instance, before taking the first taste of an alcoholic beverage, a traditional Nahua pours a dash of it on the ground as an earth offering. Gifts are also given to the earth at planting and harvesting times, "lest it become offended at being disturbed" (240–241). People are believed "to sprout from the earth like the corn plant," and thus they are returned to it on death. "The earth is womb and tomb, the provider of nourishment and all wealth, home to the ancestors, and the daily sustainer of human life" (241). In fact, the whole landscape is highly spiritualized: "Every hill, valley, spring, lake, stream, section of river, boulder, plain, grove, gorge, and cave has its proper name and associated spirit" (241). Hills and mountains are the most prominent topographic features in Nahua religion, as they "are the dwelling places of the seed and rain spirits associated with crop growth, and of powerful spirits who guard over humans" (241).

The major integrating principle of Nahua religion is a quest for balance and harmony among the supernatural forces and between them and humans, as well as among humans themselves (319; also see Sandstrom 1978, 2001). Many supernatural forces are constantly at work to upset this delicate balance or otherwise destroy the harmony that is necessary for human happiness and fertility, as well as human physical and economic well-being. Besides witches, there are various kinds of sprites, goblins, and other evil forces that inhabit such natural features as ravines, caves, sinkholes, and anthills (Ingham 1986: 103–121). There is also the Devil, who takes a variety of forms, among them a cowboy (charro), a whirlwind, and "a noisy clanking human skeleton sometimes riding in an oxcart." The Devil is a ubiquitous trouble causer who "tries to corrupt human affairs with his pride, envy, and lust and by snatching souls away from God," often in exchange for money, as well as appropriating male virility and female fertility (104–105, 108). Given his association with the wind, wealth, sin, and discord, the Devil in colonial and contemporary Nahua thought is a syncretic figure that blends European theology with folk ideas and pre-Hispanic elements. The latter probably derive from the god Tezcatlipoca, "a punitive and fear-inspiring god. . . responsible for drought, famines, and plagues. . . . He gave and took away riches and fame . . . and . . . quickened vice and sin" (109).

Among the specialists who protect humans from these dangerous forces are curers of several kinds (see Aguirre Beltrán 1963; Alvarez H. 1987; Dow 1986; Huber and Sandstrom 2001; Olavarrieta M. 1977; Ortiz de Montellano 1990: 193–235). Many curers are in fact also sorcerers who are able to cause as well as cure illness or certain bodily injuries through supernatural and magical means (see below); many others are simply herbalists. Also common are bonesetters, who not only set broken bones but also treat dislocations, sprains, and joint pain and, in general, perform chiropractic massage and body manipulation. In southern Mexico and Guatemala, many of these bonesetters employ magical and supernatural methods, but in Central Mexico they primarily use naturalistic therapies (see Paul and McMahon 2001).

As Nutini (1968b: 92–93) notes for San Bernardino Contla, Tlaxcala, contemporary Nahuas distinguish between illnesses that can be treated through modern medicine and "folk illnesses" that require a local curer's services. Folk illnesses always have supernatural or magical components, the treatment of which is outside the expertise of university-trained practitioners of scientific medicine. Prominent among these illnesses are *fright*, a form of possession in which the person loses consciousness and has a nightmare-like experience; *evil eye*, caused by envious gazes, especially upon children, who cry constantly and manifest drooping eyes and flushed cheeks; *attack of spirits*, a grave form of fright with a longer unconscious state and recurrences for several days; and *evil wind*, a very generalized cause of illness, often associated with the humors released by dead bodies or with certain animals, such as coyotes or snakes (also see Sandstrom 1978; Sandstrom 1991: 301–313).

Accounts of traditional Indian curing techniques abound in the ethnographic literature. Our example is taken from William Madsen's study of Milpa Alta, on the outskirts of Mexico City, in the 1950s. Madsen portrays Don Eusebio, a Nahua curer who specializes in "cave air," which is "caused by rain dwarfs" (Madsen 1960: 184–185). Don Eusebio "dies" twice each year so that his spirit can "go to a rain-dwarf cave to receive instruction for curing." There, the Serpent Chief of the rain dwarfs tells the assembled curers "which type of curing implements—eggs, stones, or herbs—they should use most in treating cave-air sickness" (184) and exchanges their tired old curing stones for new ones.

In the curing session that Madsen (1960: 184–185) describes, Don Eusebio began the treatment with "cleansing" the patient by rubbing his entire body with an unbroken egg, which "absorbs some of the disease in the patient's body." He then broke the egg into a glass of water and observed its movement and pattern. He noted that "the egg white rose in the shape of a whirlpool and little bubbles formed on the surface of the water," confirming his suspicion that the patient suffered from cave-air sickness. Don Eusebio then "held water in his mouth while he sucked one end of an unbroken egg held first on the patient's elbows and next on . . . [his] palms." Because the patient said his shoulder hurt, Don Eusebio sucked the same way there, and "the cave air in the patient's body passed through the egg into the water in Don Eusebio's mouth, which he spit on the floor after sucking." He then repeated the procedures using a curing stone in place of the egg, afterward blowing "through the doughnut-shaped stone on the parts of the body he had sucked." Finally, he "rubbed the patient with two other curing stones."

The foregoing case is instructive not only of traditional Indian curing techniques but also of cultural syncretism (fusion). The idea that cave air causes illness and the associated belief in rain dwarfs are of pre-Hispanic indigenous origin, as is the use of the sucking technique to "extract" intrusive objects or substances. On the other hand, divination by interpreting the patterns formed by an egg broken into a glass of water derives from sixteenth-century Spanish culture. This element is integrated so seamlessly into the curing ritual, though, that it seems perfectly "Indian" as well (see Foster 1960: passim; Quesada 1989: 69–70, 90–91).

Curers are not the only supernatural manipulators typically found in Indian communities in Central Mexico. For rural Tlaxcala, Nutini and

Roberts (1993: 39–53) single out four important Nahua supernatural personages—weathermen, sorcerers, *nahuales* (transforming tricksters), and bloodsucking witches—who either cause or remedy the discords and imbalances that disrupt human life. The basic form and attributes of all four derive from pre-Hispanic times, but they all took on European and African traits during the seventeenth century and persisted in this syncretized form into the late twentieth century. As recently as the 1960s, all four of these supernaturals were present among Indians, even most of the individuals who were making the transition to mestizos, throughout the Tlaxcala-Pueblan Valley (see Nutini and Isaac 1974: 27–148). Each is described briefly below.

Weathermen, all of whom are male, have supernatural powers to control the weather. They can stop hail, temper the torrential rain, hasten the onset of the rainy season, and control the wind in the sense of changing the course of whirlwinds or the direction of windstorms. Most weathermen acquire their powers through apprenticeship, although some are born with them; in either case, their powers come from La Malintzi and El Cuatlapanga, legendary mountain spirits and owners. These practitioners are paid for their work, either by the community or by individual field owners. Their techniques include noise (bells, rockets, rattles), prayers to the mountain spirits and Catholic saints, fasting, ritual flogging, inducing dreams, ritually harnessing the weather-controlling powers of certain animals (e.g., hummingbirds, toads, and snakes), manipulating sacred objects and talismans (e.g., black crosses, palm crosses, incense, human skulls, human and coyote bones, stone and clay figurines, human hair, and holy water), and calling forth collective action (pilgrimages, processions, ritual walking). To provide a concrete example, a weatherman protects a field against harmful natural elements with a sacred fence, which he builds "by burying clay figurines or coyote bones on the four corners of the cultivated plot"; he then sets up a black cross and an incense burner in the middle of the field, after which he recites "prescribed prayers and ritual incantations" (Nutini and Roberts 1993: 43). In addition to their main functions, as specified above, weathermen serve as prayer leaders at wakes, funerals, baptisms, and rosaries connected with the celebration of Catholic saints. This role is especially important in the many rural communities that lack a resident priest. Weathermen also officiate at a variety of other religious occasions that are hallmarks of Nahua religious practice: erection of protective crosses at certain spots (e.g., crossroads, springs, fields, haystacks, and stores), erection of burial crosses, symbolic cleansings of the sick, setting the foundation of a new house, presentation of first earrings to a baby girl, neutralizing the otherwise disastrous properties of a twin fruit or vegetable, and the like (Nutini 1984: 396; Nutini 1998; Nutini and Bell 1980: 132–134, 172–178; Nutini and Roberts 1993: 42–43).

Sorcerers are men or women (about 80 percent vs. 20 percent, respectively) who have supernatural power to do either good or evil—to cause or cure illness, alter human anatomy (e.g., break bones), cause sudden or slow death, manipulate individuals' will—by means of magical rites and ceremonies, special prayers and formulas, spells and charms, talismans, and the use of plants and animals endowed with particular magical properties. While some people are born with uncanny abilities that predispose them to sorcery—such as the ability to break eggs or glassware with their "strong sight" or to overhear conversations at great distances—sorcery powers as such are neither inherent nor hereditary but are, rather, always learned through apprenticeship. Sorcerers are public personages, known as such to all members of the community, who hire them to work either good or evil, usually after other remedies have failed. Four occasions stand out: to cure illness caused by another sorcerer, to cure ordinary illness that does not respond to either physicians or traditional curers, to cause an enemy to become seriously ill or even to die, "and to achieve success in love, sex, and the acquisition of a desirable marriage partner" (Nutini and Roberts 1993: 51). At least partly because the powers of one sorcerer can be counteracted by another, sorcerers are typically regarded as useful members of the community who perform necessary services, regardless of their good or evil nature. At the same time, they are generally thought to be very spiteful, vengeful, easily offended, and always ready to use their powers to harm others, and sorcerers who are thought to have lost control of their evil impulses are at risk of being lynched.

Nahuales are persons who have supernatural powers to transform themselves into animals, especially donkeys, turkeys, dogs, coyotes, cats, and foxes. Most rural Tlaxcalan communities are thought to have two or three nahuales, but no one is certain of their human identity, except in the rare cases in which one is caught in its animal form and successfully interrogated (see below). Like the sorcerers just described, nahuales can be of either sex, although most are men, and their powers are always learned through apprenticeship. They transform themselves into animals mainly to steal almost anything they desire (except coins, because touching metal causes them to lose control), to make fools of people who have done them wrong or simply for the fun of it through a kind of posthypnotic suggestion (e.g., by undressing in the middle of the street), to have sexual relations with men and women (who are first hypnotized or put into a deep sleep), or to play pranks such as hiding things. Nahuales are pesky but not malevolent, "for in their stealing and pranks they can only go so far, and their powers never permit them to kill" (Nutini and Roberts 1993: 45–46). On the positive side, belief in nahuales can serve to explain or excuse a great deal of abnormal behavior and odd events. On the other hand, nahuales are considered "a kind of pest that needs to be properly controlled" (46). When a person senses that an animal he or she comes upon at night is the animal form of a nahual, he or she immobilizes it by drawing a cross on the ground and sticking a knife or machete with a hat on top of it at the cross's center. If the discoverer is sufficiently strong or is with companions, he or she or they can then interrogate the nahual to determine its human identity. If the nahual-animal quickly gives up its human name, it is let go with a mild beating; if it resists, it is severely beaten or, more rarely, killed. In the latter case, the nahual's human body is found at the site the next morning, revealing its identity.

Bloodsucking witches are individuals who have supernatural powers to transform themselves into animals—most commonly turkeys but also donkeys, dogs, cats, chickens, ducks, buzzards, crows, fleas, ants, and other small animals and insects—in order to consume human blood. The great majority are women, and female witches are thought to be more powerful, evil, and bloodthirsty than male witches. They "epitomize everything inherently dreadful, loathsome, abhorrent, and hateful," personifying the evil and malicious side of the "supernatural struggle that constantly affects humanity" (Nutini and Roberts 1993: 54). Bloodsucking witches are born with their evil powers, and they are "imprinted for life with an insatiable and uncontrollable desire to drink the blood of human beings, especially of infants" (57). Furthermore, "there is no force on earth that can eradicate the[se] powers" (56). They are thought of as "recipients of a raw deal, the possessors of something that they did not want" and which they would not want to teach to anyone else. Nor is the witch's evil power passed on through heredity. Thus the power dies with the witch, but it inexplicably crops up in other unfortunate individuals.

After midnight on the last Saturday of every month, the bloodsucking witch goes to her kitchen and lights a fire of certain woods and leaves that have supernatural powers and chants magical formulas and spells. She walks over the fire three times in north-south and east-west directions and then sits on it, facing north. At this point, her lower legs and feet separate from her body. At once, she transforms herself into an animal, usually a dog, and arranges her feet and legs into a cross. She then goes out into the night, whereupon she transforms herself again, usually into a turkey, buzzard, or chicken. She is ready to begin her search for a person, typically an infant, from whom to suck blood. She usually succeeds, but if she does not, she dies at sunrise.

The most bloodthirsty witches may make as many as three additional forays for human blood each month, occasionally even during the daytime. Their thirst for blood increases sharply during the rainiest and coldest months, and most of the infant deaths attributed to their actions occur then. Of course, these are the months when the heaviest bedding is used, increasing the possibility of infant suffocation. Also, breastfeeding at night is more likely to result in asphyxia during these months if the mother falls asleep with the child at her breast under the heavy covers. More generally, choking is a constant hazard for infants, as the Nahuas have no tradition of burping them after nighttime breastfeeding.

None of these circumstances suffices, however, to explain two other salient patterns. The first is that bloodsucking witches kill twice as many female as male infants (Nutini and Roberts 1993: 165). The second is the casual disregard of protective measures against bloodsucking witches, including two methods that are thought to be completely effective: "two or three cloves of garlic wrapped in pieces of tortillas placed under the swaddling band" and "pieces of onion wrapped in pieces of tortilla [and] strewn under the crib or around the petate [sleeping mat]." Yet, except during an "epidemic" of witch attacks or when a witch is rumored to be in the vicinity, "people tend to forget" these measures, regarding them as "rather tedious to practice nightly" (70). In short, belief in bloodsucking witches that kill infants provides both psychological comfort to parents in the event of accidental or inexplicable nocturnal infant death and a socially acceptable cover for infanticide, especially of female babies. The latter might involve deliberate actions or simply be a latent consequence of the greater care generally accorded male infants, including the "more attentive and controlled" behavior of mothers when nursing male infants at night (165, 239).

Notwithstanding the foregoing traditional Indian beliefs and practices with obvious pre-Hispanic roots, which clearly set Indians off from mestizos, Indians throughout Central Mexico have long identified themselves to outsiders as Catholics (see Sandstrom 1991: 9) or, in some cases today, as other types of Christians (*evangélico, pentecostés, adventista, mormón*, etc.). In other words, Indians and mestizos do not differ in basic religious identity but rather in the form and content of religious practice. Leaving aside the recent converts to non-Catholic forms of Christianity, we can say that Indians traditionally practiced a "folk Catholicism" that departed significantly from the more formal, or orthodox, Roman Catholicism practiced by mestizos.

Indian folk Catholicism is organized at the local level only, that is, by community or neighborhoods (sections and/or barrios). Its activities are governed by an *ayuntamiento religioso*, a religious government of adult, married men selected annually by local male elders or elected in a public assembly of eligible (adult, married) men. Organizational details vary by locale and time period but have a high common denominator.

The *municipio* (township) of San Bernardino Contla (pop. 10,700), Tlaxcala, as reported by Nutini (1968b: 64–75) for the 1960s, will serve as our example. Contla's Ayuntamiento Religioso at the time consisted of two groups of officials, *fiscales* and the *cofradía*. The fiscales comprised six men by that title (see below) plus a foreman, two bellmen, two bellows operators, one waterer, and two sextons. The foreman was in charge of the fireworks that were set off for all fiestas. The bellmen rang the church bells several times each day and for fiestas, assemblies, storm warnings, and such other events as the administration of last rites to a dying person. The bellows operators had the sole function of pumping the bellows of the choir organ for every Mass. The waterer filled the parish church's baptismal font with fresh holy water each week and watered the flowers every four days. The sextons helped the priest to prepare for Mass by providing him with clean ornaments, preparing the altar, and purchasing the wine; they also helped to arrange the church for marriages, baptisms, and other special occasions.

As their title suggests, Contla's six fiscales were in charge of financial matters, among other functions. The *fiscal primero* (senior fiscal officer) was the highest religious authority in the Ayuntamiento Religioso, over which he presided, but all six of these officials cooperated in most of their functions. Each Monday, they all went door to door throughout the community asking for money donations for the parish church. Each Sunday, they escorted the priest from the sacristy to the main altar for Mass and headed all religious processions; on these occasions, each carried his *vara de mando* (staff of authority), a long wooden pole tipped with a metal cross. They also sponsored an important *mayordomía* (stewardship;

see below) and hosted a community banquet each December 25 to thank the public for their support during the previous year.

The cofradía comprised four mayordomías, religious stewardships honoring particular saints, each headed by a steward (*mayordomo*). The steward of Contla's patron saint, San Bernardino (St. Bernard), was the ranking official of the cofradía. He had the authority to reprimand the other stewards and their helpers, who consisted of one deputy (*divutado*) and one assistant (*tupil*) for each steward. The deputy served as secretary, recording all agreements reached at mayordomía meetings, for which he also provided a snack. The assistant was the mayordomía's treasurer and the guardian of its paraphernalia (ornaments, candles and candleholders, incense burners, etc.); also, each week he lit a candle before the image of the mayordomía's saint in the parish church. The deputy and the assistant, aided by two family members, carried the saint's image in all processions in which the mayordomía participated. Finally, there were two doormen (*porteros*) who opened and closed the parish church each day, tended the cemetery, made sure that the Lamp of the Holy Sacrament in the church never extinguished itself, and kept the key to the box containing such sacred paraphernalia as staffs of authority and high crosses.

Until the 1850s, when the national Reform Laws abolished their right to own communal religious property (see Chap. 3), cofradías in communities such as Contla sponsored all of the saints' celebrations with the income from their own specific lands and livestock. Community members' contributions consisted mainly or entirely of labor for cultivating or tending these properties (see Chance and Taylor 1985; Slade 1992: 3–4). Since the Reform, the sponsorship and expenses of the mayordomías responsible for these festivities have fallen to individuals who are elected annually.

Including the four mayordomías of the cofradía, Contla had a total of 146 mayordomías and 40 *hermandades* (brotherhoods), all sponsored by officers elected annually. The hermandades were structured like the mayordomías, except for two special features of the former: (1) each hermandad drew its membership from the whole community rather than from a particular neighborhood or locality; and (2) each sponsored an annual pilgrimage to the place where its saint was venerated. Through these institutions, this municipio of 10,700 people of very modest means annually staffed the whole array of religious offices—known as *cargos*, literally, "burdens"—with their attendant expenses for rockets, candles, incense, Masses, and feasts for members of the sponsoring neighborhood.

Individual officeholders spent up to five times their annual cash incomes in fulfilling their duties, raising the money through loans from real and fictive kin (compadres) and by pawning their fields (see Nutini 1968b: 50–52, 229–237; cf. Chamoux 1987: 351–366).

The awful financial burden entailed by these offices raises the question of why anyone would have agreed to serve in them. First, there was enormous social pressure to serve. Second, service in these cargos was the main avenue to prestige in Indian communities. Third, and most important in our view, such service was thought to help ensure human welfare. Men and their wives—the latter being indispensable partners who prepared festive food and helped entertain guests—assumed these burdens as a way of making the world safe for existence (after Slade 1992). In fact, this is the very core of traditional folk Catholicism.

As the foregoing suggests, the folk Catholicism of traditional Indian communities is centered on the saints, not on the formal Catholic doctrine and theology that are important in mestizo religious belief and practice. Furthermore, Indians view the saints as having direct powers of intervention, in contradiction to the formal Catholic doctrine that they are merely conduits to God. The most revered figure is always the community's patron saint, but other saints are also thought to protect individuals and communities against illness, bad weather, and economic disaster; in return, humans respect, venerate, and appease them (Slade 1992: 23–26). As the people of Contla repeatedly emphasized to Nutini in the 1960s, "We sponsor the *mayordomías* to keep the saints happy, so that they will continue to protect us"—a strictly pragmatic, nontheological approach to religion (Nutini 1968b: 77). Key Catholic supernaturals such as Jesus Christ and the Virgin Mary were "venerated . . . not because of their place in the Catholic hierarchy, but because of the traditional status of their miracles" (77). Furthermore, as Doren Slade (1992: 26) reported for Chignautla a decade later, God was "a remote abstraction" and was "unlikely to intervene as a saint would in immediate ways in an individual's life."

More generally, folk Catholicism has little place for the whole ethical and moral system of formal Catholicism, or even for such concepts as Heaven and Hell. Furthermore, neither the sacraments (such as Communion and Confession) nor attendance at Mass is very important. To make sense of the universe, the world, and human nature, the traditional Indian community relied mainly on the complex of nonorthodox ("folk") or even non-Catholic supernaturals, beliefs, and practices discussed earlier.

Modernization, Secularization, Mestizoization

Three basic concepts frame our discussion of the transformation of traditional Indian villages during the twentieth century. The first is *modernization*, which encompasses the adoption of contemporary national-urban culture, especially in the material realm (e.g., clothing, housing, furniture, household appliances, machinery) and the economy (occupations, work locations, and consumption patterns). It is also manifested in an increasing fluency in Spanish, even if an indigenous language is retained within the community and occasionally serves as a defensive barrier against outsiders (see Friedlander 1975: 87; Sandstrom 1991: 323 ff.).

The second concept, *secularization*, refers to a fundamental change in ideology, from a deeply sacred to a generally secular approach to life. Most remarkable are the changes in its religious beliefs and practices, but such seemingly unrelated institutions as politics and kinship are also typically affected deeply. In short, secularization changes a community's most basic institutions.

Modernization and secularization are causally related, with the former preceding the latter, often by a long time (Nutini and Isaac 1974; Robichaux 1994; Romero 2002). In the Tlaxcala-Pueblan Valley, for instance, there are highly modernized communities—Nahuatl is no longer spoken, most households are far more dependent on wage labor than on agricultural or artisanry, material culture is mainly store-bought—in which the mayordomías have actually increased in number and elaboration, and where kinship, compadrazgo, and local politics are still tightly integrated with folk Catholicism. At some point, however, the cumulative effects of modernization reach a critical threshold, triggering rapid secularization.

At the flashpoint, a generational divide often becomes evident: an older generation whose outside experience is relatively limited and whose identity and orientation remain local is pitted against a younger, formally schooled, Spanish-speaking generation with extensive experience in mestizo/national culture, especially through migratory wage work in urban centers (Dow 2001b). Alternatively, factions may coalesce around differences in economic orientation (commercial vs. agricultural), relative wealth, or geographic disparities (headquarters towns vs. hinterland villages) in governmental largesse (Dehouve 1976: 256–296; Friedlander

FIGURE 7.5. Distance-learning middle school (*secundaria*) in a remote, mestizoizing Nahua village in the Sierra Norte de Puebla, northeastern Puebla state. Photo by Barry Isaac.

1975: 79–83). In any case, such factional disputes erode traditional culture by undermining the community cohesion that is essential to it.

This brings us to the third concept, *mestizoization*, which is the end result of the combined modernization-secularization transition. In short, a community that was once distinctively Indian—as "Indian" was variously defined both regionally and nationally through time—becomes less and less so, ending up culturally indistinguishable from neighboring communities that were once distinctively "mestizo" in comparison. At this point, their cultural institutions and identity are regional and, to some extent, national.

To make the foregoing processes more concrete, we shall turn to Slade's (1992: 207–219) account of the modernization and secularization of Chignautla, a community in the Sierra Norte de Puebla region (northeastern Puebla state) during the 1970s and 1980s. In Chignautla, as in many other formerly traditional Indian communities, recent decades have seen a great increase in young people's commitment to wage labor in regional cities, to which they commute daily or weekly or migrate periodically. This increased outside involvement was initially impelled by land scarcity in relation to a growing population, but government programs that resulted in good roads and rural schools were also very important (see Fig. 7.5). The former greatly facilitated commuting and circular migration; the latter equipped the young with at least the rudiments of Spanish and indoctrinated them in national mestizo standards of living and values (Friedlander 1975: 128–164; Robichaux 1994: 148–151; Sandstrom 1991: 335–337; Williams G. 1963: 248–251).

Intensive engagement in wage labor, often through complicated commuting or short-term migration, has had a tremendous impact on the way time is viewed. It has led to "a preoccupation with the use of time in relation to money, since time is an essential ingredient in wage labor" (Slade 1992: 208). One result is a decline in the unpaid reciprocity that was sanctified by its importance in meeting ceremonial obligations to the saints and by its centrality to community sociability in general. Paid labor is replacing it, even in religious contexts, "because it is disrespectful to ask individuals to give up their time without compensation now that time has an established value" (208). Ceremonial life is becoming simplified in order to save time and thus money. For instance, many wedding celebrations have been shortened from three days to one, and the elaborate gift exchanges and dance performance of the ceremony with which compadrazgo was traditionally established have been abandoned (209). Also, while many young men with money are eager to serve as mayordomo, an office that involves "discrete events of short duration," they are less willing to take on other ritual offices, such as fiscal or sexton, which require greater constancy of effort during the year (208).

Even fewer time-consuming ceremonial demands are made on busy wage workers if they switch from folk to orthodox Catholicism (i.e., to the form practiced by mestizos) or to Protestantism. Either shift entails a dramatic change in emphasis: a relatively quick and inexpensive praxis of *individual* salvation replaces the costly and time-consuming *community* effort to "make the world safe for existence" and ensure "a harmonious passage through life" (209). Such shifts are facilitated by the fact that young adults "have learned alternate explanations for what occurs" (207), lessening their stock in the traditional, highly sacred worldview. They also tend to acquire a "shameful discomfort in things traditional (and therefore Indian)," making them more eager to shake off tradition and either embrace mestizo appearance, behavior, and beliefs (207; also see Friedlander 1975: 71–79) or adopt a new ethnic-religious identity that is neither traditionally Indian nor traditionally mestizo by becoming Protestants (Sandstrom 2001: 276–278; also see Dow 2001b).

Young adults' commitment to wage work outside the community also weakens the bonds of family (parent-child, sibling, extended family), neighborhood, and community, along with the reciprocal expectations that were essential to performance in traditional folk Catholicism. "It is not uncommon today for young men to leave early in the morning and return late in the evening from jobs they hold in Teziutlán," the nearest large town (Slade 1992: 214). For these individuals, daily sociality often boils down to the nuclear family, and the focus of economic welfare also becomes the individual and his or her nuclear family (also see Rothstein 1982: 39–43). Furthermore, young people's wider social field is leading them to marry outside their natal neighborhoods, which were traditionally highly endogamous, reducing the multistrandedness of community ties. Another traditional family function, educating the young, is becoming less and less important as the skills that really matter to most young people—everything from the Spanish language to industrial and commercial job skills—increasingly are imparted by public schools, employers, and job peers outside the community.

Young men are also less interested in village politics, where selection for service is based on the respect one earns through a lifetime of service to the saints. Their involvement in national culture through outside employment, coupled with increasing state involvement in municipio politics since the 1970s, has brought an increased awareness that improving local welfare requires participation in regional and national politics (also see Dehouve 1976: 235–240; Romero 2002: 263–294). That activity diverts the time and money of some of the most able and prosperous young adults away from activities with strictly community impact, including service in mayordomías (Slade 1992: 210).

The overall result is that the highly integrated fabric of traditional culture is being torn and unraveled. Several important aspects of life—politics, economics, education, and family/kinship—that traditionally were deeply embedded in religion and a sacred worldview are being disembedded from that traditional matrix. They are becoming largely separate realms of thought and action, a phenomenon peculiar to modern, postindustrial cultures (Aguirre Beltrán 1973: 128–152; Aguirre Beltrán 1979: 81–90; Isaac 2005; Polanyi 1944). Economy becomes just a way of making a living for oneself and one's nuclear family. Politics becomes strictly political, although with economic ends or implications. Education of the young becomes public rather than familial. Religion has less and less to do with these other activities. Life in general is desanctified as religion becomes largely compartmentalized in its own realm. In the foreseeable future, the saints will "still reside in the church and shrines that dot the landscape, but they will hold a position in religion rather than social life" (Slade 1992: 211). Even now, "the respect one merits and one's social standing [are] no longer confirmed by ritual rank" (211). Instead, people are increasingly ranked individually according to wealth and collectively by social class.

The foregoing account of secularization in Chignautla serves to arm us against a common misunderstanding of the phenomenon. Specifically, Slade (1992) makes clear that secularization does not mean that traditional religion is totally forsaken (cf. Robichaux 1994; Romero 2002). To the contrary, the saints usually continue to be celebrated in ways that are altered to a greater or lesser extent but still recognizably derived from past practices, and many other traditional beliefs may be retained as well (see Portal A. 1997). At the same time, though, religious beliefs and practices centered on the saints are no longer the indisputable organizers and arbiters of community and individual action. Rather, in the secularized village, the saints now "hold a position in religion rather than [in] social life" (Slade 1992: 211). This change has occurred because religion in general is increasingly compartmentalized, so that its place in the community and daily life of secularizing communities becomes more and more like the place it holds for the urban middle classes in both Mexico and the United States.

Advocates of modernization and "development" typically applaud this trajectory, for three reasons. First, it often means that the community and its members will make a larger contribution to the national economy. Second, the transformation breaks the grip of traditional village social control, allowing greater individual freedom. Third, many individuals or even whole communities experience an improvement in overall welfare, at least in the short run.

We do not dispute these possible outcomes, but we wish to point out that they can have negative as well as positive effects. For instance, greater village involvement with the national economy may increase national aggregate productivity or prosperity without doing likewise for the individuals involved, many of whom are qualified only for the hardest, dirtiest, most dangerous, and most poorly paid jobs in the national economy. Also, the regional economy can absorb only a certain number of low-skilled laborers, and once that threshold is reached, others must migrate permanently to urban centers, where their standard of living and quality of life are as apt to fall as to rise (Lewis 1961; Lomnitz 1975). Turning to another aspect, greater individual freedom can also spell greater personal isolation, even for the individuals who remain in their home communities. Slade (1992: 213), who is both a trained anthropologist and a practicing psychiatrist, notes for Chignautla that "what is being lost is not yet replaced by something else of value," that individuals' sense of emptiness "has increased their resentment at signs of success aimed at impressing others," and that the loss of respect for traditional social controls has been accompanied by higher levels of interpersonal violence and abuse. Finally, dependence on wage labor, in which men typically have a great advantage, can destroy the relatively egalitarian gender relations of traditional Indian peasant villages, reducing women to dependency on their husbands. Frances Rothstein (1982) has documented this outcome in rural Tlaxcala, and Merielle Flood (1994) and Laurel Bossen (1984) have shown it is widespread in both Mexico and Guatemala.

Temporal and Regional Variation

To illustrate the extent of regional variation in the Indian-mestizo transition, as well as to convey a sense of the time intervals involved, we briefly compare the rural communities of two regions within Central Mexico: the Tlaxcala-Pueblan Valley (central Tlaxcala and Puebla states, including their capital cities of the same names) and the Córdoba-Orizaba region of west-central Veracruz (see Maps 2 and 3). Historically, these two regions are representative of Central Mexico's two basic regional-community patterns of ethnic relations: an Indian-mestizo continuum in the Tlaxcala-Pueblan Valley and an Indian-Mestizo dichotomy in the higher elevations of the Córdoba-Orizaba region. In both regions, the great majority of the Indian population is ethnically Nahua.

The Tlaxcala-Pueblan Valley has about four hundred rural communities; the Córdoba-Orizaba region, some two hundred. Proportionately, the composition of the two regions in terms of small cities, towns, and villages is similar, except that the Tlaxcala-Pueblan Valley's settlements, which are mostly situated on level ground in the valley floor, are more nucleated. In the Córdoba-Orizaba region, in contrast, many of the rural communities are located in the mountainous and broken terrain of the *tierra templada* (temperate lands at 700–1600 m elev.) and *tierra fría* (cold lands at 1600–2800 m elev.). These upland communities are typically dispersed, with fifty meters or more between the houses located outside of a small central node (see Figs. 7.6, 7.7). Those same areas also have a proliferation of hamlets, typically called congregaciones, and rancherías, not found in the Tlaxcala-Pueblan Valley.

The two regions are somewhat different economically, especially in emphasis. The Tlaxcala-Pueblan Valley's industrial and commercial establishment is larger and more extensive, and it is also more widely distributed geographically, with medium-sized industries sometimes located in entirely rural settings. In contrast, the large industry of the Córdoba-Orizaba region is concentrated in those two cities and, besides, is less diversified, less extensive, and more regionally oriented. Finally, agriculture and ranching are much more important in the Córdoba-Orizaba region than in the Tlaxcala-Pueblan Valley (see Nutini 2005).

In 1900 these two areas were very similar in terms of ethnic composition and degree of modernization and secularization. When Frederick Starr (1900: 14–37) conducted his ethnographic survey of the Tlaxcala-Pueblan Valley in 1898, more than 70 percent of the population was Nahua. Culturally, this population lived in traditional, monolingual Indian communities almost untouched by secularization. Based on Nutini's ongoing field observations, we estimate that only about 2 percent of the valley's population was still Indian by 2000 and that Indian-mestizo differences had functionally disappeared. In contrast, the tierra templada and tierra fría portions of the Córdoba-Orizaba region retained a large percentage of Indian-traditional communities. Furthermore, the ethnic situation in much of the Córdoba-Orizaba region can still be characterized as an Indian/mestizo dichotomy, with sharply defined cultural and ethnic differences between communities or sectors within them.

By at least 1950, the rural portions of the Tlaxcala-Pueblan Valley displayed an ethnocultural continuum in which there was no sharp break between Indian and mestizo communities (see Nutini and Isaac 1974: 375–396). This does not mean that there were no remaining ethnic differences, because communities and individuals could still be placed along a continuum of modernization and secularization. What it does mean is that in the typical community participation in political, religious, and general social life was basically egalitarian and well integrated, without antagonistic sectoral interests based mainly on ethnicity. At the regional level, the situation was even more fluid. In urban and industrial contexts, the ethnocultural differences that were important in the rural hinterlands were blurred, and the rural population was perceived as a diffuse peasant mass or simply as a lower class with respect to the city.

FIGURE 7.6. Nahua house with *tabla* (plank) walls and tile roof in a *tierra fría* dispersed village in Veracruz state. Photo by Hugo Nutini.

FIGURE 7.7. Mestizo house with stuccoed and two-toned painted walls (green below and pink above) and corrugated metal roof in the *tierra templada* of Veracruz state. Photo by Barry Isaac.

THE TLAXCALA-PUEBLAN VALLEY IN THE 1950S

For the 1950s (see Nutini and Isaac 1974: 375–396), the four hundred or so rural communities in the Tlaxcala-Pueblan Valley can be classified as follows with respect to the Indian-mestizo transition: Indian-traditional (12 percent), Indian-transitional (35 percent), mestizo-transitional (45 percent), and mestizo-secularized (8 percent). This classification is based on the following variables: degree of ritual and ceremonial traditionalism, degree of belief in the non-Catholic supernatural complex (witchcraft, sorcery, nahualism, weather-making, etc.), comparative strength of the kinship and compadrazgo systems, household economy and material culture (subsistence, clothing, house construction, furniture, utensils, etc.), and language(s) habitually spoken (Nahuatl only, Nahuatl and Spanish, Spanish and Nahuatl, Spanish only).

Of course, the classification does not mean that all individuals within a community were transforming themselves in lockstep. Especially in the mestizo-transitional and mestizo-secularized communities, there were often many individuals and households that were either ahead of or behind the overall community trend. With this qualification in mind, we can proceed to a general portrait of communities in each of the four categories during the 1950s.

1. *Indian-traditional communities* were the most traditional in terms of religion. Their mayordomía systems were usually the most complex in their immediate region, and the non-Catholic supernatural complex had not changed much since Frederick Starr's ethnographic survey in 1898 (Starr 1900). Kinship remained the central institution of community life. Subsistence-oriented agriculture provided the economic base, except in a few communities that produced cottage crafts for sale (woven textiles, earthenware pottery, and wood products). Houses were constructed of adobe walls, homemade tile (*teja*) roofs, and packed-earth floors, and most furniture and household utensils were homemade. Finally, Nahuatl or Nahuatl-Spanish was the everyday language.
2. *Indian-transitional communities* were still largely traditional in terms of religion. The mayordomía system was still intact but was already exhibiting modernizing elements, such as simpli-

fied church rites, less elaborate ceremonial meals, and a more formal Catholic ambience. The non-Catholic supernatural complex remained basically unchanged. Kinship was still a central social institution, but compadrazgo had acquired more social importance in some instances—a sign that many individuals were constructing their own primary social networks through this mechanism, outside of consanguineal and affinal, or marital, kinship. The economy remained basically the same, although a few men had become wage workers who commuted daily to outside employment sites. House construction was beginning to change, with the introduction of brick or cement block walls, factory-made tile or corrugated metal (*láminas de zinc*) roofs, and factory-made tile (*baldosa*) floors. In some households, straight-backed chairs had replaced the traditional low benches and stools, and beds had replaced sleeping mats; many also had some factory-made utensils (e.g., dishes, cooking pots, forks and knives). Only middle-aged and elderly people habitually spoke Nahuatl, and it had ceased to be the everyday language of the community.

3. *Mestizo-transitional communities* were no longer traditional in terms of religion, in the sense that several elements of formal Catholicism—such as Confession, Communion, and regular attendance at Mass—had become important. In modified form, the mayordomía system reached its pinnacle of elaboration, as money earned outside the community was poured into it. The associated ceremonial meals increased in number and elaboration, and some rites and ceremonies were also added. For example, the mayordomía's image was now serenaded in the church and in the houses of the fiscales on the eve of the saint's celebration, and the priest blessed the mayordomos on their selection by the community. The non-Catholic supernatural complex was still strong but was clearly ebbing. Compadrazgo rivaled kinship in the organization of community life and had acquired several nontraditional types, such as those contracted for reasons of close friendship, a girl's fifteenth birthday, and the blessing of a new car or truck. In many communities, labor migration surpassed subsistence agriculture in economic importance. House construction began to acquire an urbanized appearance, with

factory-made components (e.g., bricks or cement blocks, roofing tiles or corrugated metal sheets, and floor tiles) and such structural features as second stories, balconies, and iron fencing. Most households also had replaced homemade furniture and utensils with factory-made products. Spanish had become the everyday language, and only old people retained some fluency in Nahuatl.

4. *Mestizo-secularized communities* were little more than rustic versions of lower- and lower-middle-class urban neighborhoods, a reflection not only of their proximity to the large city of Puebla but also of the importance of circular labor migration to Mexico City. Some of these communities retained simplified forms of the mayordomía system, in which, for instance, only the post of mayordomo was retained, such ritual occasions as the many get-togethers in private homes were eliminated, and the annual cycle of rites and ceremonies was conducted exclusively in church. Most communities, though, practiced a basically national, orthodox Catholicism. At the same time, the non-Catholic supernatural complex was still functioning somewhat, although witchcraft and sorcery were largely practices of last resort. Kinship was no longer the basic institution of community action. Compadrazgo had acquired a significant utilitarian and asymmetrical component, in the sense that ritual kin were sometimes chosen primarily to enhance economic or mobility opportunities of the godparent(s) rather than to ensure the welfare of the godchild. The mainstay of the community's economy had become labor migration and some local commerce. Housing had changed markedly; elaborate houses with gardens, balconies, and balustrades had become common, and there were also some two-story constructions. In terms of furniture, utensils, and appliances, most households had largely replaced homemade and rustic items with factory-made products. Finally, the community was now entirely monolingual in Spanish. In fact, in the most secularized of these communities, outsiders who inquired about language were commonly told that Nahuatl had never been spoken there and that only the inditos in a nearby community still spoke it.

THE TLAXCALA-PUEBLAN VALLEY TODAY: 2000–2005

The situation today is greatly different from that a mere fifty years ago, and the percentage distribution of communities in the four categories employed above demonstrates this change dramatically. Nutini's ongoing field observations indicate that about 55 percent of the valley's rural communities are now mestizo-transitional, and another 30 percent are mestizo-secularized and nearly indistinguishable from their urban social class counterparts. Indian-traditional communities now account for only about 2 percent of the valley's rural settlements, and none of them are as culturally traditional as they were fifty years ago. Indian-transitional communities have diminished to less than 15 percent, and at first blush they look more like mestizo-transitional cases. These figures reflect the fact that the majority of the valley's rural residents are now wage workers rather than peasants, and their economic interest in agriculture or husbandry, if any, is clearly secondary.

We caution that a surface of modernity quite often hides a significant retention of traditional culture, especially ideology, as evidenced most strikingly in the fairly strong persistence of belief in witchcraft and sorcery. We have observed this same situation throughout Central Mexico, indicating that the supernatural aspects of traditional culture are the last to disappear. In fact, many otherwise fully mestizoized people living in highly urban areas, even in Puebla or Mexico City, retain a belief in traditional non-Catholic supernaturalism such as witchcraft, sorcery, and nahuals (see Lagarriga 1993; cf. Portal A. 1997: 61–62, 124–125).

THE CÓRDOBA-ORIZABA REGION: 1950S–2005

Ethnic relations in the Córdoba-Orizaba region are more complicated, varying by altitude zone. At least since the 1950s, an Indian-mestizo continuum has been in place in the *tierra caliente* portion (hot lands below 700 m elev.), making that zone very similar to the Tlaxcala-Pueblan Valley in that regard, both then and at present. In contrast, an Indian/mestizo dichotomy remains in place in the tierra templada (700–1600 m) and tierra fría (1600–1800 m) zones, making them today very much like the Tlaxcala-Pueblan Valley was in the 1890s (see Nutini 2005; Nutini and Isaac 1974).

The zonal difference reflects the greater isolation of the mountainous tierra templada and tierra fría from the modernizing influences, especially good roads and accessible sites of industrial wage work, that broke down the ethnic dichotomy and replaced it with an ethnic continuum in most of Central Mexico during the twentieth century. In fact, all of the parts of Central Mexico in which an ethnic dichotomy has persisted to the present day have this same mountainous and broken topography: the Sierra de Puebla in northern Puebla state, the Sierra Madre del Sur in Guerrero state (especially the south), and the higher elevations of the Córdoba-Orizaba region (see Dehouve 1976; Nutini 2005; Nutini and Isaac 1974; Oettinger 1980). There are a few other areas of Central Mexico—most notably, central and northern Hidalgo state, northern Veracruz state, and the Sierra de Toluca in east-central Mexico state—where distinctive Indian cultures and communities persist and where ethnic relations are at least periodically antagonistic, but they lack the pervasive ethnic dichotomy of the three areas cited above (see Cervantes-Broginski 1992; Lomnitz-Adler 1992: 165–183; Martínez A. and Sarmiento 1991; Sandstrom 1991; Schryer 1990).

The Indian/mestizo dichotomy that remains in force in the Sierra de Puebla, the Sierra de Guerrero, and the higher elevations of the Córdoba-Orizaba region is a carryover from the estate stratification of colonial times. While both mestizo and Indian populations are differentiated internally by social classes and/or ranking systems, it is their separation into two overarching, endogamous estates that gives these regions their peculiar social morphology. The mestizo estate retains control, either outright or as silent partner, over extraregional commerce, modern industry, and agricultural produce dealing. Mestizos also control formal education, the parish churches, and the legal-judicial system (see Sierra 1999). For the Indian estate, local social mobility is limited not only by economic and educational disadvantages but also because known parentage automatically relegates everyone to the upper or the lower estate, with its inherent privileges or disabilities.

Gonzalo Aguirre Beltrán (1973, 1979) called such areas "regions of refuge," because their rugged terrain and/or harsh climate largely sheltered their inhabitants from modernizing forces, allowing anachronistic sociocultural patterns to persist. On the one hand, these conditions allowed the persistence of distinctively Indian languages, cultures, social structures, and ethnicities (as syncretic blends of pre- and postcolonial elements) throughout the twentieth century—an outcome regarded favorably by most anthropologists since the 1970s (see Bonfil Batalla 1996; García M.

and Medina 1983/86). On the other hand, these same conditions allowed the persistence of a colonial-era estate stratification system in which a mestizo minority retained its power position over the Indian majority.

So striking is this social arrangement to modern scholars that many have characterized the Indian and mestizo sectors as "castes," drawing an analogy with India (see Aguirre Beltrán 1973: 153–177; 1979: 93–104). We believe that the two sectors are more aptly characterized as estates, because they clearly derive from the European estate system that was transplanted to New Spain in the sixteenth century. Furthermore, this historically based view is much more in keeping with Aguirre Beltrán's (1973, 1979) most seminal idea on the topic, namely, that "regions of refuge" are zones in which older sociocultural forms retain their vitality.

Completing the Transition

Implicit in much of the foregoing discussion of the Indian-mestizo transition is a distinction between necessary and sufficient conditions, or causes. In our view, the necessary conditions are structural. The most important is ready and continuous Indian access to wage labor employment, which presupposes modern transportation systems. Also important is the fact that these jobs expose employees to national culture in an ample sense that includes not only its material components but also its intangible aspects, such as an ideology that has fewer vestiges of the colonial-era estate outlook. In practice, this stipulation means that the employment must be industrial or commercial rather than agricultural.

The sufficient conditions are expressive and ideological, amounting to a new worldview in which people no longer perceive themselves and their communities through the lens of the traditional sacred ideology. As we saw earlier, this new worldview emerges as the result of two new behavioral realities. First, more and more of the individual's activities take place outside of that traditional community context. Second, the various outside activities are carried out separately, not only from the traditional community context, but also from each other, such that economic and political activities, for instance, are separate in both senses. Even kinship becomes a partially independent arena as individuals construct their own networks of compadrazgo ties to supplement or even largely replace the traditional primary dependence on consanguineal and affinal kinship to structure sociality and economic reciprocity.

The Indian-mestizo transition also entails a fundamental, double-edged change in ethnic identity and perception. Individuals and groups cease to regard themselves as Indians, even though they remain well aware of their ethnic origins and may still adhere to some Indian customs, and they also come to be perceived by others as non-Indians. From this point forward, ethnicity is no longer the primary determinant of their placement in terms of local, regional, or national stratification. Instead, lifestyle choices, as well as economic, political, religious, and general social participation, are now primarily a matter of class, even though past ethnic disabilities may have a lingering effect in class formation and mobility.

At this point, it is important to interject two caveats. First, social class is not a new regional or even local phenomenon. Class stratification was important in many Indian communities throughout the colonial era and on into the twentieth century (Ouweneel 1995; Schryer 1990: 31–49, 96–101), although many other Indian communities displayed internal ranking but lacked social groupings with differential economic or political power (Rothstein 1982). Of course, the mestizo estate was always divided internally into classes (see Chapter 2). In short, what is new to the completed Indian-mestizo transition is the absence of overarching, ethnic-based estate stratification. The second caveat is that Indian ethnicity does not necessarily become a dead letter. Chapter 2 presented several examples of ethnic revitalization late in the twentieth century. Such ethnic revival, though, is typically inspired by regional or national politics and always occurs in the context of regional-national social class stratification (Schryer 1990: 245 ff., Vázquez L. 1992: passim). It may lead to the formation of new (real) social classes, as well as new political action blocs, but it does not replace class with ethnic stratification.

The precise point at which the Indian-mestizo transition has been completed is difficult to determine empirically, in part because there is no consistent phenotypic, or "racial," difference between Indians and mestizos and in part because the transition involves the intangible ideological shift in ethnic perception and identity. What we can say is that the threshold point is easier to determine for individuals than it is for communities. Individuals or families who have acquired mestizo status but still reside in predominantly Indian communities are easily identifiable, for two reasons. First, they have acquired some diagnostic mestizo traits, such as habitual use of Spanish and modern wardrobe (e.g., shoes rather than sandals and store-bought or tailored clothing with buttons), which set them apart from the Indian majority. Second, the latter are typically quick to identify these individuals as having made the transition, referring to them as gente de razón, gente decente, catrines, coyome, or other local terms. On the other hand, Indians who migrate permanently to large cities complete the transition, which they almost invariably had begun much earlier, soon after they settle there. In the Córdoba-Orizaba region, for example, we have not encountered any identifiable or self-identified Indians among immigrants who have resided continuously in cities for more than five years.

It is quite another matter to determine when an Indian community may be regarded as no longer Indian, because the community transition to mestizo status is usually gradual. The regional ethnic situation is also important. Where a regional Indian/mestizo dichotomy obtains, the transition is actually easier to identify, and a simple checklist of discrete, or threshold, attributes suffices: majority self-identification plus such traits as habitual language, mode of dress, house types, and occupations. Where a regional Indian-mestizo continuum exists, there is no definitive threshold that one can detect with such a checklist. Rather, the community must be placed at some point along a regional continuum of the type delineated earlier for the Tlaxcala-Pueblan Valley.

Another complication is the mixed Indian-mestizo community. In these cases, Indians and mestizos live in close proximity but remain essentially separate communities, often with separate religious and social organizations and quite often with intersecting economies over which mestizos exercise a good deal of control. Sometimes the mestizo element arose locally, perhaps only four or five generations ago. In many other instances, though, this nucleus originated with a mestizo influx from nearby cities, usually for commercial purposes. At least in the Córdoba-Orizaba region, mestizoization occurs faster in entirely Indian communities than it does in the mixed cases, doubtless because the former lack the on-site, direct control and economic exploitation of a resident mestizo sector.

The Demise of Indian Expressive Culture

Mestizoization necessarily entails the demise of the very rich Indian expressive culture that arose in the two centuries after the Spanish Conquest as a syncretic blend of Indian, Spanish, and African elements (Nutini and Bell 1980: 287–378; Nutini and Roberts 1993: 80–116). Chapter 8 provides a detailed explanation of the expressive culture concept; a thumbnail definition is that it denotes the cultural-behavioral realm that is basically noninstrumental, or nonutilitarian, in its motivation. The important point here is that differences of expressive culture—in everything from personal adornment to the details of religious practices—were the most visible markers of ethnicity for both mestizos and Indians. For the latter, folk Catholicism and other supernatural practices constituted the very core of individual and community ethnic identity and social integration.

Mestizoization eventually relegates most of this sacred core of Indian culture to the scrap heaps of "superstition," amusing folklore disconnected from daily life, and embarrassing old-fashioned ways (Friedlander 1975: 71–100; Nutini 1988: 375; Slade 1992: 206–207). Surviving practices are inevitably simplified in both outward form and depth of meaning to the individuals who strive to perpetuate them. In rural Tlaxcala, for instance, cemetery decoration for All Saints' Day and All Souls' Day (November 1 and 2) was traditionally elaborate and highly ritualized, with strict attention to types and arrangements of offerings to the dead. By the mid-1980s, however, most cemeteries in rural Tlaxcala remained drab and unkempt throughout this holiday, with fewer than half of the graves decorated—and poorly so in terms of both quantity and arrangement—by November 2. The items displayed were mostly store-bought because the knowledge required to make them at home was being lost (see Figs. 7.8–7.14). Furthermore, few people in these communities had a full working knowledge of what the traditional offerings, decorations, arrangements, and displays were supposed to denote or accomplish. In the course of this loss of traditional knowledge, the celebration had been largely desanctified and was now a festive rather than a somber occasion. Its focus had also changed. Instead of celebrating primarily the return of the souls of the dead, it had come to celebrate mainly the holiday return of the living people who had emigrated from the community (Nutini 1988: 359–376).

Such culture loss is not inherently either good or bad, although its effects can be. At issue is the speed with which functional replacements are adopted or created to foster community integration and a sense of personal purpose and satisfaction. Slade shows in her account of the mestizoization of Chignautla, Puebla, that the process can result in a sense of personal isolation, emptiness, or desperation, as well as higher levels of interpersonal violence, at least in the short run. The problem is that "what is being lost is not yet replaced by something else of value" (Slade 1992: 213).

FIGURE 7.8. Todos Santos (All Saints'/All Souls' Day), I: Traditional household altar to the dead in a Tlaxcalan village, with offerings of marigolds, *pan de muertos* (bread of the dead), fruit (oranges, plaintains, apples), bowls of turkey in mole sauce, and dried corn (to ensure a good harvest next year). Photo by Hugo Nutini.

FIGURE 7.9. Todos Santos (All Saints'/All Souls' Day), II: Traditional household altar to the dead in a Tlaxcalan village, with depictions of saints and offerings of *pan de muertos* (bread of the dead), fruit (mainly oranges and plantains), candles, and flowers (marigolds and daisies). Photo by Hugo Nutini.

FIGURE 7.10. Todos Santos (All Saints'/All Souls' Day), III: Graves decorated in traditional Indian fashion with marigold blossoms and dyed sand. Photo by Hugo Nutini.

FIGURE 7.11. Todos Santos (All Saints'/All Souls' Day), IV: Grave decorated in traditional Indian fashion with flowers (especially marigolds) and dyed sand and personalized with "Duerme M.A." (Sleep, M.A.). Photo by Hugo Nutini.

FIGURE 7.12. Fading traditions, I: Grave decorated only with marigolds for Todos Santos (All Saints'/All Souls' Day). Photo by Hugo Nutini.

FIGURE 7.13. Fading traditions, II: Household altar to the dead prepared for Todos Santos (All Saints'/All Souls' Day) but decorated carelessly and mainly with marigolds, baskets, and factory-made candles. Photo by Hugo Nutini.

FIGURE 7.14. Nahua men masquerading as *catrines* (city slickers with European clothing and facial features) during pre-Lent Carnaval in a Tlaxcalan village. Photo by Hugo Nutini.

In the best case, a new cultural synthesis will be forged quickly to provide a satisfying level of personal and group identity, community integration and participation, and a coherent philosophy of human life and experience. One suspects that this outcome is easier to achieve where the community remains rooted in the same spot throughout the transition, as in the case of formerly Indian communities that have become suburbs in the course of urban sprawl (Portal A. 1997). To a surprising extent, though, even most communities of rural-to-urban migrants eventually succeed in organizing themselves to satisfy not only essential economic but also social needs, as well as developing expressive outlets through religious participation, sports teams, home decoration, dress and adornment, and so forth (González de la Rocha 1994; Hirabayashi 1993; Lewis 1970: 413–460; Lomnitz 1975; Selby, Murphy, and Lorenzen 1990). Nevertheless, their mestizoized expressive culture pales in comparison to that of the Indian-traditional communities that most of them left behind only a few decades ago.

eight: EXPRESSION AND SOCIAL CLASS

This chapter deals with an aspect of social stratification that has received relatively little attention with regard to Mexico. We refer to *expressive culture and behavior* or, more succinctly, *expression* (see Nutini 1995, 2004, 2005; Roberts 1976; Roberts, Chiao, and Pandey 1975; Roberts and Chick 1979; Roberts and Golder 1970; Roberts and Nattrass 1980; Roberts and Sutton-Smith 1962). The hallmark of expression is that its motivation is basically noninstrumental; it is an end in itself for the individual carrying it out. At the same time, expression is closely related to social structure and can have real-world consequences. Furthermore, although expression is individually manifested, it is also shared culturally and behaviorally; in other words, it is a collective as well as an individual phenomenon.

The collective aspect of expression is what makes it useful in the analysis of social class. In a nutshell, differences between real classes are always marked by readily observable differences in expression, and even the nominal classes delineated by researchers typically entail some expressive differences. As the most immediately and directly perceived attribute of social class, expression is the most usual means by which the members of a class initially recognize and acknowledge one another and, in turn, are readily recognized as a distinctive social segment by nonmembers.

Expression is typically most pronounced in such clearly nonutilitarian aspects of culture as art, music, play, games, manners, etiquette, and adornment, but it also typically colors some aspects of warfare, economics, politics, stratification, subsistence, diet, and other mainly utilitarian arenas. Indeed, any aspect of culture or social structure may have an expressive component that configures behavior, whether temporarily or permanently, intermittently or continuously. More specifically, expression is carried out in three basic contexts: those in which behavior is primarily expressive, those in which behavior is at times expressive and at times instrumental, and those in which behavior is primarily instrumental.

Good examples of the first context are most forms of art and play (although there are professionals in both of these arenas whose goal is instrumental, making money). The traditional Japanese tea ceremony, the equestrian complex of Western aristocrats, and the indigenous Mexican cult of the dead are also examples of this first context. Most expression occurs in the second context, though, in which expressive and instrumental aims alternate or are intertwined. For instance, shopping for clothes can be alternatively expressive and instrumental, depending on clothing type or use; and food preparation for a family meal typically has both expressive and utilitarian components. The third context, in which behavior is primarily instrumental but is colored by expression, occurs less frequently and is less obvious to the casual observer, because the expressive components are often overpowered by the behavior's instrumentality. Examples are the military's special parade uniforms, as well as the hallmark colors of certain nonmilitary uniforms or aspects of them, such as the fireman's red suspenders, the traffic cop's bright blue coat, the priest's black cassock, or the physician's white smock. The names and slogans that soldiers paint on their equipment (e.g., tanks and airplanes) and ordnance (especially bombs) also exemplify this third context, as does the elaborate graffiti that urban gangs use to mark their territories.

Before defining specific kinds or types of expression, we need to introduce two more general concepts: *expressive array* and *expressive domain*. The former comprises the totality of patterns and contexts in which expression occurs in a given society or social segment. The culture of every society, as well as every social estate or real class within it, has a distinctive expressive array, although its total content and form, as well as contexts in which it is manifested, may overlap with those of adjacent social segments or cultural traditions. Thus the expressive arrays of Italians, French, Spanish, English, and Germans, for example, are all unique in content and form, but they all share the bulk of a European array. Within each of these national units, specific estates or classes (depending on time period) will have their own unique arrays while also sharing much with the societies of which they are part.

At the same time, estate or class divisions appear always to have been the most effective generators of differential expressive arrays, both within single cultural traditions (e.g., French, German, Mexican) and across them. For instance, the Mexican aristocracy's expressive array more closely resembles that of the Spanish or Italian aristocracy than it does that of, say, Mexico's plutocrats or upper-middle class. Yet about 80 percent of the Mexican aristocracy's expressive array is shared, in varying proportions, with the country's other classes. From the opposite perspective, it is the aristocracy's unique 20 percent that distinguishes it as a real class within Mexican society.

The expressive domain is the basic component of the expressive array. More specifically, it is any cultural context in which expressive behavior is realized with some degree of unity. The domain is not a fixed unit; rather, it can be aggregated or disaggregated to have broader or narrower scope, respectively, depending on viewpoint or the needs of analysis. For example, sports constitute an expressive domain in all subcultures and classes of Mexico. This domain may be broken down into the subdomains of individual and team sports; the former has such sub-subdomains as track and field, golf, and tennis, whereas the latter's sub-subdomains include soccer, baseball, American football, and the like. Track and field can be further analyzed into sprints, middle-distance running, and field events—and even further, into the 100-yard dash, mile run, shot put, and so on—each with its own expressive configuration as well as the expressive aspects that it shares with track and field as a whole.

Elsewhere, Nutini (1995, 2004) has delineated five kinds of expression: conflict, natural, terminal, palliative, and vicarious. We will discuss all but the first type, conflict expression, which is not germane to this book (see Nutini 2004: 218–219). *Natural (or inherent) expression* is a universal attribute of all societies or social groups. It is the highly visible common denominator of culture and behavior that distinguishes one society, class, or other group from another. *Terminal expression* is a last burst of refinement or creativity before the demise of a traditional institution or valued practice of a social group. The concept is exemplified in this book by the aristocracy's renaissance in Mexico City from the early 1930s to the early 1950s, when its numbers there were suddenly increased by aristocratic flight from the postrevolutionary turmoil in the provinces. For that period of about twenty-five years, the aristocracy was once again a vicarious attraction for the capital's masses and a magnet for the budding plutocracy; after that time, the public lost almost all interest, and the plutocracy began to assert itself as the new superordinate class.

Palliative expression is closely related to terminal expression, as it usually occurs in social groups that are undergoing drastic transformations. Certain forms of expression are defense mechanisms designed to palliate the pain experienced by individuals caught up in the changes. Again, the aristocracy provides the clearest examples, as when aristocratic individuals or families exalt their own class's traditional behavior—or even exaggerate certain aspects of it—in the face of the new plutocracy's expensive but "inauthentic" practices.

Finally, *vicarious expression* denotes a desire to emulate the culture of another social class. The concept has two aspects—vicarious perception and vicarious attraction—that correspond to class recognition and the desire for class mobility and come into play wherever the lifestyle or accoutrements of a different, typically higher ranking class are considered preferable. (See the final section of this chapter for an example of the much less prevalent emulation of a lower-ranking class.) Thus it is intimately associated with upward social mobility and is essential for a full accounting of it. For instance, we could not understand social climbing within the superordinate stratum on structural—that is, economic and political—grounds alone. Rather, the concept of vicarious expression is needed to explain why a rising plutocrat in possession of wealth and power that outstrip those of any aristocrat nevertheless wishes to learn aristocratic culture and transmit it to his or her children. Such a concept is also necessary to explain why most working-class parents want their children to acquire the formal education and outward behavior that will qualify them for white-collar rather than blue-collar jobs, even though the latter often pay much better.

The Upper Classes: Aristocracy, Plutocracy, Upper-Middle Class, and Political Class

For purposes of expressive analysis, the aristocracy, plutocracy, upper-middle class, and political class are best understood if treated together (see Nutini 2004, 2005). First, the plutocracy not only displaced the aristocracy as Mexico's ruling and prestige classes over the course of the twentieth century but also used the aristocracy as its model of upper-class behavior. Second, the upper-middle class was traditionally the social support group for the aristocracy and, more recently, for the plutocracy. Being socially close to these two superordinate classes, the upper-middle class developed a highly similar expressive array. Furthermore, a portion of it is a prestige class—the prestige-UMC—that still serves as the expressive model for upwardly mobile households in provincial cities, from which the aristocracy largely or entirely fled after the 1910–1920 Revolution.

The total expressive array of the upper stratum includes all major ethnographic categories, although it is quite unevenly distributed among them. The categories with the most expressive domains are material culture and technology, entertainment and recreation, and economics. Those with the least are religious organization and ritualism, kinship and social organization, and etiquette and protocol. In between are ethnicity and race, hobbies and sports, and celebrations of the life and yearly cycles.

There is also some variation among the sectors of this stratum. The most conservative is the prestige-UMC, whose array is focused on religious organization and ritualism, as well as etiquette and protocol. These are the domains that are always more prominent in groups that are no longer creating new forms of expression and whose exaggerated concern with lineage and tradition betrays their reduced economic standing. The most innovative are plutocrats, whose recently acquired wealth permits them to create expressive domains that are new to the local context, particularly in material culture and technology. The upper-middle class in general is not innovative. Instead, to the extent that their wealth permits, the vast majority of its members try to emulate the plutocracy, all the while disparaging the aristocratic models of the prestige-UMC. Finally, the small political class is expressively the poorest, although its upwardly mobile members share a large number of domains with the upper-middle class.

We can now turn to some specific aspects of superordinate expression. We have organized the discussion under three headings: the whitening syndrome, expressive emulation and provincial social mobility, and a comparison of the provincial and the Mexico City components of the national superordinate stratum.

THE WHITENING SYNDROME

The aristocracy, plutocracy, and upper-middle class perceive themselves as phenotypically white, and even the members of the latter two classes who are of Near Eastern descent quite often refer to themselves as

Europeans. This self-perception is essentially true, as very few members of these three classes exhibit Indian or African (Afro-Mexican) traits. Accordingly, plutocrats and upper-middle class people initially extend social recognition on the basis of phenotype.

The political class, in contrast, has many members who exhibit non-European phenotypes. Moreover, the members of this class tend to cultivate the image of having humble origins, and even if they are phenotypically European, they typically refer to themselves as mestizos. In turn, the rest of the superordinate stratum stereotypes the political class as a mestizo sector that is beyond their tolerable limits of non-European physical traits. Mainly for this reason, the political class is the least socially integrated sector of the superordinate stratum in provincial cities. In Mexico City, on the other hand, the political class is much more European in physical appearance and blends more easily with the other upper classes.

Nevertheless, the political class is so small—at no time having more than about 1,500 members in the whole country (Nutini 2005: 10–15)—that we can still speak of Central Mexico's superordinate sector as being primarily of European descent, despite its inclusion of a basically mestizo provincial political class. In turn, the overwhelming majority of Mexicans perceive the superordinate stratum as a whole as being the country's "whitest" sector. This perception is grounded not only in the stratum's physical appearance but also in its power and wealth, as these dimensions are typically linked in popular thinking.

More significant for understanding the mechanism of superordinate class formation is the expressive manipulation that takes place in this context. Briefly stated, physical traits that deviate from the stratum's preferred phenotype tend to be minimized or otherwise made more appealing through the whitening syndrome. The manipulations that accompany the syndrome involve self- and group-directed behavior and activities designed to induce people to regard an individual or a family as more European-appearing than is, in fact, the case. This altered perception is achieved by emphasizing cultural factors that lead people either to perceive actual physical features differently or to simply overlook them.

One of the most common strategies is to emphasize the refined behavior, good breeding, and elegance of the individual who is being whitened, playing on the racist assumption that white people are more naturally endowed with these qualities. Another strategy is to enhance the person's social background by asserting that for two or more generations his or her ancestors were of pure European stock but that some mixture with non-Europeans had occurred previously. Thus the phenotypical deviations from the European ideal are posed as recessive traits that somehow have come to the surface; in the vernacular, such a person is a "salto atrás," or throwback, a reference to one of the categories of the seventeenth-century casta system (see Chap. 3). This ruse is most successful when the individual or family being whitened is from another region, but it may also be invoked with reference to local persons. Regardless of the strategy, the aim is twofold: to induce the people of a particular social set to regard the individual or family as worthy of being accepted and to reduce the embarrassment or feeling of inferiority of the individual(s) being whitened.

The whitening syndrome is of little importance in the social interactions between plutocrats and members of the upper-middle class, given their high degree of phenotypical similarity. There are two circumstances in which it becomes important to them, however. The first involves the social inclusion of politicians whose non-European features are within the range that can be accommodated by the whitening syndrome. In fact, most of the important politicians who are sought after by the plutocracy and upper-middle class to grease the skids of business have light mestizo phenotypes. The second circumstance is the occasional marriage of one of their children to someone with a mestizo phenotype, usually the offspring of a mestizo politician or a well-to-do family of middle-class extraction. Today, these marriages are often initiated by superordinate offspring who go away to college and interact with the entire phenotypical spectrum of Mexican society. At any rate, the whitening syndrome is always stronger and more permanent in cases of intermarriage, which creates enduring kinship relations, than in cases involving only political considerations.

VICARIOUS EXPRESSION AND PROVINCIAL SOCIAL MOBILITY

Vicarious expression, or expressive emulation, underlies the fulfillment of upwardly mobile aspirations and to a significant extent shapes class consciousness. Although the process of expressive emulation is the same throughout any stratification system, the way it is enacted varies as people move from one class to another. In this section, we analyze how expressive emulation is carried out within the superordinate stratum of provincial cities and its role in achieving elite status.

Although the aristocratic hacendado class had a social presence in most provincial cities of Central Mexico until the early 1940s, it was a limited source of vicarious emulation for emerging local plutocrats. The hacendado lifestyle was impossible to replicate after the demise of the hacienda system and the remaining aristocracy's flight to Mexico City in the 1950s, and the provincial plutocracy was still too embryonic to have been directly influenced by the hacendado families before that decade. The exception is Puebla, which retained enough of these families to constitute a local aristocracy until about 1970. Elsewhere, the developing provincial plutocracy emulated the expressive complex of the prestige-UMC.

The prestige-UMC was never larger than four or five dozen households in the average provincial city. As we noted earlier, it long served as the hacendado aristocrats' social support group during the months they spent at their landed estates. By the early 1940s, it had developed a sophisticated expressive array that was mainly derived from the hacienda system. Its most notable domains extended from forms of entertainment, household decoration, and sports to presentation of self, wardrobe, and a large ensemble of behavior patterns (ranging from elegance in the celebration of events in the annual and life cycles to refined comportment at many social and religious occasions). This was the expressive array that served as the local model for the nascent plutocracy from the early 1940s until the early 1990s. Subsequently, the full complex became the exclusive preserve of the plutocracy, as neither the traditional prestige-UMC nor the upper-middle class that had developed alongside the new plutocracy was sufficiently wealthy to carry out several of these expressive domains (see below).

Another source of expressive emulation for the provincial plutocracy has been travel and business involvement abroad, especially after about 1980, when its wealth reached enormous proportions by local standards. Travel took them to Europe and other parts of the world, but their foreign business enterprises were located almost exclusively in the U.S. border states. The expressive domains that plutocrats learned abroad, directly by contact with foreign plutocrats and indirectly through other observations, are basically those that characterize plutocratic circles everywhere. In Europe, these domains were derived from vicarious emulation of the aristocracy but were subsequently modified and expanded by the plutocracy's much greater wealth. The same course was followed by Mexico's national plutocracy based largely in Mexico City, where it reached its most elaborate proportions.

By century's end, the original targets of vicarious expression—the dying aristocracy in Mexico City and the traditional prestige-UMC in provincial cities—had been marginalized in the expressive game. They simply did not have the wealth to keep up with the new plutocracy. The exclusive expressive domains of the provincial and national plutocracy are those that require an annual disposable income of more than U.S.$1 million. The richest plutocrats, especially those whose wealth exceeds U.S.$200 million, are first in various domains of conspicuous consumption, such as ostentatious mansions equipped with the most up-to-date surveillance and service gadgetry, as well as a wide range of the latest technology, from cars and airplanes to sound and visual systems.

More out of reach for the upper-middle class and even for second-rank plutocrats are expressive domains realized abroad, the most notable being traveling in grand style for months at a time (e.g., on safaris to Africa or Asia) and establishing palatial residences along the border with California, Arizona, and Texas. The latter is a trend that started modestly in the early 1970s and expanded to become a point of competition among the richest plutocrats; the value of these residences ranges from U.S.$15 million to $25 million. We should note, though, that less wealthy plutocrats, many politicians, and quite a few of the more affluent members of the upper-middle class also have residences, albeit much more modest ones, in those border states.

Compared to the provincial plutocracy, the national plutocracy of Mexico City is able to fulfill the foregoing expressive domains with much greater complexity and elaboration and also to include domains such as philanthropy, artistic exhibition and display, and other sophisticated endeavors largely absent from provincial settings. In other respects, the provincial superordinate stratum shares pretty much the same expressive array, although some expressive domains are exclusive to particular groups. For example, the provincial and national political classes have different trajectories after retiring from public office. Even the most financially successful provincial politicians do not usually become plutocrats by engaging in entrepreneurial activities, thereby generating even more wealth after retiring from politics. In contrast, successful national politicians almost invariably become high-flying plutocrats on leaving office, mainly because they have amassed much greater fortunes during their terms. On the other hand, even the rare provincial politician who achieves wealth comparable to second-rank plutocrats almost always maintains a low profile after retiring from office, mainly to avoid the scrutiny and criticism that are much more likely to occur in the relatively confined environment of provincial cities.

MEXICO CITY AND THE PROVINCES: EXPRESSIVE ARRAYS COMPARED

The provincial and capital expressive systems are highly similar in three important senses. First, their expressive arrays are similar, and all types of expression have equal functions in the two systems. Second, vicarious emulation proceeds in the same fashion in both systems. Just as the national plutocracy in Mexico City emulated the aristocracy during its period of gestation and maturation (late 1920s to late 1980s), the provincial plutocracy absorbed the basic domains of aristocratic expression, secondhand from the prestige-UMC, during its own emergent stages (early 1940s to early 1990s). In both cases, the plutocrats' goal was to achieve an elevated social status commensurate with its newly acquired great wealth and power. Third, both the aristocracy in Mexico City and the prestige-UMC in provincial cities are rapidly disappearing as functionally distinct social classes within the upper stratum.

The demise of the aristocracy and the prestige-UMC reflects the decreasing relevancy of prestige classes, which have survived mainly as an expressive model for the newly rich and powerful. They are becoming irrelevant because the Mexican stratification system is evolving from one in which expressive factors were significant in social class formation to one in which structural factors are its main determinants. This change is affecting the Mexican stratification system from top to bottom, and it is becoming increasingly like that of the more industrialized countries, especially the United States.

There are also three important differences between Mexico City and the provincial cities in terms of elite expression. First, the size of the provincial expressive array is only about half that of Mexico City's, which is also much more refined and sophisticated. More is involved here than the usual cultural differences between center and periphery or the wealth differential noted earlier. Rather, the differences reflect primarily the absence of a direct aristocratic expressive influence on the provincial plutocracy, coupled with its emulation of foreign plutocrats.

Second, neither the provincial plutocracy nor the upper-middle class in general has emulated the aristocracy's and national plutocracy's expressive emphasis on kinship, religion, and the past. Rather, the core of the provincial plutocracy's local array is material culture and technology—which its members can well afford, which the upper-middle class in general has emulated, and which the traditional prestige-UMC typically cannot afford. Indeed, material culture and technology, emulated mostly from foreign plutocratic models, are the domains in which both the provincial and the national plutocracies are creating their own expressive array.

Third, conspicuously absent or diminished among the provincial upper classes are the refined collections, fine cuisine, decoration and display, and etiquette and protocol that are diagnostic domains of the superordinate expressive array in Mexico City. More specifically, collecting by the provincials is for the most part confined to cars and other technological objects; they have little interest in collecting the paintings, antique furniture, pre-Hispanic objects, and other fine arts that grace the houses of the superordinate stratum in Mexico City. Instead, the provincial household may contain very expensive decorative items but often has a kitschy (*cursi*) appearance; it lacks the striking elegance and concern with decoration and display that characterize most superordinate households in Mexico City. Also, the traditional Mexican haute cuisine, in which aristocratic households in the capital traditionally excelled, does not exist in the provinces; in fairness, we should note that this art is now dying out in the capital as well. Fourth, the provincial upper classes lack and sometimes even scorn the keen sense of etiquette and protocol of the traditional elites, such as table seating order, proper tea service, and specialized clothing for social occasions and sports. The provincial prestige-UMC has preserved them to some extent, however, by virtue of its own traditions and its history of close contact with hacendado families.

The Solid-Middle Class

Solid-middle class individuals and families are consumed with material concerns, always looking to get ahead economically and to avoid going down in the social scale. More than any other social class in the whole stratification system, the SMC is concerned with making sufficient money to satisfy vicarious modes of expression that they observe directly from the upper-middle class and indirectly from television, newspapers, and magazines, as well as from limited travel outside Mexico, primarily to the U.S. border states. As we saw in Chapter 5, the SMC is the most upwardly striving sector of Mexican society, with only a minority of members who are not trying to climb socially. Apart from its dedication to vicarious expression, the SMC shares in the natural expression of the other middle classes, by which we mean that their basic arrays include the same sports, many forms of entertainment, and many domains of expression associated with urban living (e.g., patronizing exclusive stores, attending musical or stage events, and sponsoring art exhibitions).

SMC vicarious expression is centered on the most visible domains: house, interior decoration, wardrobe, personal demeanor, proper speech, and public comportment. While their vicarious emulation may be influenced by what they see on television and read in newspapers and magazines, the immediate input is what they directly observe or imagine that upper-middle-class people do. In their attempt to become more like them, SMC individuals or families are hoping to enhance their chances of being accepted by them.

If their upward striving is to be successful, SMC people must avoid being scorned as *arribistas* (social climbers) with kitschy tastes. Thus they usually do not begin making a concerted effort to emulate the upper-middle class until they have achieved a certain economic threshold: a home in an elite residential section of the city and other readily visible symbols of affluence, such as expensive cars, the latest household appliances, and enrollment of their children in the "best" local schools. Reaching this threshold may require many years of hard work. Thereafter, families who play the upward mobility game well are quickly accepted; acceptance for others is slower and for some never proffered. After three or four years of unsuccessful effort, rejected families typically turn vociferously egalitarian.

It is typically the SMC wife, rather than her husband, who initially urges that the couple should make a concerted effort at upward mobility. She does so on the basis of her exposure to upper-middle-class behavior at social, religious, and entertainment events. Usually, her husband readily agrees, and together they decide on a specific strategy. If they do not already live in an elite neighborhood, their first step will be to buy or, preferably, build a house in such a setting.

This first step is easy, compared to the task of outfitting the house with the proper furniture, basic accessories, and art. These purchases require the advice of an interior decorator, preferably one from Mexico City. There is considerable risk that decorators from the megalopolis will both grossly overcharge their provincial customers and convince them to buy expensive but kitschy items that would be difficult to sell to the more sophisticated customers in the capital. For the upwardly mobile members of the provincial SMC, however, a gaudily decorated house is not necessarily a drawback, because many of their betters in the local upper-middle class will have fallen into the same trap in their own upward strivings.

Along with acquiring and decorating a new house, the couple—especially the wife—will begin to practice what they have observed of upper-middle-class personal demeanor, dress (tailor-made clothing, natural fibers, etc.), and patterns of public speech (e.g., using precise diction [*hablado* instead of *hablao*] and generally avoiding vulgar expletives and popular slang). They also begin to inform themselves systematically about appropriate behavior, through reading the social sections of newspapers and magazines and by observing equivalent details in television programs.

These steps having been accomplished, the SMC couple invites one or more upper-middle-class families to their home for an event, such as a cocktail party, specifically to demonstrate that they run a proper household and behave as properly as those whom they are trying to emulate and impress. Previously, the two households will have had casual or business contacts, and frequently their children attend the same school. If the invitation is reciprocated, it is a sure sign of acceptance that generally leads to a permanent relationship.

The next step is taken by the upper-middle-class family and is aimed at generating acceptance for the SMC family. The means include invitations to important events in the life or annual cycle, introductions to prominent upper-middle-class families, and, in general, facilitation of interaction of the SMC couple and their children with their upper-middle-class counterparts. Once the SMC family has been well accepted in their new social milieu, intermarriage may follow, signaling full incorporation into the upper-middle class.

From beginning to end, the process may take as little as five years or as long as ten. It is complete once the SMC family both considers itself and is perceived as upper-middle class. In other words, upward mobility entails both actually belonging, in terms of displaying the material and behavioral accoutrements, and being perceived as belonging to the higher social class.

The whitening syndrome always accompanies the expressive emulation process when the SMC individuals' appearance departs from European phenotypes. The syndrome has the same two components described for the upper classes: efforts of the upwardly mobile to encourage perception of themselves as being more European than they actually are and collusion by members of the superior class to facilitate this perception.

The Provincial Lower-Middle and Working Classes

We deal here only with the provincial situation because Mexico City is too diversified for succinct treatment. In the provincial context, the lower-middle and working classes are similar in expressive behavior. The loci and emphases of expression are somewhat different, however, largely because the working class is generally closer culturally and socially to the village situation.

Provincial lower-middle- and working-class households, like their SMC counterparts, are very concerned with material acquisition, but their expressive emulation is subordinated to the requirements of securing what they regard as a proper standard of living: decent housing, necessary household appliances, adequate clothing, appropriate diet, and enough money for basic forms of entertainment, such as an occasional movie. The SMC families with whom they interact are one source of their rather limited vicarious emulation, but much more important are newspapers, magazines, television, and direct observations during their occasional trips to Mexico City. On the other hand, upward mobility is not a primary concern for most lower-middle- and working-class families, and when this concern does arise, it is directed more by the desire to improve their economic lot than by expressive emulation.

The exceptions to the foregoing are mostly the relatively affluent lower-middle-class owners of small shops, many of whom not only identify with the SMC but also aspire to attain that status. This small group, probably no more than 5 percent of their class in the average provincial city, assiduously emulates the SMC, just as the latter expressively emulates the upper-middle class. Moreover, the material domains and patterns of behavior required for upward mobility are basically the same in both cases. Entry into the SMC is faster, however, because SMC families are less uppity and fastidious.

The lower-middle-class effort to move into the SMC is fraught with the danger of expressive blunders, owing to its members' lower degree of formal education and lesser exposure to sociocultural situations outside of their own class. Upwardly mobile families engage in expressive emulation especially in such domains as household decoration, personal behavior, and wardrobe. In many lower-middle class (and some working-class) families, college-educated offspring play a significant role in this expressive transformation, influencing their parents to make changes in these domains. They must do so cautiously, though, because they risk derision from both the SMC and those within their own class if they appear to be putting on airs.

We now turn to the specific domain of household decoration, dealing first with the working class. In the main room (not necessarily a living room) of the working-class house, decoration plays a minor role. Typical are wall calendars, clocks, family photographs, religious icons, and such trinkets as seashell ashtrays. Furnishings in this main room are sparse, typically including a table, a breakfront (*trastero*) to store dishes and cups, several metal store-bought or wooden homemade chairs, and occasionally a trunk and/or a sofa-chair. Finally, the abode itself is a more important domain of expression than its interior decoration. If they inhabit a house, families typically decorate the outside with potted plants and vines, or if there is sufficient outdoor space, they might plant a small garden. If they live in an apartment, they typically use storage trunks or build alcoves and shelves to relieve the cramped appearance of the small spaces.

The transition to lower-middle-class status is marked by significant changes in household decoration. In fact, household decoration increases in expressive significance as people move up the social scale, and it is the most important diagnostic trait of class membership in the middle stratum. Of most importance here, the main room of the house becomes a living room furnished with store-bought sofas, sofa-chairs, upholstered chairs, a center coffee table, and, occasionally, a breakfront. The walls might be decorated with posters, bucolic paintings on velvet, or tanned pelts of wild animals.

The passage to SMC status is marked by further elaboration in household decoration. The living room furniture is more elegant, and there is a significant concern with blending the colors and shades of furniture and the curtains, this last item generally being absent from lower-middle-class houses, the windows of which may occasionally have *visillos* (common lace curtains). Also, oil paintings and watercolors by local artists may now decorate the living room walls.

Turning to religious expression, the only major differences between the lower-middle and working classes occur in the physical manifestations of Catholicism. For example, working-class families prefer the rural, folk Catholic form and decoration of the household altar to the saints of their devotion—complete with candles, statues and pictures of saints, wooden or metal crosses, incense burners, and so on (see Nutini 1988: 186–196; Sandstrom 1991: 111, 217), whereas lower-middle-class families, most of whom are more than a generation removed from their rural origins, do not. Also, religious rites and ceremonies take place almost exclusively in church for lower-middle-class families, whereas many of them still are carried out at home in the working class. On the other hand, Catholic beliefs and ideology are the same in both classes. Furthermore, for both classes, the cult of the saints and the traditional religious covenant binding individuals and the deity remain basically unchanged from the folk context (see Chap. 7), except that the covenant no longer has a collective component, becoming centered on the individual worshiper instead.

The expressive realization of compadrazgo, kinship, and celebrations connected with the life and annual cycles is the same (except as noted above) in both lower-middle and working-class families—and, again, is quite close to the rustic folk situation. They evoke the highly ritualized nature of personal interaction in these aspects of social and religious life, which urban living has changed but not appreciably secularized. The behavioral ideal of lower-middle- and working-class urbanites, most of whom are less than three generations from their village roots, retains an expressive component that changes only if the transition is made to the SMC. In that event, compadrazgo, kinship, and the fulfillment of the life and ritual cycles cease to be highly sacred institutions with strong spiritual compulsion behind them. Instead, they become regulated by orthodox Catholicism and by economic considerations that minimize cost and/or promote the individual's or household's welfare.

Finally, the whitening syndrome occurs among the upwardly mobile families of the lower-middle class but not as prominently as in the superordinate stratum and the SMC. It is diminished by the tendency of most such lower-middle-class families to gravitate toward SMC families who are phenotypically most similar to them, that is, more mestizo in appearance, in the hope of more ready acceptance. On the other hand, the current generation of lower-middle-class college students is less worried about phenotype and thus much less likely to give it an expressive role in its quest for upward mobility. Rather, the aim is to generate the perception that they are as competent in the professions or in business as the SMC or the upper-middle class. This attitude strikes many SMC and upper-middle-class individuals as uppity, a reflection of their racist view that only persons with basically European phenotypes have an inherent capacity to succeed in the professions and big business.

More generally, the whitening syndrome in the lower-middle and working classes simply reflects a deep-seated tendency in Mexican culture to favor European-appearing individuals. For example, lighter-skinned children are typically considered prettier and are often treated preferentially by their parents, and they also may be more sought after as potential spouses when they reach adulthood. In fact, the racism that both underlies and reinforces the whitening syndrome is present at all levels of the Mexican stratification system and is an obstacle to be overcome in the ongoing struggle to build a more egalitarian and just society. As we made clear in Chapter 2, however, Mexican racism pales when compared to that of the United States or, for that matter, of such other Latin American countries as Guatemala, Brazil, Bolivia, Ecuador, or Peru.

Downward Emulation

Thus far, we have treated expressive emulation exclusively in terms of upward social mobility. That is indeed its typical context, but Central Mexico also presents a peculiar twist in the opposite direction. We refer to postrevolutionary, governmentally promoted vicarious emulation of selected cultural aspects of the region's lowest-ranking social aggregate—the traditional village Indians. In this case, the desired outcome was not social mobility but rather increased personal authenticity through tangible identification with the nation's pre-Hispanic roots. The most notable manifestations of this phenomenon occurred around the mid-twentieth century, during the heyday of *indigenismo* (Indianism) and the attempt to create an authentic Mestizo Mexico.

As we noted in Chapter 2, postrevolutionary politicians and intellectuals promoted indigenismo and mestizaje in an attempt to forge a new, non-European national identity. Making the idea of a Mestizo Mexico broadly palatable required rehabilitating the Indian part of the mixture after some four centuries of official and intellectual Eurocentricity. Anthropologists, painters and muralists, novelists, journalists, choreographers, cinematographers, politicians, and a host of other middle-class (and a few elite) intellectuals quickly volunteered or were enlisted in this effort. So successful were they that their intellectual and artistic creations featuring Indian artifacts and themes became iconic symbols of Mexicanness, both at home and abroad. The use of "Indian" foods, clothing, adornment, decorations, and names for one's children penetrated deeply into the Mexican middle classes for a time, occasionally to the point of fervent anti-Hispanicism (see Friedlander 1975). Among other things, it has resulted in the large number of middle-class people with such names as Cuauhtemoc and Xóchitl even today and, for a time, in a personal style we might call the "Frida Kahlo neo-Indian look." Collecting and displaying pre-Hispanic artifacts of all kinds but especially of ceramics (everything from spindle whorls to vases and pots) also became fashionable among the well-to-do.

Few of these individuals had a deep knowledge about or empathy with traditional village Indian culture. In actuality, they did not need either, because indigenismo—itself largely a middle-class movement, albeit one strongly encouraged by the government for its own purposes—presented them with an idealized and nonthreatening preselection of disconnected traits that they could embrace either singly or together and without disrupting any facet of their largely urbanized, industrialized, and commercialized lifestyles.

Another group of downward emulators are the millions of middle-class foreign tourists, mostly from the United States and Western Europe at mid-twentieth century but today from all over the world, who also define Mexicanness largely in terms of its Indian cultures, both prehistoric and contemporary. To authenticate their status as international travelers who have acquired exotic knowledge and tastes, these tourists have purchased many millions of such iconically "Indian" items as onyx carvings, obsidian-handled letter openers, dolls dressed in colorful costumes, high-crowned hats, woven bulrush mats, ceramic objects with rustic decorations, women's shawls and full-length pleated skirts, men's serapes, or multicolored blankets to be used as sofa or sideboard throws. They also have snapped millions of photographs of "Indian" markets, festivals, dance performances, and the like.

That these "Indian" material items, theatrical performances, and cultural tropes have little connection with the overwhelmingly modernized Mexican nation or the daily life of the great majority of its citizens has not dampened their appeal to the international visitors. It is doubtful that many of these visitors fail to notice this disconnectedness. It is more likely that they have this awareness but dismiss it as irrelevant, because they are searching for the very same kind of Mexicanness that the Mexican promoters of indigenismo sought to create, namely, connectedness to the country's "authentic" roots.

CONCLUSION

In the course of this book, we have portrayed the evolution of Central Mexico's social stratification system from the moment of the Spanish Conquest through the end of the twentieth century. The major turning points were the de jure abolition of estate stratification on independence from Spain in 1821 and its de facto replacement with social class stratification following the 1910–1920 Revolution. This was so even in most of the countryside, although in a few relatively isolated zones—so-called refuge regions—vestiges of the estate system survived up to the end of the twentieth century. Following the Revolution, social mobility resulted in a substantial middle stratum but not the middle-class majority that social philosophers have proclaimed as the national ideal ever since the Reform period of the 1850s. Instead, Central Mexico finished the twentieth century with a lower-stratum majority.

In this chapter, we explore two aspects of social class in Central Mexico at the beginning of the twenty-first century. The first is the erosion of many of the visible hallmarks of class membership during the second half of the twentieth century, especially in the middle and lower strata. Thus the middle and lower classes that social scientists delineate today are mostly nominal distinctions that facilitate social analysis rather than "real" groupings with distinctive lifestyles, class consciousness, and internal social cohesion (see Portes 2003). The second matter we entertain here is the persistence of a poor, lower-stratum majority in Central Mexico despite considerable geographic and social mobility during the twentieth century. To anticipate, we envisage a lower-stratum majority in Central Mexico for at least the next several decades.

Real versus Nominal Social Classes

In Mexico, as well as in the rest of the Americas and in Europe, the social classes that replaced the estates and subestates of the previous stratification system were initially as readily visible as the estates had been. In other words, they were real (rather than nominal) classes with clear differences in occupation, formal training, diet, wardrobe, house type, residential zone, and expressive culture. During the second half of the twentieth century, however, many of these once-clear differences were eroded or even erased. Mass education, mass communications media, mass production of goods and services, mass geographic mobility, and substantial social mobility led to an unprecedented extent of cultural blending, or hybridization, across social systems, countries, even whole continents (see García Canclini 1990). In the process, many of the formerly reliable and readily visible signs of class membership either disappeared or became unreliable indicators of social placement. In terms of wardrobe, for example, the lower classes dressed up, adopting the garments or styles of the urban middle classes, while many members of the upper classes dressed down by adopting those same garments or styles in daily life. Denim jeans and khaki pants became Mexico's (and much of the world's) everyday wear, first for men and then, although still to a lesser extent, also for women.

In the Córdoba area of central Veracruz, for instance, we know several wealthy men, each worth U.S.$10–50 million dollars, whose daily wear is faded blue jeans and print work shirts, probably purchased at Wal-Mart (Walmex) or equivalent stores, and whose daytime vehicles are road-weary pickup trucks. In other words, in their informal, workaday public presentation, they are difficult to distinguish from many members of the lower-middle and working classes. Of course, if we followed them home at the end of the workday, we would be confronted with their obviously upper-class residential style and expensive expressive culture that would be beyond the financial reach of the nonrich. At the same time, however, many of the kitchen appliances and much of the home entertainment equipment found in these elite homes are now also present in most homes in all classes, although usually in less expensive models.

The comparable melding of consumption patterns and even of worldviews within the United States has led some social scientists to proclaim the death of social classes in postindustrial societies. For example, the anthropologist Walter Goldschmidt (1999: 64) has asserted that "social classes do not exist" in the present-day United States, a position he first espoused a half century earlier (Goldschmidt 1955; cf. Goldschmidt 1950). The same conclusion about the United States is announced by the title of the sociologist Paul Kingston's book, *The Classless Society* (2000).

Of course, these authors recognize the existence of economic inequality and differential social status in the United States. They argue, however, that such differences, even if they are great, do not automatically establish social classes in any "real," or existential, sense. It is crucial to keep in mind that the "classless" quality that they assert for the present-day United States refers to an absence of classes within their "realist orientation to class analysis." This viewpoint holds that "real" social classes—in contrast to researcher-designated, nominal social classes—exist only where "there are relatively discrete, hierarchically ordered social groups, each with distinctive cultural experiences" (Kingston 2000: 16). A real class is "a substantial group having common economic circumstances and relatively distinct life experiences" (53); in other words, it has a distinctive subculture.

Kingston (2000: 168–178) cannot find empirical evidence of any real classes in the present-day United States, not even at the very top or the very bottom. Goldschmidt (1955: 1215) once argued—correctly, in our view—that social class is more perceptible "at either end of the hierarchy than it is in the middle" in the United States. Nevertheless, his viewpoint generally coincides with Kingston's, because he argues that any definable classes in the contemporary United States are "analytical and not in the culture" (Goldschmidt 1999: 62)—in short, nominal rather than real.

In this book we have suggested that the "classless society" model has increasing validity in present-day Central Mexico. This is not to say that there are no real social classes there, however, as real classes quite clearly still exist at the very top and, in a more restricted sense, at the very bottom of the Central Mexican stratification system (cf. Goldschmidt 1955: 1214–1215). At the top, we find the socially cohesive and highly self-aware aristocracy, plutocracy, political class, and prestige-UMC, the cream of the upper-middle class. All told, these upper classes constitute less than 1 percent of the country's population (see Table 0.1), and since the Revolution, they have resided almost entirely in the country's larger cities, especially Mexico City. The aristocracy is disappearing as a distinctive class component of this upper stratum, and the upper-middle class is in decline as a cohesive unit, but the plutocracy and the political classes remain highly distinctive, real classes.

At the very bottom of Central Mexico's stratification system, we also find real social classes, but these are exclusively in the countryside and strictly localized. We refer to the remaining Indian-traditional villagers, whose shared agrarian rootedness and sacred institutions provide internal social cohesion to the whole village or to a class (or classes) within it and whose overt ethnicity still provides them with a protective barrier against national-mestizo society. All told, ethnic Indians constitute only about 10 percent of the national population, and probably no more than 25 percent of them still reside in the traditional villages we have in mind here. Lest we be misunderstood, we reiterate that we are speaking of these villagers as constituting real social classes only at a strictly localized, municipio level. On a national, state, or regional scale, in contrast, there are no real social classes based on ethnicity, Indian or otherwise, nor do we see any possibility even of constructing meaningful nominal ethnic classes at those levels.

In the remaining 95 percent or more of present-day Central Mexican society, we have distinguished five classes: upper-middle (excluding the prestige-UMC at its apex, as explained above), solid-middle, lower-middle, working, and marginal. Their proportionate representation in the Central Mexican population is roughly as follows: upper-middle class, 2 percent; SMC, 10 to 15 percent (highest in Mexico City); lower-middle class, 20 to 25 percent; working class, 30 to 35 percent; marginal class, 25 to 30 percent (see Table 0.1). These divisions do not exhaust the possibilities, of course. For instance, in some rural areas it might be possible to distinguish a peasant (small-scale agrarian) and/or a ranchero (medium-scale agrarian) class, and perhaps one or the other would still be a real class. While conceding that possibility, if not at present then certainly in the recent past, we caution that both peasants (except the remaining Indian-traditional villagers) and rancheros have lost or are losing their distinctive, occupation-derived lifestyles and social cohesion in most of Central Mexico (see Kearney 1999; Lomnitz-Adler 1992: 183–186).

In terms of the real/nominal distinction, the lower-middle, working, and marginal segments are clearly nominal classes. Of course, this characterization does not mean that these distinctions are made willy-nilly. In fact, each of these classes can be seen as occupying a loosely defined economic (occupational and/or financial) and political (power) position within its locale or in the Central Mexican stratification system as a whole, and internally each has a common denominator of other cultural traits (consumption patterns, religious practices, kinship organization, expressive culture, etc.). At the same time, however, these groupings lack both social cohesiveness and consistency in life experiences or subculture (after Goldschmidt 1955, 1999; Kingston 2000: 53). Rather, their constituent individuals and households share life experiences and cultural traits or patterns to varying extents, both with each other and with adjacent groupings. Not surprisingly, these nominal classes are also largely lacking in class consciousness.

On the other hand, the prestige-UMC is arguably a real class. The case is strongest with regard to the provincial cities of a few decades ago, where this class remained both socially cohesive and distinctive in its aristocratized expressive culture, where it still provided the other middle segments with their most usual models for upward mobility, and where it was still cultivated by the local plutocracy. The case is weaker today, especially in Mexico City and perhaps in some of the larger provincial cities, where the upper-middle class is rapidly losing these very distinctive attributes. We will return to this last point in a moment.

The SMC is more problematic, because the case could be made for it as either a real or a nominal class. We have characterized it as a collection of professionals, owners of medium-sized businesses, medium-sized farmers, middle-level bank officials, and local, state, and federal government bureaucrats. We also noted that the SMC is virtually indistinguishable from the main component of the upper-middle class in terms of residence, kinship, and household organization. These characteristics, considered alone, make a strong case for the SMC as a nominal class. On the other hand, most SMC individuals have a good sense of their relative socioeconomic standing; they speak of themselves as the sector that makes the social machinery work, contrasting their own honesty, sincerity, and hard work with the dishonesty, cynicism, and graft of the upper stratum. In other words, they express the consciousness of kind that we would expect of a real class. Yet, in another odd twist, they typically make no effort to organize themselves for political, civic, or charitable action. They are, rather, inert critics of "the system," typically abstaining from participation in civil society.

The contradictions do not stop there. The SMC, despite its biting criticism of its socioeconomic betters, is the most upwardly striving component of the entire stratification system. When Mexicans poke fun at social climbers, they usually have in mind the SMC, and the trait they most ridicule is its members' obsessive efforts to "improve" themselves, an expression of their longing for upper-class acceptance and their fear of losing status among their peers (see Careaga 1974: 63–71). This is precisely the kind of insecurity expressed through emulative consumerism and other attempts at status enhancement that we would expect in a pecking order consisting of a gradient of statuses but not of real classes (see Goldschmidt 1955, 1999). In short, the SMC members' great insecurity about who they are and what they want to be, socially, combined with their disinclination to organize themselves for any civic purpose, undermines the argument for regarding them as constituting a real social class. Thus we believe the best solution is to treat the SMC as a nominal class.

In contrast, the real classes of the upper stratum show none of the middle-class status insecurity displayed by the SMC. Although the plutocratic class's rise during the second half of the twentieth century was accompanied by self-conscious striving in the form of expressive emulation of the dying aristocracy and, more recently, by a fascination with expensive consumer items, plutocrats have a keen sense of their superordinacy. This self-assuredness was a hallmark of the aristocracy during its heyday, of course. This secure awareness of their social distinctiveness and superiority allowed both the aristocracy and the prestige-UMC element of the old regime, as well as today's plutocrats, to associate freely with people of the middle and lower strata on many social occasions without discomfort or loss of status.

Ironically, such fluidity of interaction is more characteristic of relatively rigid stratification systems with superordinate real classes than it is of looser, more fluid systems with nominal classes such as we find in the United States today. In the more rigid systems, the enduring boundaries are so evident that relaxed interaction with socially inferior persons poses no threat to the superordinate individuals or groups. Because no one could lose sight of the obvious social differential, no one stands to either lose or gain status through such casual contact. In Mexico, the saying *juntos pero no revueltos*—together but not scrambled—captures the easy ambience of socially mixed gatherings.

Whether the self-assuredness of the upper stratum will long endure is now in doubt, however. The prestige classes, with their distinctive expressive culture that served as a model for the newly rich and powerful, are losing their importance in the Mexican stratification system. The clear trend is toward the demise of the old aristocracy in Mexico City and of the prestige-UMC in provincial cities as distinctive social classes within the upper stratum. They are becoming irrelevant because the expressive arrays that announced and reinforced their dominance until the mid-twentieth century (e.g., lineage, refined behavior, tradition) are rapidly declining in importance for social class formation.

Simply put, claims to upper-class status today are only rarely rooted in prestigious landed wealth or buttressed by documented antiquity or a heraldic tradition stretching back to the Spanish Conquest or even to late-medieval Spanish nobility and gentry. Quite the contrary, the plutocracy that is now the dominant element of the upper stratum is of mid- to late-twentieth-century origin and is invested mainly in large-scale and often far-flung commercial, industrial, and financial operations. Its prosperity depends on the manipulation of all these assets as fungible wealth, not as heirlooms or patrimony to be preserved and displayed as hallmarks of an exalted heritage. Not surprisingly, the stratification system is changing to one in which such structural factors as power, wealth, formal education, and occupation are the main determinants of class membership.

In short, the system is becoming more and more like that of the fully industrialized countries. Thus Central Mexico seems eventually destined to become as "classless," that is, as lacking in real (vs. nominal) classes, as the United States is said to be at present. If so, the Mexican upper classes will probably become less certain of their social superiority and, accordingly, less inclined to associate casually with members of inferior social classes.

The Enduring Lower-Stratum Majority

Central Mexico ended the twentieth century with an urban, lower-stratum majority. Economists disagree on just how much of this population is "poor," but most studies showed a national poverty rate of 45 percent or higher during the last half of the twentieth century. Furthermore, poverty was clearly increasing at century's end, as even the federal government's preferred measuring method shows that the national poverty rate climbed from 44.2 percent in 1992 to 53.8 percent in 2000. On the other hand, Mexico's leading poverty researcher, Julio Boltvinik, has consistently argued for much higher rates. His studies revealed a national poverty rate of 75.3 percent and an urban rate of 69.1 percent in 2000, up from 61.7 in 1989 (Damián and Boltvinik 2003: 528).

These figures are surprising, even shocking, in light of the tremendous social mobility that followed the 1910–1920 Revolution and continued at a rapid pace through midcentury, probably reaching a peak in the 1960s. Thus the question that has to be answered is, Why didn't Mexico as a whole and especially its core area, Central Mexico, end the century with a middle-class majority? Five answers come readily to mind.

First, Mexico entered the twentieth century with a minuscule upper class and a very small middle class, together probably constituting only about 15 percent of Central Mexico's population, while the remaining 85 percent was lower class and mostly impoverished (cf. Granato and Mostkoff 1990; Stern 1994). In other words, Mexico had a very long way to go if it was to become the predominantly middle-class country envisioned by pre-Revolution social philosophers.

Second, much of the social mobility that indeed occurred during the last two-thirds of the twentieth century was movement from the marginal to the working class. We do not want to make light of this kind of mobility, which lifted many households from extreme poverty (in which life's most basic needs could be met inconsistently or, in many cases, never adequately) into moderate poverty (in which comforts were relatively few but basic physical needs were regularly met, albeit minimally). Our point is, rather, that this considerable mobility did not contribute to the formation of a middle-class majority.

Third, after midcentury, the urban lower classes were continuously replenished by waves of impoverished immigrants from the countryside. This phenomenon was largely the result of government policies that sacrificed agricultural prosperity to industrial growth by suppressing producer prices for basic foodstuffs in order to curtail urban pressure for higher wages. It is true that many families in the post-Revolution generation of rural-to-urban émigrés experienced genuine upward mobility in their new setting. By midcentury, however, urban demand for low-skilled labor was largely saturated. Thus the continuing migration stream converted rural poverty into urban poverty at least as often as it led to upward mobility.

Fourth, middle-class formation was slowed, even blocked in many instances, by the "permanent crisis" that began with the 1982 "debt crisis" and continued through the December 1994 "peso crisis" and on into the twenty-first century. In both cases, the peso had to be sharply devalued on the international money market. Devaluation drove up the cost of both imported finished goods and domestic manufactures with imported components. The result was runaway inflation. To illustrate, a visitor to Mexico City could live modestly but comfortably on 100 pesos per day, including a simple but clean and safe hotel room with bath, in the early 1960s; by the early 1990s, in contrast, admission to a pay toilet in the city cost 1,000 pesos. Through it all, the corrupt and state-controlled labor unions that served as gatekeepers to formal sector employment kept wages low, ostensibly to promote industrial and commercial growth but at the same time enriching the upper-class investors in those sectors. Thus "the great majority of people in Mexico, those born after 1980, have experienced stagnation of real income throughout their entire lifetime" (Griffin and Ickowitz 2003: 577). In the 1993–2003 period, in fact, most Mexicans experienced a decline in real wages (adjusted for inflation), regardless of whether they were blue-collar or white-collar workers (Polaski 2003: 24).

Fifth, and finally, achieving or maintaining middle-class status has always been harder in Mexico than in the United States. In the first place, salaries for the same or comparable middle-class jobs are much higher in the United States—more than eleven times higher in 1994, when Rani Schwartz (1994: 38–39, 162–165) did a comparative study. At the same time, "the level of prices in Mexico is similar to that of the United States, in the products that the middle class consumes and which characterize it as such" (36). This is generally true even if the products are manufactured in Mexico by subsidiaries of U.S. companies, because transportation costs of components, tariffs and value-added taxes, fewer economies of scale, and market bottlenecks add to the prices of Mexican products, even if they are made with cheaper labor. In fact, some middle-class "essentials" are actually more costly in Mexico. For instance, when gasoline cost $1.00 per gallon in most of the United States, it cost $1.44 in Mexico; when installation of a telephone in the United States averaged about $42, it cost $478 in Mexico City; and comparable automobiles were two or three times as expensive in Mexico (see Schwartz 1994: 36–43, 159–161). Furthermore, bank credit is costly and difficult to obtain, and credit card interest is typically two or three times higher than in the United States.

Long-Term Continuities

We do not claim to be clairvoyant, but we foresee no major changes in the class structure of Central Mexico in the near future. In other words, we think that Central Mexico will have a lower-stratum majority for several more decades. Five factors lead us to this conclusion.

First, the urban, lower-stratum majority almost certainly will continue to be replenished—overwhelming any loss through upward mobility—by the migration of the rural poor to the cities, where almost all of them will join the poorest sectors. Owing to neoliberal trade policies, Mexico lost 1.3 million agricultural jobs (including self-employment) from the beginning of 1994 through the end of 2002 (Audley 2003: 6; Polaski 2003: 19–20; also see Echánove and Steffen 2003). By mid-2003 about one thousand people were abandoning the countryside each day (Ruiz and García 2003).

A major cause of this situation is NAFTA, the 1994 North American Free Trade Agreement involving Mexico, the United States, and Canada. This treaty liberalized trade by reducing or eliminating most tariffs and quotas but did not compensate for major economic imbalances among the constituent economies. For instance, agricultural production in the United States continues to be very heavily subsidized at the same time that the large size of U.S. farms and agribusinesses allows them to achieve economies of scale that are not possible for most of their Mexican counterparts. The result is that U.S. agricultural products—even maize, the hallmark of Mexican agriculture—enter the Mexican market at prices below local production cost (see Chollett 1999; McDonald 1994). Thus NAFTA not only has widened Mexico's agricultural trade deficit with the United States but also is "the most significant factor in the loss of agricultural jobs in Mexico" (Polaski 2003: 20). Furthermore, neither NAFTA nor other neoliberal measures have enabled the Mexican economy to provide enough formal sector jobs to keep up with rising demand, let alone to reverse the downward trend in real wages (Audley 2003).

Second, the Mexican government's "export economy" drive, a major component of neoliberalism since the beginning of the De la Madrid administration (1982–1988), does not seem destined to lead to sustained economic growth. A major aspect of it is the *maquiladora* (assembly plant) program, which is concentrated in clothing, electronics, and automobile components. This program, created in 1965 "to allow tariff-free and tax-free imports of materials and components into Mexico for assembly and re-export to the United States" (Polaski 2003: 15), led to the employment of over 1.3 million people at its peak in 2001. Although the maquiladoras have added about 550,000 workers since NAFTA took effect in 1994, their workforce actually declined by about 250,000 jobs between the beginning of 2002 and May 2003 (Polaski 2003: 15–16). This loss was largely due to international competition, especially from China, where wages are much lower (see Turati 2003).

The most serious limitation of the maquiladora is inherent: the manufacturing components are imported, limiting maquiladora feedback to the rest of the economy. "In this model, the spillover effect . . . is very limited. . . . Forward and backward linkages . . . are not created, limiting the multiplier effect of any growth in exports" (Polaski 2003: 16). A case in point is the huge, ultra-modern Volkswagen México plant in Puebla, which employs about 25,000 workers directly and perhaps another 50,000 indirectly in companies elsewhere in Mexico that supply the factory. These suppliers, though, "are virtually all foreign-owned and import most of the materials they use. The value Mexico adds to the . . . [cars] it exports is mainly labor" (Rosenberg 2002: 32). In short, even this large "manufacturing" plant operates basically like a maquiladora, assembling imported components. Thus it remains an economic island that has little stimulus value for the rest of the economy. "In spite of the fact that Mexico has been host to many car plants," laments an economist at the Universidad Autónoma de Puebla, "we [still] don't know how to build a car" from scratch (Rosenberg 2002: 32). To make matters worse, the rest of the manufacturing sector (i.e., outside of the maquiladoras) increasingly shows the same pattern of importing the components for its products intended for export, either because the components are not available in Mexico or because Mexican suppliers are losing out to foreign suppliers (Polaski 2003: 16–17). Not surprisingly, "overall employment in nonmaquiladora manufacturing in Mexico was lower in 2003 than in 1994, except in microenterprises, which are mainly in the informal sector" (15).

Third, while it is impossible to predict the long-term impact of globalization on the Mexican economy, the results thus far are not encouraging. We have already pointed out that both the maquiladora and nonmaquiladora manufacturing sectors are suffering the negative impact of cheaper production costs in other countries. China has become a major competitor, and in 2003 it displaced Mexico as the second-largest exporter to the United States (Polaski 2003: 17). Mexican goods are also experiencing Chinese competition in internal markets. For instance, imported Chinese "clones" of such hallmark Mexican craft goods as basketry, ceramics, and women's shawls are now underselling those produced in Mexico, threatening the livelihood of the millions of Mexicans who earn part or all of their livings from home or workshop manufacture of these items for the tourist trade (Solís 2005). Such unfavorable competition is not likely to abate. Even the net trade surplus with the United States that Mexico has achieved under NAFTA most likely "will erode as other low-wage countries gain similar access" to the U.S. market as free-trade agreements proliferate (17).

Fourth, the neoliberal model of economic development calls for deregulation not only at home, through reducing the role of government in manufacturing and marketing, but also internationally, through reducing such traditional trade restrictions as tariffs and quotas. The goal is to embrace globalization through "free trade." Whether or not neoliberalism is the best method of world engagement is a policy matter that is worth debating, but globalization itself is a fact of life—and has been for the past five hundred years or so—that must be accommodated in some fashion. Any argument either for or against globalization as such is moot. Rather, debate has to center on the conditions under which countries or economic sectors engage the world economy. While it is true that "no nation has ever developed over the long term without trade," it is also true that "the United States, Germany, France and Japan all became wealthy and powerful nations behind the barriers of protectionism," while "East Asia built its export industry by protecting its markets and banks from foreign competition" (Rosenberg 2002: 30; also see Reynolds 2003). Yet such powerful international institutions as the World Trade Organization and the International Monetary Fund, which are largely controlled by wealthy, powerful countries that can impose their decisions on the world's poor and weak countries, have adopted the mantra of global "free trade." In our view, expecting Mexico to become an economic winner in the global arena after lowering all its protective barriers is analogous to expecting a turtle to win a battle with wolves after removing its shell.

Fifth, Central Mexico appears to be on the verge of losing its role as the engine of the country's economy. The 1982 debt crisis and nationalization of banks and the 1994 peso crisis all had tremendously adverse consequences for Central Mexico (especially its political and economic hub, Mexico City), loosening its grip on the national economy. At the same time, the neoliberal policies put in place after 1982 have generally stimulated the export manufacturing and agribusiness economy of northern Mexico while dampening productivity and growth in the central and southern parts of the country, where agricultural enterprises were generally smaller and where industry had been heavily dependent on governmental subsidies and co-investment (see Loaeza 2001; Trejo and Jones 1998).

If these regional trends continue, as we expect, then the North will become progressively wealthier, Central Mexico will be drained of much of its economic vitality, and the South will sink further into poverty. At the end of the twentieth century, it was already possible to discern "the potential segmentation of the country into a rich and democratic north and a poor, violent, and autocratic south" (Trejo and Jones 1998: 95). In this climate, the most likely outcome for the middle stratum of the class structure is shrinkage in the South, stability or modest shrinkage in Central Mexico, and expansion in the North.

REFERENCES

Aguilar M., Alonso

1983 *Estado, capitalismo y clase en el poder en México.* Mexico City: Editorial Nuestro Tiempo.

Aguirre Beltrán, Gonzalo

1963 *Medicina y magia.* Mexico City: Instituto Nacional Indigenista.

1972 *La población negra de México.* Mexico City: Fondo de Cultura Económica.

1973 *Regiones de refugio: El desarrollo de la comunidad y el proceso dominical en Mestizoamérica.* 2nd ed. Mexico City: Instituto Nacional Indigenista.

1979 *Regions of Refuge.* Monograph No. 12. Washington, DC: Society for Applied Anthropology.

Aguirre Beltrán, Gonzalo, and Ricardo Pozas Arciniega

1973 *La política indigenista en México: Métodos y resultados.* 2nd ed. Serie de Antropología Social, No. 21. Mexico City: Instituto Nacional Indigenista.

Alba Vega, Carlos, and Dirk Kruijt

1995 "El significado del sector informal y la microempresa en América Latina y en México." Pp. 141–171 in *Micro y pequeña empresa en México: Frente a los retos de la globalización*, ed. Thomas Calvo and Bernardo Méndez. Mexico City: Centro Francés de Estudios Mexicanos y Centroaméricos.

Aldana Martínez, Gerardo

1994 *San Pablo Ixayoc: Un caso de proletarización incompleta.* Mexico City: Universidad Iberoamericana.

Alvarez Heydenreich, Laurencia

1987 *La enfermedad y la cosmovisión en Hueyapan, Morelos.* Mexico City: Instituto Nacional Indigenista.

Anderson, Rodney D.

1974 "Mexican Workers and the Politics of Revolution, 1906–1911." *Latin American Historical Review* 54: 94–113.

Anguiano, Arturo

1975 *El estado y la política obrera del cardenismo.* Mexico City: Ediciones Era.

Arizpe, Lourdes

1985 *Campesinado y migración.* Mexico City: Secretaría de Educación Pública.

Aron, Raymond

1966 "Social Class, Political Class, Ruling Class." Pp. 201–210 in *Class, Status, and Power: Social Stratification in Comparative Perspective,* ed. Reinhardt Bendix and Seymour M. Lipset. New York: Free Press.

Audley, John J.

2003 "Introduction." Pp. 4–8 in *NAFTA's Promise and Reality,* by Demetrios G. Papademetriou, John J. Audley, Sandra Polaski and Scott Vaughan. Washington, DC: Carnegie Endowment for International Peace.

Avila Sánchez, Héctor

2002 *Aspectos históricos de la formación de las regiones en el estado de Morelos (desde sus origines hasta 1930).* Cuernavaca: Universidad Nacional Autónoma de México, Centro Regional de Investigaciones Multidisciplinarias.

Barba de Piña Chan, Beatriz

1960 "Bosquejo socio-económico de un grupo de familias de la Ciudad de México." *Anales del Instituto Nacional de Antropología e Historia, 1957–1958* 11: 87–152.

Bartra, Roger

1975a (ed.) *Caciquismo y poder política en el México rural.* Mexico City: Siglo XXI.

1975b "Campesinado y poder político en México." Pp. 5–30 in *Caciquismo y poder política en el México rural,* ed. Roger Bartra. Mexico City: Siglo XXI.

Basave Benítez, Agustín

1992 *México mestizo: Análisis del nacionalismo mexicano en torno a la mestizofilia de Andrés Molina Enríquez.* Mexico City: Fondo de Cultura Económica.

Bazán Longi, Homero

2003 "Esos fachosos perseguidos." *El Universal* (Mexico City), August 2, 2003, p. C5.

Benería, Lourdes, and Martha Roldán

1987 *The Crossroads of Class and Gender: Industrial Homework, Subcontracting, and Household Dynamics in Mexico City.* Chicago: University of Chicago Press.

Berdan, Frances F.

1982 *The Aztecs of Central Mexico: An Imperial Society.* New York: Holt, Rinehart & Winston.

1986 "Enterprise and Empire in Aztec and Early Colonial Mexico." Pp. 281–302 in *Economic Aspects of Prehispanic Highland Mexico,* ed. Barry L. Isaac. Greenwich, CT: JAI Press.

Boltvinik, Julio

2000 "Incidencia e intensidad de la pobreza en México." Pp. 191–243 in *Pobreza y distribución del ingreso en México,* ed. Julio Boltvinik and Enrique Hernández Laos. Mexico City: Siglo XXI.

2002 *Poverty Measurement Methods—An Overview*. New York: United Nations Development Programme, Poverty Reduction Series. www.undp.org/poverty/publications/povred/PovertyMeasurementMethods.pdf.

2003 "Welfare, Inequality, and Poverty in Mexico, 1970–2000." Pp. 385–446 in *Confronting Development: Assessing Mexico's Economic and Social Policy Challenges*, ed. Kevin J. Middlebrook and Eduardo Zepeda. Stanford, CA: Stanford University Press.

Bonfil Batalla, Guillermo

1996 *México Profundo: Reclaiming a Civilization*. Trans. Philip A. Dennis. Austin: University of Texas Press.

Bonnassie, Pierre

1991 *From Slavery to Feudalism in South-Western Europe*. Trans. Jean Birrell. Cambridge: Cambridge University Press.

Bossen, Laurel H.

1984 *The Redivision of Labor: Women and Economic Choice in Four Guatemalan Communities*. Albany: State University of New York Press.

Bourdieu, Pierre

1973 "Cultural Reproduction and Social Reproduction." Pp. 71–112 in *Knowledge, Education, and Cultural Change: Papers in the Sociology of Education*, ed. Richard Brown. London: Tavistock.

Bourdieu, Pierre, and Jean-Claude Passeron

1990 *Reproduction in Education, Society and Culture*. Trans. Richard Nice. London: Sage.

Bracho, Teresa

2000 "Poverty and Education in Mexico: 1984–1996." Pp. 249–284 in *Unequal Schools, Unequal Chances*, ed. Fernando Reimers. Cambridge, MA: Harvard University Press.

Brading, D. A.

1980a (ed.) *Caudillo and Peasant in the Mexican Revolution*. Cambridge: Cambridge University Press.

1980b "Introduction: National Politics and the Populist Tradition." Pp. 1–16 in *Caudillo and Peasant in the Mexican Revolution*, ed. D. A. Brading. Cambridge: Cambridge University Press.

Brumfiel, Elizabeth M.

1987 "Elite and Utilitarian Crafts in the Aztec State." Pp. 102–118 in *Specialization, Exchange, and Complex Societies*, ed. Elizabeth M. Brumfiel and Timothy K. Earle. Cambridge: Cambridge University Press.

Buve, Raymond

1980 "State Governors and Peasant Mobilisation in Tlaxcala." Pp. 222–244 in *Caudillo and Peasant in the Mexican Revolution*, ed. D. A. Brading. Cambridge: Cambridge University Press.

1984a (ed.) *Haciendas in Central Mexico from Late Colonial Times to the Revolution*. Amsterdam: Centrum voor Studie en Documentatie van Latijns Amerika.

1984b "Agricultores, dominación política y estructura agraria en la Revolución mexicana: El caso de Tlaxcala (1910–1918)." Pp. 199–271 in *Haciendas in Central Mexico from Late Colonial Times to the Revolution*, ed. Raymond Buve. Amsterdam: Centrum voor Studie en Documentatie van Latijns Amerika.

Careaga, Gabriel

1974 *Mitos y fantasías de la clase media en México*. Mexico City: Editorial Joaquín Mortiz.

Carmack, Robert M., Janine Gasco, and Gary H. Gossen, eds.

1996 *The Legacy of Mesoamerica*. Upper Saddle River, NJ: Prentice-Hall.

Carrera, Magali M.

2003 *Imaging Identity in New Spain: Race, Lineage, and the Colonial Body in Portraiture and Casta Paintings*. Austin: University of Texas Press.

Carrera Stampa, Manuel

1954 *Los gremios mexicanos: La organización gremial en Nueva España*. Mexico City: Ibero América de Publicaciones.

Carrión, Jorge, and Alonso Aguilar M.

1972 *La burguesía, la oligarquía y el estado*. Mexico City: Editorial Nuestro Tiempo.

Carroll, Patrick J.

2001 *Blacks in Colonial Veracruz: Race, Ethnicity, and Regional Development*. 2nd ed. Austin: University of Texas Press.

Caso, Alfonso

1948 "Definición del indio y lo indio." *América Indígena* 8: 239–247.

Caso, Alfonso, Silvio Zavala, José Miranda, and Moisés González N.

1973 *La política indigenista en México*. 2nd ed. Serie de Antropología Social, No. 20. Mexico City: Instituto Nacional Indigenista.

Castellanos Guerrero, Alicia

1994 "Asimilación y diferenciación de los indios en México." *Estudios Sociológicos* 34: 101–127.

Castillo Palma, Norma Angélica

2001 *Cholula: Sociedad mestiza en ciudad india*. Mexico City: Universidad Autónoma Metropolitana-Iztapalapa.

Cervantes-Braginski, María Teresa

1992 "San Pedro Arriba: Modernization and Secularization in a Mexican Village." Ph.D. dissertation, University of Pittsburgh.

Chamoux, Marie-Noelle

1987 *Nahuas de Huauchinango*. Mexico City: Instituto Nacional Indigenista.

Chance, John K.

2000 "The Noble House in Colonial Puebla, Mexico: Descent, Inheritance, and the Nahua Tradition." *American Anthropologist* 102: 485–502.

Chance, John K., and William Taylor

1985 "Cofradias and Cargos: An Historical Perspective on the Mesoamerican Civil-Religious Hierarchy." *American Ethnologist* 12: 1–26.

Chant, Sylvia

1991 *Women and Survival in Mexican Cities*. Manchester: Manchester University Press.

Chávez Carbajal, María Guadalupe
1995 "La gran negritud en Michoacán, época colonial." Pp. 79–131 in *Presencia africana en México*, ed. María Martínez Montiel. Mexico City: Consejo Nacional para la Cultura y las Artes.
Chollett, Donna L.
1999 "Global Competition and Community: The Struggle for Social Justice." *Research in Economic Anthropology* 20: 19–47.
Collier, George A.
1994 "Reforms of Mexico's Agrarian Code: Impacts on the Peasantry." *Research in Economic Anthropology* 15: 105–127.
Contreras Suárez, Enrique
1978 *Estratificación y movilidad social en la Ciudad de México*. Mexico City: Universidad Nacional Autónoma de México.
Cope, R. Douglas
1994 *The Limits of Racial Domination: Plebian Society in Colonial Mexico City, 1660–1720*. Madison: University of Wisconsin Press.
Cordry, Donald, and Dorothy Cordry
1968 *Mexican Indian Costumes*. Austin: University of Texas Press.
Cornelius, Wayne A., Jr.
1973 "Contemporary Mexico: A Structural Analysis of Urban Caciquismo." Pp. 135–150 in *The Caciques*, ed. Robert Kern and Ronald Dolkart. Albuquerque: University of New Mexico Press.
Cortés, Fernando
2003 "El ingreso y la desigualdad en su distribución. México: 1997–2000." *Papeles de Población* 35: 137–152.
Cortés, Hernán
1971 *Letters from Mexico*. Trans. and ed. A. R. Pagden. New York: Grossman.
Couturier, Edith Boortein
1976 *La Hacienda de Hueyapan, 1550–1936*. Mexico City: Secretaría de Educación Pública.
Crawford, M. H., P. L. Workman, C. McLean, and F. C. Lees
1976 "Admixture Estimates and Selection in Tlaxcala." Pp. 161–168 in *The Tlaxcaltecans: Prehistory, Demography, Morphology and Genetics*, ed. Michael H. Crawford. Publications in Anthropology, No. 7. Lawrence: University of Kansas.
Crompton, Rosemary
2000 "The Gendered Restructuring of the Middle Classes: Employment and Caring." Pp. 165–183 in *Renewing Class Analysis*, ed. Rosemary Crompton, Fiona Devine, Mike Savage, and John Scott. Oxford: Blackwell and Sociological Review.
Crompton, Rosemary, and John Scott
2000 "Introduction: The State of Class Analysis." Pp. 1–15 in *Renewing Class Analysis*, ed. Rosemary Crompton, Fiona Devine, Mike Savage, and John Scott. Oxford: Blackwell and Sociological Review.
Crompton, Rosemary, Fiona Devine, Mike Savage, and John Scott, eds.
2000 *Renewing Class Analysis*. Oxford: Blackwell and Sociological Review.

Cross, John C.

1998 *Informal Politics: Street Vendors and the State in Mexico City*. Stanford, CA: Stanford University Press.

Damián, Araceli, and Julio Boltvinik

2003 "Evolución y características de la pobreza en México." *Comercio Exterior* 53(6): 519–531.

De la Fuente, Julio

1973 *Educación, antropología y desarrollo de la comunidad.* 2nd ed. Serie de Antropología Social, No. 4. Mexico City: Instituto Nacional Indigenista.

De la Peña, Sergio

1982 *La formación del capitalismo en México.* 9th ed. Mexico City: Siglo XXI.

Dehouve, Danièle

1976 *El tequio de los santos y la competencia entre los mercaderes.* Mexico City: Instituto Nacional Indigenista.

Delgado Moya, Rubén

2004 *Constitución política de los Estados Unidos Mexicanos, comentada.* Mexico City: Editorial SISTA.

Díaz Barriga, Miguel

1996 "Necesidad: Notes on the Discourses of Urban Politics in the Ajusco Foothills of Mexico City." *American Ethnologist* 23: 291–310.

Domínguez Ortiz, Antonio

1973 *Las clases privilegiadas en la España del antiguo régimen.* Colección Fundamentos 31. Madrid: Ediciones ISTMO.

Doremus, Anne

2001 "Indigenismo, Mestizaje, and National Identity in Mexico during the 1940s and 1950s." *Mexican Studies/Estudios Mexicanos* 17: 375–402.

Dow, James W.

1986 *The Shaman's Touch: Otomí Indian Symbolic Healing.* Salt Lake City: University of Utah Press.

2001a "Protestantism in Mesoamerica: The Old within the New." Pp. 1–23 in *Holy Saints and Fiery Preachers: The Anthropology of Protestantism in Mexico and Central America*, ed. James W. Dow and Alan R. Sandstrom. Westport, CT: Praeger.

2001b "Demographic Factors Affecting Protestant Conversions in Three Mexican Villages." Pp. 73–86 in *Holy Saints and Fiery Preachers: The Anthropology of Protestantism in Mexico and Central America*, ed. James W. Dow and Alan R. Sandstrom. Westport, CT: Praeger.

Dow, James W., and Alan R. Sandstrom, eds.

2001 *Holy Saints and Fiery Preachers: The Anthropology of Protestantism in Mexico and Central America.* Westport, CT: Praeger.

Durán, Diego

1994 *The History of the Indies of New Spain.* Trans. Doris Heyden. Norman: University of Oklahoma Press.

Echánove, Flavia, and Christina Steffen

2003 "Coping with Trade Liberalization: The Case of Mexican Grain Producers." *Culture & Agriculture* 25(2): 1–12.

Enríquez Rosas, Rocío

2003 "El rostro actual de la pobreza urbana en México." *Comercio Exterior* 53(6): 532–539.

Epstein, Steven A.

1991 *Wage Labor and Guilds in Medieval Europe.* Chapel Hill: University of North Carolina Press.

Flood, Merielle K.

1994 "Changing Gender Relations in Zinacantán, Mexico." *Research in Economic Anthropology* 15: 145–173.

Forbes

1994a "The Billionaires" (ed. Graham Button). Vol. 154, no. 2 (July 18): 134–135, 154–219.

1994b "Billionaires in the Making" (Michael Schuman). Vol. 154, no. 2 (July 18): 146–148.

1995 "A Tough New World" (Christopher Palmeri and Kerry A. Dolan). Vol. 156, no. 2 (July 17): 122–124.

1996–2007 www.forbes.com/lists billionaires (*Forbes* online).

Foster, George M.

1960 *Culture and Conquest: America's Spanish Heritage.* Publications in Anthropology, No. 27. New York: Viking Fund.

Friedlander, Judith

1975 *Being Indian in Hueyapan: A Study of Forced Identity in Contemporary Mexico.* New York: St. Martin's Press.

Frye, David

1996 *Indians into Mexicans: History and Identity in a Mexican Town.* Austin: University of Texas Press.

Gall, Olivia

1999 "Racismo, modernidad y legalidad en Chiapas." *Dimensión Antropológica* 15: 55–86.

García Canclini, Néstor

1990 *Culturas híbridas: Estrategias para entrar y salir de la modernidad.* Mexico City: Grijalbo and Consejo Nacional para la Cultura y las Artes.

García Mora, Carlos, and Andrés Medina, eds.

1983/86 *La quiebra política de la antropología social en México.* 2 vols. Mexico City: Universidad Nacional Autónoma de México.

Gibson, Charles

1964 *The Aztecs under Spanish Rule.* Stanford, CA: Stanford University Press.

1967 *Tlaxcala in the Sixteenth Century.* Stanford, CA: Stanford University Press.

1973 "Caciques in Postconquest and Colonial Mexico." Pp. 18–26 in *The Caciques,* ed. Robert Kern and Ronald Dolkart. Albuquerque: University of New Mexico Press.

Gilbert, Dennis, and Joseph A. Kahl

1987 *The American Class Structure: A New Synthesis*. Chicago: Dorsey Press.

Gillian, Angela

1976 "Clase, raza y etnicidad en Brazil y México." *Nueva Antropología* 5: 91–103.

Godínez S., Pedro M., and Donaciana Martín C.

1991 "Migración." Pp. 164–172 in *Nos queda la esperanza: El Valle del Mezquital*, ed. Carlos Martínez Assad and Sergio Sarmiento. Mexico City: Consejo Nacional para la Cultura y las Artes.

Goldschmidt, Walter

1950 "Social Class in America: A Critical Review." *American Anthropologist* 52: 483–489.

1955 "Social Class and the Dynamics of Status in America." *American Anthropologist* 57: 1209–1217.

1999 "Dynamics of Status in America." *Anthropology Newsletter* 40(5): 62, 64.

Gómez Carpinteiro, Francisco Javier

1998 *Tanto que costó: Clase, cultura y nueva ley agraria en un ejido*. Mexico City: Instituto Nacional de Antropología e Historia.

González Cosío, Arturo

1976 *Clases medias y movilidad social en México*. Mexico City: Editorial Extemporáneos.

González de la Rocha, Mercedes

1994 *The Resources of Poverty: Women and Survival in a Mexican City*. Oxford: Blackwell.

González Navarro, Moisés

1970 "*Mestizaje* in Mexico during the National Period." Pp. 145–169 in *Race and Class in Latin America*, ed. Magnus Mörner. New York: Columbia University Press.

Granato, Stephanie, and Aída Mostkoff

1990 "The Class Structure of Mexico, 1895–1980." Pp. 103–115 in *Society and Economy in Mexico*, ed. James Wilkie. Berkeley: University of California Press.

Griffin, Keith, and Amy Ickowitz

2003 "Confronting Human Development in Mexico." Pp. 577–595 in *Confronting Development: Assessing Mexico's Economic and Social Policy Challenges*, ed. Kevin J. Middlebrook and Eduardo Zepeda. Stanford, CA: Stanford University Press.

Guerrero, Raúl

1985 *El pulque*. Mexico City: Editorial Joaquín Mortiz.

Harvey, H. R.

1972 "The Relaciones Geográficas, 1579–1586: Native Languages." Pp. 279–323 in *Handbook of Middle American Indians*, vol. 12, ed. Howard F. Cline. Austin: University of Texas Press.

Henao, Luis Emilio

1980 *Tehuacán: Campesinado e irrigación*. Mexico City: Editorial Edicol.

Hernández Laos, Enrique, and Jorge Velázquez Roa

2003 *Globalización, desigualdad y pobreza: Lecciones de la experiencia mexicana*. Mexico City: Universidad Autónoma Metropolitana.

Herrera Feria, María de Lourdes

1990 "Trabajadores prófogos y endeudados en la región de Atlixco, durante la segunda mitad del siglo XIX." Pp. 143–150 in *Origen y evolución de la hacienda en México: Siglos XVI al XX*, ed. María Teresa Jarquín Ortega. Toluca: El Colegio Mexiquense.

Hicks, Frederic

1999 "The Middle Class in Ancient Central Mexico." *Journal of Anthropological Research* 55: 409–427.

Hirabayashi, Lane

1993 *Cultural Capital: Mountain Zapotec Migrant Associations in Mexico City*. Tucson: University of Arizona Press.

Huber, Brad R., and Alan R. Sandstrom, eds.

2001 *Mesoamerican Healers*. Austin: University of Texas Press.

INEGI [Instituto Nacional de Estadística, Geografía e Informática]

2003 *Mujeres y hombres en México 2003*. Aguascalientes, AGS: INEGI.

Ingham, John M.

1986 *Mary, Michael, and Lucifer: Folk Catholicism in Central Mexico*. Austin: University of Texas Press.

Isaac, Barry L.

1986 "Notes on Obsidian, the Pochteca, and the Position of Tlatelolco in the Aztec Empire." Pp. 316–343 in *Economic Aspects of Prehispanic Highland Mexico*, ed. Barry L. Isaac. Greenwich, CT: JAI Press.

2005 "Karl Polanyi." Pp. 14–25 in *A Handbook of Economic Anthropology*, ed. James G. Carrier. Cheltenham: Edward Elgar.

Israel, J. I.

1975 *Race, Class and Politics in Colonial Mexico, 1610–1670*. Oxford: Oxford University Press.

Jacobs, Ian

1980 "Rancheros of Guerrero: The Figuroa Brothers and the Revolution." Pp. 76–91 in *Caudillo and Peasant in the Mexican Revolution*, ed. D. A. Brading. Cambridge: Cambridge University Press.

Jarquín Ortega, María Teresa, ed.

1990 *Origen y evolución de la hacienda en México: Siglos XVI al XX*. Toluca: El Colegio Mexiquense.

Jiménez Guillén, Raúl, and Genoveva Márquez Ramírez

2003 *Los egresados como reflejo de la calidad académica: El caso de la Universidad Autónoma de Tlaxcala*. Tlaxcala: Universidad Autónoma de Tlaxcala.

Katz, Friedrich

1974 "Labor Conditions on Haciendas in Porfirian Mexico: Some Trends and Tendencies." *Hispanic American Historical Review* 54: 1–47.

Kearney, Michael

1999 "Neither Modern nor Traditional." Pp. 69–79 in *Identities on the Move*, ed. Liliana R. Goldin. Albany: State University of New York, Institute of Mesoamerican Studies.

Kicza, John E.

1999 "Formación, identidad y estabilidad dentro de la élite colonial mexicana en los siglos XVI y XVII." Pp. 17–34 in *Beneméritos, aristócratas y empresarios*, ed. Bernd Schröter and Christian Büschges. Madrid and Frankfurt: Iberoamericana and Veruert Verlag.

Kingston, Paul W.

2000 *The Classless Society*. Stanford, CA: Stanford University Press.

Knight, Alan

1991 "Land and Society in Revolutionary Mexico: The Destruction of the Great Haciendas." *Mexican Studies/Estudios Mexicanos* 7(1): 73–104.

1994 "Peasants into Patriots: Thoughts on the Making of the Mexican Nation." *Mexican Studies/Estudios Mexicanos* 10(1): 135–161.

Konrad, Herman W.

1980 *A Jesuit Hacienda in Colonial Mexico: Santa Lucía, 1576–1767*. Stanford, CA: Stanford University Press.

1990 "El peonaje por deudas y la tienda de raya en la hacienda colonial: Interpretaciones pasadas y presentes." Pp. 127–136 in *Origen y evolución de la hacienda en México: Siglos XVI al XX*, ed. María Teresa Jarquín Ortega. Toluca: El Colegio Mexiquense.

La Botz, Dan

1992 *Mask of Democracy: Labor Suppression in Mexico Today*. Boston: South End Press.

1997 "Fidel Velázquez Sánchez: Embodiment of State-Unionism." *Mexican Labor News and Analysis* 2 (June 22): Special Issue ("Fidel Velázquez Obituary").

Lagarriga Attias, Isabel

1993 "El nahual y el diablo en la cosmovisión de un pueblo de la Ciudad de México." *Anales de Antropología* 30: 277–288.

Laurell, Asa Cristina

2003 "The Transformation of Social Policy in Mexico." Pp. 320–349 in *Confronting Development: Assessing Mexico's Economic and Social Policy Challenges*, ed. Kevin J. Middlebrook and Eduardo Zepeda. Stanford, CA: Stanford University Press.

Laurin-Frenette, Nicole

1976 *Las teorías funcionalistas de las clases sociales: Sociología e ideología burguesa*. Madrid: Siglo XXI.

Leal, Juan Felipe, and Margarita Menegus

1995 *Hacendados y campesinos en la Revolución Mexicana: El caso de Tlaxcala, 1910–1920*. Mexico City: Universidad Nacional Autónoma de México.

León, Nicolás

1924 *Las castas del México colonial o Nueva España*. Mexico City: Museo Nacional de Arqueología, Historia y Etnografía.

Lewis, Laura A.

2000 "Blacks, Black Indians, Afromexicans: The Dynamics of Race, Nation, and Identity in a Mexican *moreno* Community (Guerrero)." *American Ethnologist* 27: 898–926.

Lewis, Oscar

1951 *Life in a Mexican Village: Tepoztlan Restudied.* Urbana: University of Illinois Press.

1961 *The Children of Sánchez: Autobiography of a Mexican Family.* New York: Random House.

1970 *Anthropological Essays.* New York: Random House.

Loaeza, Soledad

2001 "México: La rebelión de las élites." *Estudios Sociológicos* 19: 363–380.

Lockhart, James

1991 "Españoles entre indios: Toluca a fines del siglo XVI." Pp. 52–116 in *Haciendas, pueblos y comunidades,* ed. Manuel Miño Grijalva. Mexico City: Consejo Nacional para la Cultura y las Artes.

1992 *The Nahuas after the Conquest.* Stanford, CA: Stanford University Press.

Lockhart, James, and Enrique Otte

1976 *Letters and People of the Spanish Indies: Sixteenth Century.* Cambridge: Cambridge University Press.

Lomnitz, Larissa Adler de

1975 *Cómo sobreviven los marginados.* Mexico City: Siglo XXI.

Lomnitz-Adler, Claudio

1992 *Exits from the Labyrinth.* Berkeley: University of California Press.

2001 *Deep Mexico, Silent Mexico.* Minneapolis: University of Minnesota Press.

Machuca Ramírez, Jesús Antonio

1998 "Nación, mestizaje y racismo." Pp. 37–74 in *Nación, racismo e identidad,* ed. Alicia Castellanos Guerrero and Juan Manuel Sandoval Palacios. Mexico City: Editorial Nuestro Tiempo.

MacLachlan, Colin M., and Jaime E. Rodríguez O.

1980 *The Forging of the Cosmic Race: A Reinterpretation of Colonial Mexico.* Berkeley: University of California Press.

Madsen, William

1960 *The Virgin's Children: Life in an Aztec Village Today.* Austin: University of Texas Press.

Margolies, Barbara Louise

1975 *Princes of the Earth: Subcultural Diversity in a Mexican Municipality.* Washington, DC: American Anthropological Association.

Marín Bosch, Miguel

1999 *Puebla neocolonial, 1777–1831: Casta, ocupación y matrimonio en la segunda ciudad de Nueva España.* Zapopan: El Colegio de Jalisco.

Martín Casares, Aurelia

2000 *La esclavitud en la Granada del siglo XVI: Género, raza y religión.* Granada, Spain: Universidad de Granada.

Martínez, Fabiola

2004a "Desencanto y frustración de asalariados, saldo de cuatro sexenios neoliberales." *La Jornada* (Mexico City), December 12, Política section. www.jornada.unam.mx.

2004b "El salario mínimo se incrementará en promedio 1.7 pesos en 2005." *La Jornada* (Mexico City), December 17, Sociedad y Justicia section. www.jornada.unam.mx.

Martínez Assad, Carlos, and Sergio Sarmiento, eds.

1991 *Nos queda la esperanza: El Valle del Mezquital.* Mexico City: Consejo Nacional para la Cultura y las Artes.

Martínez Maranto, Alfredo

1995 "Dios pinta como quiere: Identidad y cultura en un pueblo afromestizo de Veracruz." Pp. 525–571 in *Presencia africana en México*, ed. María Martínez Montiel. Mexico City: Consejo Nacional para la Cultura y las Artes.

Martínez Montiel, María, ed.

1995 *Presencia africana en México.* Mexico City: Consejo Nacional para la Cultura y las Artes.

McDonald, James H.

1994 "NAFTA and Basic Food Production: Dependency and Marginalization on Both Sides of the US/Mexico Border." *Research in Economic Anthropology* 15: 129–143.

Medellín, Rodrigo A.

1988 *Sanctorum: Resurgimiento campesino en un pueblo de Tlaxcala.* Mexico City: Secretaría de Educación Pública.

Medina, Andrés

1998 "Los pueblos indios en la trama de la nación: Notas etnográficas." *Revista Mexicana de Sociología* 60(1): 131–168.

Mertens, Hans-Günther

1989 "Los peones de las haciendas de trigo en el Valle de Atlixco a fines del porfiriato." Pp. 149–217 in *Paternalismo y economía moral de las haciendas mexicanas del porfiriato*, ed. Herbert J. Nickel. Mexico City: Universidad Iberoamericana.

Meyer, Jean

1986 "Haciendas y ranchos, peones y campesinos en el porfiriato: Algunas falacias estadísticas." *Historia Mexicana* 35: 477–509.

Meyer, Michael C., and William L. Sherman

1991 *The Course of Mexican History.* New York: Oxford University Press.

Miller, Simon

1995 *Landlords and Haciendas in Modernizing Mexico: Essays in Radical Reappraisal.* Amsterdam: Centro de Estudios y Documentación Latinoamericanos.

Molina Ludy, Virginia, and Kim Sánchez Saldaña

1999 "El fin de la ilusión: Mobilidad social en la Ciudad de México." *Nueva Antropología* 55: 43–55.

Mondragón Barrios, Lourdes

1999 *Esclavos africanos en la Ciudad de México: El servicio doméstico durante el siglo XVI.* Mexico City: Ediciones Euroamericanas and Consejo Nacional para la Cultura y las Artes.

Mörner, Magnus

1967 *Race Mixture in the History of Latin America.* Boston: Little, Brown.

Naveda Chávez-Hita, Adriana
1987 *Esclavos negros en las haciendas azucareras de Córdoba, Veracruz, 1690–1830*. Jalapa: Universidad Veracruzana.
Nickel, Herbert J.
1987 *Relaciones de trabajo en las haciendas de Puebla y Tlaxcala (1740–1914)*. Mexico City: Universidad Iberoamericana.
1988 "Agricultural Laborers in the Mexican Revolution (1910–40): Some Hypotheses and Facts about Participation and Restraint in the Highlands of Puebla-Tlaxcala." Pp. 376–416 in *Riot, Rebellion, and Revolution: Rural Social Conflict in Mexico*, ed. Friedrich Katz. Princeton, NJ: Princeton University Press.
1989a (ed.) *Paternalismo y economía moral de las haciendas mexicanas del porfiriato*. Mexico City: Universidad Iberoamericana.
1989b "Elementos de la economía moral en las relaciones laborales de las haciendas mexicanas." Pp. 15–68 in *Paternalismo y economía moral de las haciendas mexicanas del porfiriato*, ed. Herbert J. Nickel. Mexico City: Universidad Iberoamericana.
1996 *Morfología social de la hacienda mexicana*. 2nd ed. Mexico City: Fondo de Cultura Económica.
Nierman, Daniel, and Ernesto H. Vallejo
2003 *The Hacienda in Mexico*. Austin: University of Texas Press.
Notimex
2007 "Laboran 500 mil personas en comercio ambulante en DF: UNAM." *El Universal* (Mexico City), July 25. www.eluniversal.com.mx/notas/vi438984.html.
Nutini, Hugo G.
1968a "A Synoptic Comparison of Mesoamerican Marriage and Family Structure." *Southwestern Journal of Anthropology* 23: 383–404.
1968b *San Bernardino Contla: Marriage and Family Structure in a Tlaxcalan Municipio*. Pittsburgh, PA: University of Pittsburgh Press.
1984 *Ritual Kinship: Ideological and Structural Integration of the Compadrazgo System in Rural Tlaxcala*. Princeton, NJ: Princeton University Press.
1988 *Todos Santos in Rural Tlaxcala: A Syncretic, Expressive, and Symbolic Analysis of the Cult of the Dead*. Princeton, NJ: Princeton University Press.
1995 *The Wages of Conquest: The Mexican Aristocracy in the Context of Western Aristocracies*. Ann Arbor: University of Michigan Press.
1997 "Class and Ethnicity in Mexico: Somatic and Racial Considerations." *Ethnology* 36: 227–238.
1998 "La transformación del tezitlazc o tiempero en el medio poblano-tlaxcalteca." Pp. 159–170 in *La cultura plural: Reflexiones sobre diálogo y silencios en Mesoamérica (homenaje a Italo Signorini)*, ed. Alessandro Lupo and Alfredo López Austín. Mexico City: Universidad Nacional Autonóma de México.
2000 "Native Evangelism in Central Mexico." *Ethnology* 39: 39–54.
2004 *The Mexican Aristocracy: An Expressive Ethnography, 1910-2000*. Austin: University of Texas Press.

2005 *Social Stratification and Mobility in Central Veracruz.* Austin: University of Texas Press.

Nutini, Hugo G., and Betty Bell

1980 *Ritual Kinship: The Structural and Historical Development of the Compadrazgo System in Rural Tlaxcala.* Princeton, NJ: Princeton University Press.

Nutini, Hugo G., and Barry L. Isaac

1974 *Los pueblos de habla náhuatl de la región de Puebla y Tlaxcala.* Mexico City: Instituto Nacional Indigenista.

1977 "Ideology and the Sacro-Symbolic Functions of Compadrazgo in Santa María Belén Azitzimititlán, Tlaxcala, Mexico." *L'Uomo* 1(1): 81–121.

Nutini, Hugo G., and Timothy D. Murphy

1968 "Labor Migration and Family Structure in the Tlaxcala-Pueblan Area, Mexico." Pp. 80–103 in *Essays in Honor of Ralph L. Beals,* ed. Walter Goldschmidt. Berkeley: University of California Press.

Nutini, Hugo G., and John M. Roberts

1993 *Bloodsucking Witchcraft: An Epistemological Study of Anthropomorphic Supernaturalism in Rural Tlaxcala.* Tucson: University of Arizona Press.

Ochoa, Enrique C.

2000 *Feeding Mexico: The Political Uses of Food since 1910.* Wilmington, DE: Scholarly Resources.

Oettinger, Marion

1980 *Una comunidad tlapaneca: Sus linderos sociales y territoriales.* Mexico City: Instituto Nacional Indigenista.

Olavarrieta Marenco, Marcela

1977 *Magia en los Tuxtlas.* Mexico City: Instituto Nacional Indigenista.

Olivares, Enrique

1978 "Gobierno, corrupción y sindicalismo (un movimiento encadenado)." Pp. 58–100 in *La burguesía mexicana: Cuatro ensayos,* 3rd ed., by Ramiro Reyes Esparza, Enrique Olvares, Emilio Leyva, and Ignacio Hernández G. Mexico City: Editorial Nuestro Tiempo.

Olivé Negrete, Julio César, and Beatriz Barba de Piña Chan

1960 "Estudio de las clases sociales en la Ciudad de México, con vista a caracterizar a la clase media." *Anales del Instituto Nacional de Antropología e Historia, 1957–58* 11: 153–195.

1962 Estudio de clases sociales en la Ciudad de México: experiencias con un grupo obrero." *Anales del Instituto Nacional de Antropología e Historia, 1961* 14: 219–281.

Oppenheimer, Andrés

1996 *Bordering on Chaos.* Boston: Little, Brown.

Ortner, Sherry B.

1998 "Identities: The Hidden Life of Class." *Journal of Anthropological Research* 54: 1–17.

Ortiz de Montellano, Bernard R.

1990 *Aztec Medicine, Health, and Nutrition.* New Brunswick, NJ: Rutgers University Press.

Ouweneel, Arij
1995 "From *tlahtocayotl* to *gobernadoryotl*: A Critical Examination of Indigenous Rule in 18th-Century Central Mexico." *American Ethnologist* 22: 756–785.
Palmer, Colin A.
1976 *Slaves of the White God: Blacks in Mexico, 1570–1650*. Cambridge, MA: Harvard University Press.
Pardinas, Juan
2004 "Fighting Poverty in Mexico: Policy Challenges." Pp. 65–86 in *Mexico under Fox*, ed. Luis Rubio and Susan Kaufman Purcell. Boulder, CO: Lynne Rienner.
Paré, Luisa
1975 "Caciquismo y estructura de poder en la Sierra Norte de Puebla." Pp. 31–61 in *Caciquismo y poder política en el México rural*, ed. Roger Bartra. Mexico City: Siglo XXI.
1977 *El proletariado agrícola en México ¿Campesinos sin tierra o proletarios agrícolas?* Mexico City: Siglo XXI.
Paredes Martínez, Carlos, and Blanca Lara Tenorio
1995 "La población negra de los valles centrales de Puebla: Orígenes y desarrollo hasta 1681." Pp. 19–77 in *Presencia africana en México*, ed. María Martínez Montiel. Mexico City: Consejo Nacional para la Cultura y las Artes.
Paul, Benjamin D., and Clancy McMahon
2001 "Mesoamerican Bonesetters." Pp. 243–269 in *Mesoamerican Healers*, ed. Brad R. Huber and Alan R. Sandstrom. Austin: University of Texas Press.
Pérez-Rocha, Emma, and Rafael Tena
2000 *La nobleza indígena del centro de México después de la conquista*. Mexico City: Instituto Nacional de Antropología e Historia.
Perkins, Stephen M.
2007 "The House of Guzman: An Indigenous Cacicazgo in Early Colonial Central Mexico." *Culture and Agriculture* 29(1): 25–42.
Perrucci, Robert, and Earl Wysong
2003 *The New Class Society: Goodbye American Dream?* Latham, MD: Rowman & Littlefield.
Polanyi, Karl
1944 *The Great Transformation: The Political and Economic Origins of Our Time*. New York: Holt, Rinehart & Winston.
Polaski, Sandra
2003 "Jobs, Wages, and Household Income." Pp. 11–37 in *NAFTA's Promise and Reality*, by Demetrios G. Papademetriou, John J. Audley, Sandra Polaski, and Scott Vaughan. Washington, DC: Carnegie Endowment for International Peace.
Poniatowska, Elena
1975 *Massacre in Mexico*. Trans. Helen R. Lane. New York: Viking Press.
Portal Ariosa, María Ana
1997 *Ciudadanos desde el pueblo: Identidad urbana y religiosidad popular en San Andrés Totolte-*

pec, Tlalpan, México, D.F. Mexico City: Consejo Nacional para la Cultura y las Artes and Universidad Autónoma Metropolitana.

Portes, Alejandro

2003 "La persistente importancia de las clases: Una interpretación nominalista." *Estudios Sociológicos* 21(61): 11–54.

Portes, Alejandro, and Kelly Hoffman

2003 "Latin American Class Structures: Their Composition and Change during the Neoliberal Era." *Latin American Research Review* 38: 41–82.

Portocarrero, Gonzalo

1999 "La ambigüedad moral del humor y la reproducción del racismo: El caso de la china Tudela de Rafael León." *Dimensión Antropológica* 15: 27–53.

Provost, Paul Jean

1975 "Culture and Anti-Culture among the Eastern Nahua of Northern Veracruz, Mexico." Ph.D. dissertation, Indiana University.

Puga, Cristina

1993 *México: Empresarios y poder*. Mexico City: Universidad Nacional Autónoma de México.

Quesada, Noemí

1989 *Enfermedad y maleficio: El curandero en el México colonial*. Mexico City: Universidad Nacional Autónoma de México.

Rajchenberg S., Enrique

1995 "Tradición e identidad: La clase obrera de Orizaba (1900–1920)." *Estudios Sociológicos* 38: 395–407.

Ramírez Rancaño, Mario

1984 "Un frente patronal a principios del siglo XX: El centro industrial mexicano de Puebla." Pp. 17–45 in *Clases dominantes y estado en México*, ed. Salvador Cordero H. and Ricardo Tirado. Mexico City: Universidad Nacional Autónoma de México.

1990 *El sistema de haciendas en Tlaxcala*. Mexico City: Consejo Nacional para la Cultura y las Artes.

Rendón Corona, Armando

2001 "El corporativismo sindical y sus transformaciones." *Nueva Antropología* 59: 11–30.

Rendón Garcini, Ricardo

1989 "Aportación al estudio de las relaciones económico-morales entre hacendados y trabajadores: El caso de dos haciendas pulqueras en Tlaxcala." Pp. 69–91 in *Paternalismo y economía moral de las haciendas mexicanas del porfiriato*, ed. Herbert J. Nickel. Mexico City: Universidad Iberoamericana.

Restrepo, Iván, and José Sánchez Cortés

1972 *La reforma agraria en cuatro regiones*. Mexico City: Secretaría de Educación Pública.

Reynolds, Clark W.

2003 "A Comparative Perspective on Mexico's Development Challenges." Pp.

596–605 in *Confronting Development: Assessing Mexico's Economic and Social Policy Challenges*, ed. Kevin J. Middlebrook and Eduardo Zepeda. Stanford, CA: Stanford University Press.

Roberts, John M.

1976 "Belief in the Evil Eye in World Perspective." Pp. 223–278 in *The Evil Eye*, ed. Clarence Maloney. New York: Columbia University Press.

Roberts, John M., Chen Chiao, and Triloki N. Pandey

1975 "Meaningful God Sets from a Chinese Personal Pantheon and a Hindu Personal Pantheon." *Ethnology* 14: 121–148.

Roberts, John M., and Garry E. Chick

1979 "Butler County Eight Ball: A Behavioral Space Analysis." Pp. 65–99 in *Sports, Games and Play: Social and Schological Viewpoints*, ed. Jeffrey H. Goldstein. Hillsdale, IL: Lawrence Erlbaum.

Roberts, John M., and Thomas V. Golder

1970 "Navy and Polity: A 1963 Baseline." *Naval War College Review* 23: 30–41.

Roberts, John M., and Susan M. Nattrass

1980 "Women and Trapshooting: Competence and Expression in a Game of Physical Skill with Chance." Pp. 262–291 in *Play and Culture*, ed. Helen B. Schwartzman. West Point, NY: Leisure Press.

Roberts, John M., and Brian Sutton-Smith

1962 "Child Training and Game Involvement." *Ethnology* 1: 166–185.

Robichaux, David

1994 "Clase, percepción étnica y transformación regional: Unos ejemplos tlaxcaltecas." *Boletín de Antropología Americana* 30: 143–157.

Robins, Wayne

1994 "El indigenismo posrevolucionario mexicano y la cuestión de las tierras de los pueblos indígenas." *Nueva Antropología* 46: 25–37.

Rodríguez López, María Teresa

1988 *Preservación de la lengua materna*. Mexico City: Instituto Nacional Indigenista.

Romer, Marta

1998 "Reproducción étnica y racismo en el medio urbano: un caso de migrantes mixtecos en la zona metropolitana de la Ciudad de México." Pp. 231–248 in *Nación, racismo e identidad*, ed. Alicia Castellanos Guerrero and Juan Manuel Sandoval Palacios. Mexico City: Editorial Nuestro Tiempo.

Romero, Osvaldo

2002 *La Malinche: Poder y religión en la región del volcán*. Tlaxcala: Universidad Autónoma de Tlaxcala.

Rosenberg, Tina

2002 "The Free-Trade Fix." *New York Times Magazine*, August 18, pp. 28–33, 50, 74–75.

Rothstein, Frances A.

1982 *Three Different Worlds: Women, Men, and Children in an Industrializing Community*. Westport, CT: Greenwood Press.

Rubio, Luis

1998 "Coping with Political Change." Pp. 5–36 in *Mexico under Zedillo*, ed. Susan Kaufman Purcell and Luis Rubio. Boulder, CO: Lynne Rienner.

Ruiz, José Luis, and Ariadna García

2003 "Abandonan el campo mil personas cada día." *El Universal* (Mexico City), July 22, p. A1.

Ruvalcaba Mercado, Jesús

1983 *El maguey manso: Historia y presente de Epazoyucan, Hgo.* Mexico City: Universidad Autónoma Chapingo.

Sahagún, Bernardino de

1979 *General History of the Things of New Spain (Florentine Codex), Book 8: Kings and Lords*, 2nd ed., trans. A. J. O. Anderson and Charles E. Dibble. Santa Fe, NM: School of American Research.

Saldívar, Américo

1977 "Diferencias ideológicas entre obreros y empleados." Pp. 193–215 in *Migración y desigualdad social en la Ciudad de México*, ed. Humberto Muñoz, Orlandina de Oliveira, and Claudio Stern. Mexico City: El Colegio de México and Universidad Nacional Autónoma de México.

Salvucci, Richard J.

1987 *Textiles and Capitalism in Mexico: An Economic History of the Obrajes, 1539–1840*. Princeton, NJ: Princeton University Press.

Samstad, James G.

2001 "El movimiento obrero mexicano después de Fidel Velázquez." *Nueva Antropología* 59: 31–52.

Sanderson, Susan R. W.

1984 *Land Reform in Mexico: 1910–1980*. Orlando, FL: Academic Press.

Sandstrom, Alan R.

1978 *The Image of Disease: Medical Practices of Nahua Indians of the Huasteca.* Monographs in Anthropology, No. 3. Columbia: University of Missouri Press.

1991 *Corn Is Our Blood: Culture and Ethnic Identity in a Contemporary Aztec Indian Village.* Norman: University of Oklahoma Press.

2001 "Conclusion: Anthropological Perspectives on Protestant Conversion in Mesoamerica." Pp. 263–289 in *Holy Saints and Fiery Preachers: The Anthropology of Protestantism in Mexico and Central America*, ed. James W. Dow and Alan R. Sandstrom. Westport, CT: Praeger.

Santiago Cruz, Francisco

1960 *Las artes y los gremios en la Nueva España.* Mexico City: Editorial Jus.

Schryer, Frans J.

1990 *Ethnicity and Class Conflict in Rural Mexico.* Princeton, NJ: Princeton University Press.

Schwartz, Rami (with Salomón Bazbaz Lapidus)

1994 *El ocaso de la clase media.* Mexico City: Grupo Editorial Planeta.

Selby, Henry A., Arthur D. Murphy, and Stephen A. Lorenzen

1990 *The Mexican Urban Household: Organizing for Self-Defense.* Austin: University of Texas Press.

Shadow, Robert D., and María J. Rodríguez V.

1995 "Historical Panorama of Anthropological Perspectives on Aztec Slavery." Pp. 299–323 in *Arqueología del norte y del occidente de México,* ed. Barbro Dahlgren and María de los Dolores Soto de Arechavaleta. Mexico City: Universidad Nacional Autónoma de México.

Sierra, Augusto Santiago

1973 *Las misiones culturales.* Mexico City: Secretaría de Educación Pública.

Sierra, María Teresa

1999 "Racismo y derecho: La justicia en regiones indígenas." *Dimensión Antropológica* 15: 87–111.

Simpson, Lesley Byrd

1982 *The Encomienda in New Spain.* Berkeley: University of California Press.

Slade, Doren L.

1992 *Making the World Safe for Existence: Celebration of the Saints among the Sierra Nahuat of Chignautla, Mexico.* Ann Arbor: University of Michigan Press.

Smith, Michael E.

1998 *The Aztecs.* Oxford: Blackwell.

Solís, Juan

2005 "Pretende Fonart evitar 'clonación' de artesanías." *El Universal* (Mexico City), August 5, Cultura section, p. 2.

Sorokin, Pitirim A.

1947 *Society, Culture, and Personality: Their Structure and Dynamics.* New York: Harper & Brothers.

Starr, Frederick

1900 *Notes upon the Ethnography of Southern Mexico,* vol. 1. Davenport, IA: Davenport Academy of Sciences.

Stern, Claudio

1994 "La desigualdad socioeconómica en México: Una revisión de las tendencias, 1895–1992." *Estudios Sociológicos* 35: 421–434.

Taylor, William B.

1979 *Drinking, Homicide and Rebellion in Colonial Mexican Villages.* Stanford, CA: Stanford University Press.

Teichman, Judith A.

1995 *Privatization and Political Change in Mexico.* Pittsburgh, PA: University of Pittsburgh Press.

Tobler, Hans Werner

1980 "Conclusion: Peasant Mobilisation and the Revolution." Pp. 245–255 in *Caudillo and Peasant in the Mexican Revolution,* ed. D. A. Brading. Cambridge: Cambridge University Press.

Trejo, Guillermo, and Claudio Jones

1998 "Political Dilemmas of Welfare Reform: Poverty and Inequality in Mexico." Pp. 67–99 in *Mexico under Zedillo*, ed. Susan Kaufman Purcell and Luis Rubio. Boulder, CO: Lynne Rienner.

Trejo Delarbre, Raúl, and José Woldenberg

1984 "Las desigualdades en el movimiento obrero." Pp. 229–256 in *La desigualdad en México*, ed. Ronaldo Cordero and Carlos Tello. Mexico City: Siglo XXI.

Tuma, Elias

1965 *Twenty-six Centuries of Agrarian Reform: A Comparative Analysis*. Berkeley: University of California Press.

Turati, Marcela

2003 "Preocupa futuro comercial." *Reforma* (Mexico City), August 12, p. 5A.

Valdés, Luz María

1995 *Los indios en los censos de población*. Mexico City: Universidad Nacional Autónoma de México.

Valdivia Dounce, Teresa

1996/1999 "Estado, ley nacional y derecho indígena." *Anales de Antropología* 33: 319–341.

Vázquez León, Luis

1992 *Ser indio otra vez: la purepechización de los tarascos serranos*. Mexico City: Consejo Nacional para la Cultura y las Artes.

Villoro, Luis

1950 *Los grandes momentos del indigenismo en México*. Mexico City: El Colegio de México.

Vincent, Theodore G.

2001 *The Legacy of Vicente Guerrero, Mexico's First Black Indian President*. Gainesville: University Press of Florida.

Viqueira, Carmen, and José I. Urquiola

1990 *Los obrajes en la Nueva España, 1530–1630*. Mexico City: Consejo Nacional para la Cultura y las Artes.

Von Mentz, Brígida

1999 *Trabajo, sujeción y libertad en el centro de la Nueva España: Esclavos, aprendices, campesinos y operarios manufactureros, siglos XVI a XVIII*. Mexico City: CIESAS (Centro de Investigaciones y Estudios Superiores en Antropología Social).

Warman, Arturo

1980 *"We Come to Object": The Peasants of Morelos and the National State*. Trans. Stephen K. Ault. Baltimore, MD: Johns Hopkins University Press.

Warner, William Lloyd

1960 *Social Class in America*. New York: Harper & Row.

1963 *Yankee City*. New Haven, CT: Harcourt Brace.

Whiteford, Andrew H.

1960 *Two Cities of Latin America: A Comparative Description of Social Classes*. Bulletin No. 9. Beloit, WI: Logan Museum of Anthropology.

Williams García, Roberto
1963 *Los tepehuas.* Xalapa: Universidad Veracruzana.
Womack, John, Jr.
1969 *Zapata and the Mexican Revolution.* New York: Alfred A. Knopf.
Zavala, Silvio
1967 *Los esclavos indios en Nueva España.* Mexico City: El Colegio Nacional.
Zea, Leopoldo
1968 *El positivismo en México: Nacimiento, apogeo y decadencia.* Mexico City: Fondo de Cultura Económica.

INDEX

Note: Numbers in bold refer to figures, maps, and tables.

Breinigsville, PA USA
03 October 2010

246576BV00001B/6/P

9 780292 723511